810.9005
G 96a

71697

DATE DUB			
GAYLORD M-2			PRINTED IN U.S.A.

WITHDRAWN

The Angry Decade

By

Leo Gurko

HARPER COLOPHON BOOKS
Harper & Row, Publishers
New York, Evanston & London

CARL A. RUDISILL LIBRARY
LENOIR RHYNE COLLEGE

FOR

MIRIAM, STEPHEN, AND JANE

810.9005
96a
71697
Nov., 1970

THE ANGRY DECADE.   Copyright 1947 by Leo Gurko. All
rights reserved. No part of this book may be used or reproduced in
any manner whatsoever without written permission except in the
case of brief quotations embodied in critical articles and reviews.
For information address Harper & Row, Publishers, Incorporated,
49 East 33rd Street, New York, New York. 10016.

This book was originally published by Dodd, Mead and Company,
New York, and is here reprinted by arrangement.

First HARPER COLOPHON edition published 1968 by Harper &
Row, Publishers, Incorporated, New York, New York.

Library of Congress Catalog Card Number: 68–19708

ACKNOWLEDGMENTS

I wish to thank the following publishers and authors for permission to use extracts from their books:

The John Day Company for the selection from *Where Life Is Better*, by James Rorty; Doubleday & Company for the extract from *Barren Ground*, by Ellen Glasgow, copyright 1926, 1933 by Ellen Glasgow; Duell, Sloan and Pearce for the poem by E. E. Cummings, copyright 1939-40; Kenneth Fearing for the selections from *Poems* and *Dead Reckoning. A Book of Poetry*; Harcourt, Brace and Company for the selections from *Language in Action*, by S. I. Hayakawa, *Middletown in Transition*, by Robert S. Lynd and Helen Merrell Lynd, and the poem by Horace Gregory; Harper & Brothers for the selections from *The Web and the Rock*, by Thomas Wolfe, copyright 1939 by Maxwell Perkins; Alfred A. Knopf, Inc. for the poem from *Harmonium*, by Wallace Stevens, copyright 1923, 1931 by Alfred A. Knopf, Inc.; Little, Brown & Company for the selection from *So Little Time*, by John P. Marquand; Robert M. McBride & Company for the selection from *World Diary: 1929-1934*, by Quincy Howe; Random House, Inc. for the selections from *Absalom, Absalom!*, by William Faulkner; Rinehart & Company for the selection from *The Fall of the City*, A Verse Play for Radio, copyright 1937 by Archibald MacLeish; Charles Scribner's

v

Sons for selections from *Look Homeward, Angel,* by Thomas Wolfe, and *For Whom the Bell Tolls,* by Ernest Hemingway; The Vanguard Press for the selections from *Studs Lonigan,* by James T. Farrell, copyright 1935 by The Vanguard Press, Inc.; Yale University Press for the selections from *Theory of Flight,* by Muriel Rukeyser.

After the lapse of a generation, I wish once again to thank Robert E. Grayson, librarian of the *New York Herald Tribune,* for providing me with access to its back files. That distinguished newspaper is now, unhappily, defunct. My gratitude once more goes to my wife for the critical care she lavished on my manuscript.

LEO GURKO

PREFACE TO THE PAPERBACK EDITION

T HE period from the stock market crash to Pearl Harbor was one of the liveliest and most dramatic in recent American history. This book is a social and literary account of that period, and seeks to capture its spirit through the chief historical and literary events.

The Angry Decade was first published in 1947. Returning to the book after twenty years, I remain in sympathy with its selective blending of literature and history, and reaffirm its conclusions. Some of my individual judgments have inevitably changed. I think better of Faulkner's *Sanctuary*, and less highly of Ellen Glasgow. That I could have compared Thomas Wolfe to Balzac and Dostoevsky seems to me preposterous. I should not now so exclusively equate Hemingway with a love of violence and a sense of life emptiness. Erskine Caldwell has faded from view, though he was a luminary of the 30's. I would have subdued the tone of his portrait had I the advantage of hindsight. The novels of Howard Fast and Albert Maltz are overpraised. Clifford Odets' play *Waiting for Lefty* was certainly thrilling to watch in the ambience of 1935, but it reads today like the crudest kind of left-wing propaganda. In chapter eight, I certainly should have mentioned the hysterical internment of the Nisei during World War II as an element in our attitude toward the Japanese enemy. By and large, however, there are no fundamental themes I would alter.

The 30's were preeminently our age of social consciousness. The crises of the time made this inevitable. The great depression, with thirteen million unemployed at its peak, forced a grudging awareness of the "dismal" science of economics and the economic process. Japanese aggression in Manchuria and China, the rise of Hitler and Nazism in Europe, destroyed the isolationist cocoon of the 20's and made the country unhappily conscious of foreign affairs. The phenomenal growth of the trade-union movement, encouraged by the New Deal and nurtured by such dynamic and charismatic leaders as John L. Lewis and Walter Reuther, turned labor for the first time in American history into a major force in public life and thus radically altered the power arrangements of the nation.

The domestic scene was dominated by the potent figure of FDR. He converted the governing process into an instrument of salvation for millions of his followers, and was so great a political virtuoso that he transformed politics itself into an art that riveted the attention even of the millions who disliked or were repelled by him. He did not eliminate unemployment. His policies were a success at some points, a failure at others. But as a dramatic spectacle, his performance in office was a smash hit everywhere. It proved irresistibly fascinating both to Roosevelt's numerous admirers and to his less numerous but no less passionately aroused detractors.

The attention of everyone was forced outward, away

from the private self, away from the intensely personal pursuit of excitement, pleasure, sex, or art that marked the 20's, to preoccupation with history, economics, politics, and collective action. The needs of the psyche were subordinated to the operations of society. Competition was a traditional sacred cow in America. Cooperation now began rivaling it as a working idea. All this was reflected in the literature. The decade began with *The 42nd Parallel* and ended with *The Grapes of Wrath*. John Dos Passos' first trilogy, *U.S.A.*, was a great literary "spectacular" of the 30's, an imaginative explanation of how the first thirty years of the century paved the way for the great collapse. The figures in *Tobacco Road* were seen against the rural Georgia slums they embodied. The early heroes of Thomas Wolfe began as radical individualists, wrapped up in an incessant, narcissistic contemplation of their own vitality and genius, but the later ones were forced out of themselves into their first tentative, painful collisions with the depression and fascism.

The 30's were the great creative years in Faulkner's career. *Sanctuary*, published at the beginning of the decade, works its way into the world of bootleggers, gangsters, brothels, and small-town criminal procedures. *The Hamlet*, at the end, introduces the Snopeses, those irresistible representatives of the new industrialism, soulless and commercialized, creeping over the face of the countryside like a swarm of resurrected Old Testament locusts. Even Hemingway was nudged out of the separate peace Tenente Henry had concluded with the first World War. For a time after *A Farewell to Arms*, that supreme tribute to isolationism and privacy that brought the 20's to their end, Hemingway continued to ply the trade of romantic individualism. Two of his books in the early 30's were, respectively, a manual on Spanish bullfighting and an account of a hunting trip in Africa. But by 1937 he had produced what amounted to a depression novel, *To Have and Have Not*, which concluded with the hero's dying plea for collective action. The plea was not convincing, a circumstance much less significant than the fact it was made at all. The Spanish Civil War completed the process of social involvement for Hemingway. In *For Whom The Bell Tolls*, at the conclusion of the decade, he registers his disillusionment with politics, both Loyalist and Franco-ist. But he does so only after a detailed analysis of political issues and an intimate confrontation with them.

Even the writers who began with a stylistic commitment to the private life and the interior consciousness found it hard to resist the pressure the 30's exerted upon them. Two of these in particular, Nathanael West and Henry Roth, did not appear in my original text. Regarded from the perspective of the 60's, they assume a greater significance than they possessed at the time. Early in the 30's, West came back from Paris, his head swimming with the new theories of surrealism. In 1933 *Miss Lonelyhearts* appeared, a masterful little exercise in hallucination. Its newspaper columnist is seen going slowly mad not only through psychotic images exploding in his brain but in the genuine breakup of the world he inhabits, the world of anger, misery, religious fanaticism, and despair pouring into him through the letters of his anguished readers. This was not the unreliable testament of a madman but a true account of the 30's on the nightmarish side. West broadened his account in *The Day of the Locust*, his last novel (1940). It was a Dantesque vision of Hollywood, populated with rampant egotisms in perpetual collision, climaxed by a riot at a movie premiere where a savage crowd of movie worshipers seek to devour the very stars they worship. America's breaking-up is West's unwavering theme, brilliantly rendered by the techniques of surrealism, itself devoted to the idea that the only meaningful act is the act of annihilation.

An equally powerful practitioner of surrealism was Henry Roth, whose single novel, *Call It Sleep*, came out late in 1934. It was well reviewed and instantly forgotten. It remained in limbo for thirty years and then was enthusiastically rediscovered. Roth shared West's conviction that the frenzy of the mind is an analogue of the cosmic frenzy. Here, the impressionable consciousness of an immigrant boy thrust into the ghettos of Brooklyn and the East Side progresses in visionary bursts that fuse his bruised feelings and palpitating senses with the equally bruised, equally palpitating kaleidoscope of the swarming New York life in the first decade of the century.

The novel, like its youthful hero, breaks out of the dark basements, the crowded streets, the railroad yards with their awesomely flashing third rails, to the rooftops, the high places, and finally heaven itself, where some renewed covenant with God is established. While the characters in West are either dying or dead, twitching automata going through their last uncontrollable spasms, Roth's are consumed by an excessive energy that drives them to explosive reaches beyond their finite selves. West's vitality resides in his imagination, Roth's in his story, yet both link the fevered mind and the fevered world into sequences of interpenetrating energy and meaning. In an age openly devoted to the documentary, the socio-political, the immediately factual apprehension, they record obscure psychological disturbances. But their presence lends the angry decade one of its most authentic grace notes.

The reader is asked to bear in mind that since the book was written in the mid-40's, some of the time references are those of that period, not the present. Also, a number of the people described as still alive and functioning have since died.

New York
1967

CONTENTS

OVERTURE

CERTAIN things spring to mind when the 1930's are mentioned: the depression, *Gone with the Wind*, the mellifluous voice of Franklin D. Roosevelt over the radio, *Anthony Adverse*, the rise of Hitler, *The Grapes of Wrath*. It was the decade of men selling apples on street corners and the Bonus March on Washington, of Benny Goodman and the jitterbugs, of the Dust Bowl, the T.V.A., and the great Ohio River flood. It saw the growth of the picture magazines and the phenomenal spread of *The Reader's Digest*. It was the decade of the New Deal, Huey Long, Technocracy, and the repeal of Prohibition.

The radio was one of the centers of the 30's. It broadcast operas, symphony concerts, and every variety of jazz to the far ends of the country. It sponsored the news analysts—H. V. Kaltenborn, Gabriel Heatter, Lowell Thomas, Edwin C. Hill, and Raymond Gram Swing—who brought the wide world into every man's home. Without it, Father Coughlin would not have reached his vast audience so quickly, and President Roosevelt would have lost one of his most powerful modes of communication. It made Bing Crosby and Bob Hope household names, and unfolded dramatic events like the abdication speech of King Edward VIII and the crises in Central Europe before the ears of millions. It launched "Information Please" and other quiz programs, the singing commercials, "Invitation to Learning," the soap operas, the experimental plays of the Columbia Workshop, Charley McCarthy, the town cries of Alexander Woollcott, the exciting new techniques of Norman Corwin and Arch Oboler, the Lone Ranger and Major Bowes.

As pervasive as the radio programs were the movies of the 30's, ranging from the vast outpouring of purely "escapist" and "entertainment" films to Pare Lorentz's *The Plough that Broke the Plains* and *The River*. It was the time when Walt Disney rose to prominence, George Arliss served as a one-man biographical guide to history, Shirley Temple assumed a special rôle as America's favorite child actress, and Dr. Kildare became the country's best-known physician. It was the period of *The Informer* and *It Happened One Night*, of Mae West and *Mr. Deeds Goes to Town*, of the newsreels and The March of Time, of the G-men and the gang leaders. It was the era of the filming of *Gone with the Wind*, when it seemed as though half the nation was absorbed in the pursuit of an actress to play Scarlett O'Hara. The talkies were perfected then, and technicolor introduced, the Nazis attacked and democracy consciously defended, horse operas and lush musicals produced in droves.

It was the era when pictures in *Life* magazine, condensed articles in the digest magazines, cartoons political and non-political, comic strips, spot broadcasts, quick documentaries, and inspirational books, provided the public with a tremendous number of shortcuts to a world which had grown too complicated in meaning and too accelerated in pace to be studied at leisure.

In literature, it was the age of John Steinbeck and Thomas Wolfe, William Faulkner and John P. Marquand, James Farrell, Erskine Caldwell, William Saroyan, Richard Wright. Proletarian fiction flourished during the 30's, as did the historical novel and the detective story, though they had their beginnings long before. *Tobacco Road* was the decade's longest-running play, Maxwell Anderson, Robert Sherwood, and Clifford Odets its most prolific playwrights. Carl Sandburg and Stephen Vincent Benét continued their respective poetic definitions of democracy. It was the time of *Winterset, U.S.A.,* and *For Whom the Bell Tolls, Life Begins at Forty* and *The Importance of Living,* the WPA writers' projects and the Group Theater. *The New Yorker* proceeded on its urbane and sophisticated way, as did its principal contributors, James Thurber and E. B. White, Robert Benchley and S. J. Perelman, with their several varieties of humor. Hart Crane committed suicide near the beginning of the decade, Edward Arlington Robinson died in the middle, and Archibald MacLeish abandoned poetry for political dispute toward the end. It was a period in literature when anger and whimsy. social significance of the heaviest sort and humor of the lightest, Studs Lonigan and Walter Mitty, flourished side by side.

II

From the crash of stock market prices in October, 1929, to the crash of bombs on Pearl Harbor in December, 1941, America endured twelve of the most turbulent years of her history. That they were years of high tension and social shock, of shrill clamor, of violent shifts in focus and sudden fractures in the fabric of the country, is abundantly evident. Their essential personality and the forces that impelled them are less so. The chroniclers of the period, among them the Beards, James Rorty, Louis Adamic, Gilbert Seldes, the Lynds, and Carey McWilliams, stress its frenzy and confusion. Yet it was also an age of buoyancy, of intermittent faith and spasmodic optimism. It passed from the despair of 1931-33 to the crusading hopes of the New Deal, from the struggle for economic stability at home to the war against fascism abroad. Frenzy and disorderliness were recurring overtones, but only overtones; they were not the themes or the substance.

Frenzy of a kind also marked the 20's, but at their base the two decades were quite different. Disillusioned by the first World War, the 20's spent themselves in the pursuit of their own great self-created illusion: that the problems of life could all be solved by the acquisition of enough money. To be sure, the articulate figures of the time did not think so. H. L. Mencken fostered the notion that life in America was stupid, Sinclair Lewis that life was drab, Ernest Hemingway that life was empty. The cul-

tural campaigns of the age warred against the "booboisie,"
against the Philistinism of Gopher Prairie, and sought new
sensations in French bistros and Spanish bull rings. But
the rebels and protesters, though they commanded a wide
audience, remained in the minority.

The critiques of the 20's, which were largely negative
in character, began aiming, in the 30's, at positive solu-
tions, at affirmations of various kinds, political in some instances, personal in others.[1] It was the era of Sandburg's
The People, Yes and Sherwood's *Abe Lincoln in Illinois*,
of Steinbeck's impassioned tales of the underprivileged and
Wolfe's pursuit of wind-grieved ghosts within the periphery of a loneliness without end. Spurred by disasters unknown to the 20's, it was no longer content with sum-
maries of life's shortcomings; it insisted on their elimination. The 30's wanted employment and peace, the employment that had been crippled by the depression, the
peace threatened by the Nazis. These were its twin passions; most Americans prized them above luxury, above
bigger and better mechanical gadgets.

If the economics of the decade made jobs the first
issue, its politics made peace the second. The Nye Munitions Committee, functioning in 1935, investigated prof-
iteering in munitions during World War I and did severe
damage to the shreds of surviving belief in the idealism
of that war. The Oxford Peace Pledge movement in England, binding British youth never to fight again, reverber-

---

[1] In the foreword to his *Intellectual America*, Oscar Cargill refers aptly
to the leading spirits of the two eras as "iconoclasts" and "shapers."

ated through the pro-peace youth groups of the United
States. But the peace movement was complicated by the
fact that Nazism, vastly more hideous than the old imperialism, was the growing enemy, thereby setting at odds
the experience of the past and the menace of the present,
and begetting a mass of political confusion by creating a
hostile counterpoint between the pacifist and anti-fascist
impulses.

It was indeed a decade of strange bedfellows, of jock-
eying for position, and intense opportunism. Between September, 1939, and June, 1941, the Hearst press, the Republicans, and the Communists were against intervention in
the European war, against Roosevelt and the "war-
mongers." At the same time *The New York Times* and
The New Republic were for all-out aid to England. In
1937, during one of the most serious of the business "recessions" that marked the Roosevelt Administration, the
Communists were accusing Roosevelt of budget-paring
and Wall Street of deliberately sabotaging the national
economy in order to discredit the New Deal. Hearst was
attacking Roosevelt for not paring the budget enough. The
Republicans were crying that private enterprise could no
longer endure New Deal regimentation. *The New York
Times* and *The New Republic* parted ways on the issue,
one moving to the right, the other treading gingerly to the
left. As the ultimate symbol of the reversals of that volatile
time, there stood John L. Lewis and his numerous peregri-
nations, from C.I.O. organizer in 1935 to Republican
campaigner in 1940, from self-proclaimed leader of Amer-

ican youth in 1937 to caller of coal strikes in 1943, with youth at the battlefronts.

It was a decade of preoccupation with foreign affairs, which served in the long run to siphon off discontent at home. Though Roosevelt's policies adrenalized American economy, American economic life did not improve essentially; moreover, it proceeded in leaps and jerks, sudden recessions alternating with abrupt advances. The illusion of prosperity was more real than prosperity itself. In this state of affairs, the growth of European fascism played an increasing psychological rôle once it became obvious that another world war was inevitable and that fascism was a manifestly greater menace even than hard times. Hence the extraordinary effect of the Spanish Civil War upon the American consciousness. This miniature prelude to World War II produced an enormous body of public debate, private polemics, reportage, and one extensive novel, *For Whom the Bell Tolls*, written by the great American fictional expert on war and violence.

The civil war in Spain dramatized also the confusions and contradictions produced at home by the mounting tensions in Europe. A Gallup poll taken in 1937 to sound out the American public on the question of Spain indicated that 65 per cent of those expressing an opinion sympathized with the Spanish republic, and wished for its success in the war against Franco; a year later, this percentage had risen to 75. Yet in 1937 the government of the United States extended the Neutrality Act to cover Spain and thus prevented the Spanish government from obtaining arms and supplies in America.

Sharp as was the impact of the Spanish war upon America, it was mild in comparison with the pressure of events in Europe between March, 1938, and September, 1939, the period that began with the last stages of the Austrian crisis, continued climactically through the Czech and Polish crises, and reached the final boil with the outbreak of the second World War. It was a day-to-day affair. The press and the radio gave minutely detailed accounts of events in Central Europe on what was at times an hour-to-hour basis. What Hitler said to Schuschnigg, the activities of the Austrian Nazis and Dr. Seyss-Inquartt, the rumors about German troop concentrations on the border, the *Anschluss* itself, the vast drama of Czechoslovakia with its Henleins, Runcimans, Beneses, and Neville Chamberlains intermingled in a nightmare kaleidoscope, the capitulation at Munich with its corollary farce of "Peace in our time," the seizure of Prague, and the dramatic events of the summer of 1939 revolving about Poland, dominated the American scene to such a degree that today it is difficult to remember what simultaneous events were occurring here at home. The questions of whether there would be another war and whether we could stay out of it became the issues of the moment, beside which all else paled. The fate of the millions of unemployed was temporarily forgotten, for their future, as well as that of their more fortunate countrymen, was being determined overseas.

With the outbreak of the war in Europe, there ensued

a kind of suspension of the national life, which even the debate in 1940 over the third term failed seriously to challenge. The country was more concerned over the fall of France than over the chances of Wendell Willkie, more over the coming German invasion of England than over the prospects of Roosevelt winning another easy victory. The debate over selective service, the appearance of Lend-Lease, the activities of the America First Committee, blotted out the purely domestic issues that had occupied the center of the national stage since the great crash. Tempers ran as high as ever but along different lines. It was evident that the program of America as the Arsenal of Democracy would temporarily solve the problem of unemployment in a more thoroughgoing way than any of the earlier pulmotor processes of the New Deal.

It was evident, too, from the re-election of Mr. Roosevelt that the chief ground swell of public opinion was in favor of continued intervention on the side of the Allies. While the America First Committee did a tremendous amount of campaigning during 1941, and Senators Wheeler and Nye a great deal of orating in the Senate, the bulk of the people, though lacking in spectacular media of communication, approved the naval convoying of our supply ships, the expansion of Lend-Lease, the occupation of Iceland, our assumption of firmness in the negotiations with Japan. 1941 was a year of shrill polemics which repeated in the debate on foreign affairs the astonishing formula of the 30's: the disagreement between the vocal, well-organized minority and the unorganized and relatively uncommunicative majority. It was the Landon-Roosevelt campaign all over again, where Landon received the support of 85 per cent of the newspapers and Roosevelt was elected by the greatest landslide in American history.

The America of 1941 was in some ways the Europe of 1939, a continent living not in the complexities of its present but in the uncertainties of the future. Few wanted war; nearly all felt it to be inevitable. Every speech of the President's was awaited with growing foreboding, and heard with relief when it did not bring the dread pronouncement. The isolationists received so wide a hearing not because they expressed the convictions of the majority but because they dangled before the public's eye the only comforting illusion of the day. It was good to hear from any source that we need not get involved even when it was becoming increasingly plain that nothing in the world could prevent it.

The shock of December 7 was not that we were at war but that the great blow came from Japan. The country was prepared for war with Germany, but for years had been lulled into believing that the Japanese would never dare attack us. It was the whole people as well as the occupants of Pearl Harbor who were caught off guard. But in the shock of that disaster a momentary unity seized the country, a phenomenon so novel that it deserves recognition as a sort of landmark to end the period that began with the crash of the great bull market.

III

The great bull market—that wave of the 20's which seemed at the time to be the eternal wave of the future as well. It has been the fashion to regard the boom as a disastrous period in American history, a calamitous era of false prosperity scarred by a vicious pursuit of Mammon. This theory, in the light of subsequent events, is as superficial as it is puritanical. We have a passion for moral judgments, and love to punish ourselves for our failures by regarding them as sins. But much of the prosperity of the 20's was not false but real, based as it was to a considerable degree upon an expansion of the productive capacities of the country.

As for the paper profits of the bull market, they were a brutally effective way of demonstrating one grave shortcoming of our economic life: the absence of any functioning system of checks and balances. Without a lid on speculation, without scrupulous investigation of security issues, there was little to prevent these cyclical market inflations in which the rich would become momentarily richer and the poor would be dazzled by the false prospect of escaping from their poverty. This unhealthy condition had long since been removed from American political life, which, in its triangular division of power and intricately devised control of each branch of the Federal government by the other two, has for more than a century and a half successfully prevented the appearance of tyranny and the usurpa-

tion of power by demagogues or oligarchs. This represented
sound forethought on the part of the founding fathers.
There had been no similar provision for the economic life
of the young republic, hence the lag of economic justice
behind political, hence the growing concentration of wealth
and its abuse. While elections became increasingly free,[2]
markets did not. While there have been hardly any political *coups d'état* in our history, there have been a great
many economic ones. Panics, bank failures on a huge scale,
periodic depressions, economic buccaneering on an epic
plane, the spread of monopolies and cartels, have coexisted
with a refreshing absence of political adventurism in the
Federal government and, the South apart, the careful preservation of the basic political rights of the people.

There had been steps taken toward the imposition of
legal checks upon this unregulated economic process: the
Interstate Commerce Commission was formed in 1887, and
the Sherman and Clayton Anti-Trust Acts were adopted
in 1890 and 1914. But the country's expanding economic
activities continued to outstrip the legal restraints upon
them. They became greatly inflated during the first World
War and swelled into the great speculative bubble of the
20's. With the crash and the paralytic despair that followed it, conditions grew ripe for the first time in American history for the establishment of a system of economic
controls similar in function to the political controls set up
after the Revolutionary War. In this sense, some of the

---

[2] With the gradual removal of such restrictions as property qualifica-
tions, indirect elections, race and sex bars.

legislative reforms of the New Deal, far from laying the groundwork of fascism, as John T. Flynn believes, introduced into the economic life of the country the same practices that had long governed its political life. The insurance of bank deposits, the supervision of the stock exchange, the right of workers to organize and bargain collectively, were primary elements in an economic Bill of Rights, and now, a decade later, are accepted as such by nearly everyone. The great bull market is to be seen in this perspective: it was the necessary prelude to a basic and durable change in the life of the nation. It was a disaster, but a disaster that led irresistibly to a constructive end.

To say only that much is to strip this vast phenomenon to its bald philosophical essentials. It says nothing of the agony and intensely involuted drama of a generation of human beings shaken from familiar moorings and groping their way toward what they hoped would be a new security, proceeding from depression to war with scarcely an interlude, scarcely a breathing spell to take hold of the present and assay the future. The decade of the 30's was uniquely one in which time outran consciousness, in which the sequential stages of depression and of reform appeared too rapidly to allow for accurate fathoming. Hence, the misery of the country was equaled only by its bewilderment. It was this mixture of wretchedness and confusion that helped induce the paralysis which seized America from 1930 to 1933, when the newspapers and President Hoover assured one another that things would get better any minute now, while the great bulk of the people sank into a lethargic despair from which they were drawn at last by the anxious hope with which they greeted in March, 1933, the advent of a new President.[8]

In 1930, nobody believed the slump was permanent, a conviction reinforced by occasional advances of the stock market and the usual unwillingness to accept the hard fact that standards of living were sinking. The country began pulling the blankets over its head and living in an atmosphere of hothouse unreality. These were years of anguish and illusion.

In March, 1933, a new President entered the White House and set into motion that intricate series of events known conglomerately as the New Deal. The whole country, like a huge ship capsized and half-gutted in a river bed,

[8] The feelings with which Mr. Roosevelt was greeted grew even stronger during his first year in office. Quincy Howe, in his *World Diary: 1929-1934*, describes one manifestation during the spring of 1934:

". . . the President's personal popularity had never stood higher. The following letter from the correspondence columns of the *New York World-Telegram* written by an anonymous C.W.A. worker who attended Secretary of the Treasury Woodin's funeral in the middle of May expressed the feelings of millions of inarticulate Americans at that time:—

" 'I sat in the church waiting to see him [Roosevelt] . . .

" 'I respected . . . Mr. Woodin as a superior man, but I must confess my attention was riveted on that phenomenal person who had made it possible for me to laugh, to speak up to my friends in full confidence of my potency as a provider, even to permit me to think of the possibility of marriage.

" 'The services were over. The congregation stood at attention as Mr. Roosevelt walked slowly up the steps and out the door. In reality I could see him no longer, but it appeared to me I could see him through the panels, walking back to his task to work new miracles.

" 'To him I am merely a figure on a sheet of statistics, but I shall always see him as one who, though a simple American, is yet more than a man.' "

was lifted from the orgy of wishful thinking that had endured for more than three years. As an uplifter of morale, there had been few movements like the New Deal in American history. It galvanized everyone by its furore of activity: it revived the banks, blanketed the country with codes and projects, poured floods of money into the pockets of people who had none and a very great deal into the pockets of those who had, paid farmers not to produce, supported students in college, channeled poolroom youth into the CCC camps, drew unemployed writers and painters into the WPA, and gave the starving a guarantee that they would not perish. Led by the President, with his famous "fireside chats," its spokesmen delivered encouraging and triumphant speeches over the radio. It created a great hustle-bustle, a vast to-do, and in the commotion and general uproar, the mood of the nation passed from the gloom of the Hoover era to an argumentative buoyancy which helped create the conviction that things had improved basically, though it was not yet clear that they had. These were the years of animation and reform. They came to an end toward the close of 1937.

Two events early in that year sealed off the highwater mark of the New Deal. The great campaign to pack the Supreme Court had raged for months and at last had been defeated. Though the President in the end had his way through resignations and fresh appointments, and the Court ceased to invalidate reform measures, it was apparent that he had reached the limit of revising the administrative structure of the country. The second catalytic event was the business recession, sharp enough to scare a great many people into believing 1929 was setting in again. The effect on the New Deal was profound: instead of boldly striking out again in further aggressive pump-priming, it drew in its horns, began shaving the Federal budget, approaching business as shrilly but with less assurance than before, and in general assuming the defensive. The crisis of the Spanish War, the ominous events in central Europe, the growing evidence of Japan's designs in China, accelerated this drawing-in process. Though Dr. New Deal (as Roosevelt himself referred to it) was not officially buried until the end of 1943, he was as good as dead by the end of 1937.

Early in 1938, the Austrian *Anschluss* ushered in that long series of crises which sputtered like a string of giant firecrackers until they exploded with a terrific roar on December 7, 1941. Those four years of growing involvement in foreign affairs were a prelude of tense waiting for the trial to come. In them, the Roosevelt-Willkie campaign of 1940 was as engulfed as the Roosevelt-Landon campaign of 1936 had been in the tidal wave of the New Deal.

The years 1929 through 1941 divide themselves into the triple sections of the depression, the New Deal, and the threat of war. The period began with the greatest of domestic crises and ended with the greatest of foreign crises; within the outer limits of these twin disasters, it ran the gamut of lesser extremes. It began under the aegis of Hoover and ended under that of Roosevelt. It began by believing that prosperity would return overnight of its own volition, and ended by feeling that if left to its own devices prosperity would never return. In foreign affairs, it began with suspicion of England, sympathy for Germany, amiability toward the Japanese, and marked hostility toward the Soviet Union; in twelve years each of these attitudes had been completely reversed. It was an age of interlocking currents and sudden tears in the social fabric, of strange alliances and frequent *crises de nerfs*. So much happened to it that the mere preservation of sanity was in some ways its most notable achievement, a tribute to the infinite capacity of human nature to absorb punishment. Like the Abbé Siéyès after the French Revolution, anyone who was asked what he had done during the 1930's could reply adequately, "I survived."

That in itself was a sufficient accomplishment.

1: THE CRASH AND THE END OF SATIRE

IN THE UNCLOUDED summer of 1929, the great millennium of peace and prosperity seemed to have arrived in America at last. People were clearly not in the mood for another war. They were reading *All Quiet on the Western Front* and *A Farewell to Arms*, disillusioned commentaries on the first World War. John Steinbeck, who was to become the great socially conscious writer of the coming period, had just made his literary début with *Cup of Gold*, a novel about Sir Henry Morgan, the buccaneer, which hardly anyone read. That may have been due partly to Sir Henry arriving at the melancholy conclusion that all his wealth and power had not been worth amassing, which must have struck the average reader in the summer of 1929 as romantically silly. That summer, too, had seen the appearance of another first novel, which made a far greater impact. It exploited no childish notions about the follies of materialism; its author had indeed a remarkable appetite for the solid things in life: food, people, self-fulfillment. It was an extraordinarily energetic though imperfect saga of the loneliness of the human soul. The book was Thomas Wolfe's *Look Homeward, Angel.*

1929 was also the year that witnessed the beginning of the conversion of Sinclair Lewis, the decade's great fictional satirist. His *Dodsworth*, published in that year, was almost the first important novel in American literature to display the virtues of the businessman and to suggest that the brave new world might be built by him. In seven years, Lewis's satirical cycle had swung about from the futility of George F. Babbitt to the usefulness of Sam Dodsworth.[1] *Dodsworth* and its hero did little to disturb the strong faith of most Americans in things as they were, and served to introduce the Lewis who, in the 30's, was to descend fretfully into weak apologetics for the very Main Streets he had once so aggressively denounced.

It was in the fall of 1929, too, that William Faulkner published another of his revolving novels, *The Sound and the Fury*, about the turgid decadence of a Southern family. If Lewis was retrenching, Faulkner very decidedly was not. If Lewis was turning about to protect the civilization he had been belaboring, Faulkner was whetting his knife to continue thrusting at its vitals. The effect was not particularly painful to the vast reading public of the North and West, to whom the South was a rather unreal place compounded of soft voices, mint juleps, and hot-tempered passion. Since terror is never very terrible when it happens to someone else, the public could be titillated by the pain and irony in Faulkner, while remaining, in its own mind

[1] Of course, Lewis had a considerable affection from the very beginning for some aspects of life on Main Street and for a variety of Main Streeters, but this affection tended to be recessive in the satirical novels of the 20's and first began growing dominant with *Dodsworth*.

at least, perfectly protected from them. But this was still the glazed season of 1929 when Faulkner had not yet developed from an *enfant terrible* to a slashing chronicler of a civilization which he found stagnant and dying.

It was also the season of *They Stooped to Folly*, as refined a study of the South as Faulkner's was rough. Ellen Glasgow, too, was aware of the deficiencies of her province but she was also aware of its virtues. This comedy of manners, like all her books, established a neat antithesis between the younger and older generations, between the spokesmen for Civil War gallantry and the spokesmen for the new freedom; the whole tableau, in the French classical style, exquisitely polished and formal. Miss Glasgow is cautious where Faulkner is bold, tentative where he is dogmatic, ladylike where he is uncouth. Her characters, like his, are quiveringly sensitive, but where his are forever plumbing the soft pulpy folds of their subconscious, hers are forever anatomizing their overt reflections and conscious memories. The figures in *They Stooped to Folly* are so many butterflies pinned to a mat, each in his symbolical place: Milly, the young rebel, having a baby out of wedlock for Love's sake; Martin, the young war casualty, tormented and confused; Mary Victoria, ruthlessly consecrated to Moral Uplift; Virginius, doubting yet clinging to the old tradition; his wife Victoria, good but not sensual; Mrs. Dalrymple, sensual but not good. The novel, elegant as a ballet, is a supreme tribute to the clarity Art can impose upon Life. The conclusion Miss Glasgow is forever arriving at, that there is something to be said for and against both sides, has the unsurprising vagueness of the glittering generality. *They Stooped to Folly* was decidedly one of the better literary things in life during the last summer of the 20's. It was pro-youth but not too pro-youth, satirical but not too satirical, and struck a nice balance between the sexes and generations. Poised and graceful, it was on the best-seller list in the early autumn.

II

On October 19 of that same autumn, the sluice gates of Wall Street began opening. On October 23, the flood of selling caused the whole price structure of the stock market to collapse with a record number of almost thirteen million shares unloaded. Several days later, a curtain opened on the turbulent decade to come with the climax of the strike trial in Gastonia, an event so blatantly unjust to the strikers that conservative newspapers editorialized against "class justice" making a mockery of the North Carolina judiciary. On October 27, the newspapers noted signs of Wall Street's recovery and credited President Hoover with allaying fear. But on October 29, one of the black days in American history, the bottom fell out of the market again with a new high of sixteen million shares traded. And on November 3, three books [2] were reviewed which, with significant unison, attacked the machine age. On the 17th of November the *New York Herald Tribune*

[2] They were *Our Business Civilization* by J. T. Adams, *This Ugly Civilization* by Ralph Borsodi, and *Dance of the Machines* by Edward J. O'Brien.

could still write that "Business is sound and prosperity remains. . . . The President's optimism and confidence are well-founded. . . . Fortunately the disturbance of today does not go deep into business fundamentals." This was how the crash seemed to the press and the country in November and December, 1929, and on through 1930 and 1931, with the vast bulk of the people nursing the illusion that good times were hovering around the nearest corner.

In March, 1930, during the first gyrations of wishful thinking about the crash, the public was being amused by the latest performance of H. L. Mencken. His *Treatise on the Gods*, the philosophical counterpart of *Elmer Gantry*, was an attack upon religion and the religious impulse, based on the familiar premise that men are spiritual cowards and hence must invent a God to bear for them the responsibilities of life. It was the sort of book that could be popular only during an era of material prosperity, for only then can a people afford to be amused by assaults upon their convictions and shibboleths. Mencken derided not only religion and religious institutionalism, but democracy and the masses as well. The American public, however, secure in its feeling that democracy under the aegis of Harding, Coolidge, and Hoover was working well, laughed at his wit and ignored his cynicism.

What was true of the 1920's was true even more conspicuously of that equally prosperous period two hundred years before, when Jonathan Swift was launching his even more violent satires against the England of the 1720's and the human species in general. Those bitter works, *A Mod-*

est Proposal and *The Drapier's Letters*, were read with amusement, and *Gulliver's Travels*, for all its bloodcurdling doctrine, was enshrined almost at once as a children's classic. Mencken, in the latest of his satires, remained, like Swift, a phenomenon of prosperity. With the depression, he retired to Baltimore, to the relative mildness of his inquiries into the American language, and the writing of his paneled autobiography. A satirical attack upon religion in 1932 or 1933 would have been simply pointless bad taste, for a country hungry and insecure was in no mood for laughter and even less inclined to tolerate an exposure of inadequacies all too painfully evident. Mencken, a superb master of the art of split-second public timing, withdrew from the scene at the very last graceful moment.

Not everyone, however, read the times so well. In September, 1929, Messrs. Woll and Green of the American Federation of Labor were publicly expressing worry over technological unemployment—six weeks before the beginning of the greatest period of non-technological unemployment in American history. Ramsay MacDonald, the British Prime Minister, was staking his belief in world peace on naval disarmament conferences. Aristide Briand was talking about the United States of Europe, and the British were announcing that they had lost their fear of submarines. American newspapers were saying that American prosperity was due not to luck but to our genius for taking advantage of favorable opportunities. In October, with MacDonald and President Hoover conferring on the banks of the Rapidan, the Jews were looking to the Prime

Minister for aid in the latest Zionist crisis, a process that kept repeating itself until the British quit Palestine. France was withdrawing the last of her troops from the Rhineland and beginning work on the Maginot Line. Professor Snedden of Columbia, by way of proving that politicians have no monopoly on error, was predicting that nursery schools were only a passing fad and that "the child's place is in the home until he is nine or ten."

The convictions of that year ran parallel courses in politics and literature. The average American was anti-war, and devoured Hemingway and Remarque. He looked naturally to the bankers and industrialists for leadership, and found Sinclair Lewis's Sam Dodsworth admirable. Despite Henry Ford, Bishop Cannon, and the Anti-Saloon League, the American was by and large against Prohibition and found the alcoholic literature of Hemingway and F. Scott Fitzgerald altogether palatable.

If his serious convictions were being epitomized in fiction, his lighter moods are to be traced in the best sellers on the non-fiction list. These were headed by the crackerbarrel humor of Chic Sale in *The Specialist* and what passed for crackerbarrel humor in Calvin Coolidge's *Autobiography*. Abbé Dimnet, in *The Art of Thinking*, was teaching the American how to think in a few easy lessons, just as ten years later Mortimer J. Adler was to teach him how to read in a few somewhat harder ones. He was conquering new worlds with Richard Halliburton, learning how to perfect his contract bridge from the experts, storming Olympus with William Bolitho in *Twelve Against the*

Gods, and reliving the triumphs of Eddie Cantor in his *Caught Short,* the inevitable memoir of the successful entertainer.

The American of 1929 was an admirable fellow, with a large capacity for enjoying life. There was room in his experience for the most searching satire upon himself which he took without malice and with relatively unclouded laughter. If he lived in a fool's paradise and nursed illusions, they were at least the right illusions. He believed, as had the eighteenth century, that man was a reasonable animal, had learned the last of his bitter lessons in the first World War, and was now on the final lap of creating a just and abundant society. The problem of bread was already solved; the problem of war was on the verge of solution. There was no limit to the intense dazzle of the millennium directly ahead. Belief in the idea of progress and the good life was never stronger. If the Arabs were slaughtering Jews in Palestine, if there was labor trouble in Gastonia, if William B. Shearer was suing certain shipbuilding firms for back pay incident to his services as a propagandist against naval disarmament at the Geneva Disarmament Conference in 1927, if one had to flout the law by frequenting speak-easies and patronizing bootleggers—well, these were minor irritations in a world that was essentially on the right track. It is easy to label the American of that period as an empty and egotistical materialist. But he was not a gourmandising decadent, feasting on rich food, swilling rare drinks, pursuing new sensations, like the Romans before the fall. There was no "after me the

deluge" feeling. His materialism was benevolent and for-
ward-looking, previsioning a future that would engulf
everyone in a tide of lasting prosperity. His heart was in
the right place, even though the specific things he lived by
gave off the wrong glitter: radios, automobiles, chromium
kitchens, brass plumbing, stocks and bonds, and real estate.
Even Babbitt, that representative symbol of the 20's, had
a dim perception of values beyond the appetites of the moment and made a few vague but perceptible gestures in
the direction of a better world.

The oversimplification of our judgment of the American of 1929 grew in direct ratio to the intensity of the depression. The deeper it became the more odious and superficial he seemed. Today, it is possible to see him in more
accurate perspective: more naïve than odious, more dizzy
with success than soulless. Bernard DeVoto in his *The
Literary Fallacy* argues that literature is a false index to its
times.[3] Yet Babbitt and Will Kennicott remain uncannily
accurate portraits of the average American of the 20's,
with his personal warmth and vague benevolence as well as
his Philistinism.

At best, materialism was only a thick crust which
served to cover the times in the eye of history. Beneath
this crust were millions of Americans whose lives had no
connection with the boom, to whom the stock market and

[3] But he himself had unintentionally disproved this point of view in his
novel, *We Accept with Pleasure*, which appeared ten years earlier. That book
was an accurate index to its time and place, upper class Boston in the post-
war 20's, with its characteristic moods and experiences.

the ecstasy of swift riches were only phrases in the press. The vast rural population, sequestered in the remote regional areas of the country, New England, the backwoods of Kentucky and Tennessee, the mountains of Arkansas, the unending plains before the Rockies, were no more hedonistic or moneygrubbing than they had been a century before. To them as to many others even in the great cities, the problems of living were as baffling and unchanged as ever. Loneliness, the aching of the soul, the mystery of the universe, while invaded by science and in part illumined by psychiatry, had not loosened their grip on human nature. In an essay on Flaubert, Edmund Wilson remarked that merely to have the right political opinions is not enough to solve the difficulties of existence. One might add as a comment on the 20's that merely to have enough money is not enough to solve them either. Neither a large bankroll nor a formulated political philosophy *per se* transfers one to the Elysian fields of this earth, as the 20's believed in the case of the first and the 30's in the second.

III

If the America of Gopher Prairie, of the fat boys and the big money, was being defined by Sinclair Lewis and John Dos Passos, the America underneath the materialist crust was being fiercely recorded by Thomas Wolfe in the first of his soul journeys in search of an end to solitude. So intense was the blaze of *Look Homeward, Angel* that it pierced to some degree even the benevolent smugness of

1929. With all its shortcomings, it was the nearest thing to a literary thunderbolt in the twentieth century. The grandioseness of the book was in itself breath-taking. Wolfe sought to capture not merely infinity in space (for what else can one call his huge assemblage of ravines, mountains, cataracts, and plains of the American continent?) but infinity in time as well.

"Each of us is all the sums he has not counted: subtract us into nakedness and night again, and you shall see begin in Crete four thousand years ago the love that ended yesterday in Texas.

"The seed of our destruction will blossom in the desert, the alexin of our cure grows by a mountain rock, and our lives are haunted by a Georgia slattern, because a London cutpurse went unhung. Each moment is the fruit of forty thousand years. The minute-winning days, like flies, buzz home to death, and every moment is a window on all time."

He wrenched from the subcellars of consciousness the memories of earliest time, natal and prenatal, seeking out even the sensations of the month-old Eugene Gant surrounded by adult ogres in the miasmic world of infancy. But nothing so clearly indicated the profoundly agitated life under the shell of prosperity than the novel's projection of the loneliness and sorrow of the human soul, the ceaseless quest for friends, brotherhood, love, and the sense of belonging. That these things remained beyond the grasp of young Gant, and convincingly so, was a significant indication that the boom, for all its magnitude, remained dissociated from the emotional dislocations of the time.

Though *Look Homeward, Angel* was filled with bombast, wordiness, verbal egotism, in it Wolfe expressed his feelings in a prose that had not been heard since Melville. He restored to American writing what had been lacking since the days of *Moby Dick:* luxuriance and a sense of splendor.

"He brought back the width of the desert; the vast yellow serpent of the river, alluvial with the mined accretions of the continent; the rich vision of laden ships, masted above the sea-walls, the world-nostalgic ships, bearing about them the filtered and concentrated odors of the earth, sensual negroid rum and molasses, tar, ripening guavas, bananas, tangerines, pineapples in the warm holds of tropical boats, as cheap, as profuse, as abundant as the lazy equatorial earth and all its women; the great names of Louisiana, Texas, Arizona, Colorado, California; the blasted fiend-world of the desert, and the terrific boles of trees, tunnelled for the passage of a coach; water that fell from a mountain-top in a smoking noiseless coil, internal boiling lakes flung skywards by the punctual respiration of the earth, the multitudinous torture in form of granite oceans, gouged depthlessly by canyons, and iridescent with the daily chameleon-shift beyond man, beyond nature, of terrific colors, below the un-human iridescence of the sky."

Wolfe, like Melville, lifted literature to the realm of metaphysics, raising the great questions of the meaning of existence and man's place in the universe. This is why Eugene Gant is a kind of *Übermensch*, oversized spiritually as well as physically, too large for Altamont (Asheville) and

Old Catawba (North Carolina), not understood by the mortals who surrounded him. He, more than the table-thumping chest-beaters of Jack London, is the indigenous American superman, as large and sensual as the country itself. To be sure, he is the superman still adolescing but his Gargantuan appetite for love and food is already matched by his Gargantuan capacity for suffering, and the lineaments of his maturity are already plain.

The cultist idolaters of Wolfe tended to see only his superhumanism, his detractors only the adolescence. Actually his canvas was so wide-sweeping and his energy so carnivorous that one can find in him fuel for any thesis. From one angle, he was a sort of literary Nazi: a hot mixture of energism, mysticism, egocentrism, repetitious cascades of words that blot out sense (like the speeches of Hitler), anti-Semitism, anti-Negroism, anti-feminism. This is probably what the Nazis thought they saw when they made him their favorite contemporary American author and lionized him during his stay in Germany, where he went to spend the royalties from the German translation of his books. Yet he was also a Sinclair Lewis of sorts, satirizing materialism in the deep South. Like Dos Passos, he caught the rhythm of American life. Like Sandburg, he had a passion for the physical vastness of the country. Like Fitzgerald, he was the melancholy apostle of a sad lost youth. Violence, gruesomeness, and sensuality magnetized him, as they did Hemingway. But the wonder of being alive, the cosmic loneliness of all of us, exhaled in torrents of words, were the particular ingredients of Wolfe, filling every pore of *Look Homeward, Angel.*

The novel dispels the easy illusion that during the boom people in America did nothing but play the stock market, patronize bootleggers, and go in for fads like mah jong and crossword puzzles. If Gilbert Seldes' estimate that no more than two and a half million people were involved in the stock market at its peak is correct, then *Look Homeward, Angel* is as accurate a guide to the America of its time as the newspaper headlines, the "flapper" cartoons, and the movies of "flaming youth."

The life of a country is a series of changing surfaces and shifting accents. The emotions do not change, their overt expressions do. It is when the outward aspects of things are mistaken for their essence that errors in judgment are bred. This happened to the America of 1929, whose surface gyrations were mistaken for the substance, and has, as a consequence, received so bad a press during the past fifteen years. The stock market was only an overt symbol of the time, an institution actively involving a relatively small section of the country, and by no means the chief index to the lives of the great bulk of the people (especially those who were already beginning to suffer from the unemployment swell that set in as early as 1927), and the millions of villagers and small-towners to whom Wall Street was, if anything, a symbol of iniquity. Since they were less inundated by floods of bonds, coupons, refrigerators, and automobiles, the lineaments of their inner lives were more discernible. They suffered, lusted, procreated, were lonely, endured humiliations, escaped into the fantasies so richly provided by the movies and radio, and in general sweated through the toilsome process of learning how to live and how not to live with one another, as do most generations always. If the external events, the press, the economics of 1929, show us the pneumatic outlines of the boom, the literature of that year, Bernard DeVoto to the contrary, is a main avenue of entry into the nation teeming beneath the surface symbolism. Ellen Glasgow and Sinclair Lewis, and, on a larger scale, William Faulkner and Thomas Wolfe, all of whom wrote novels of considerable importance in the months immediately preceding the crash, should reduce the temptation to facile pigeonholing. Though they are not free of exaggeration and caricature, they create an intriguing mosaic of America on the edge of the great calamity that introduced the new decade.

2: PROSPERITY AROUND THE CORNER

IN A SCUFFLE, sometimes a man will receive a serious blow on the head which, in the heat of combat, he does not feel. Days and weeks may pass, and all will seem well. Roughly speaking, this was the state of the country in 1930 and 1931. In the fall of 1929 it had suffered a grave shock, but its conduct during the next two years was predicated on the belief that the shock, to begin with, was inconsequential and in any event would soon wear off. This is the unanimous testimony of the historians of the time. Reactions in Middletown,[1] for example, were standard:

"Middletown entered 1930 prepared for the best. There had been a stock-market crash to be sure but . . . local bankers were predicting a boom in the spring. . . .

"One of the most illuminating aspects of this early period of the depression was the reluctance of Middletown's habits of thought to accept the fact of 'bad times' . . . one does not like to admit that the techniques and institutions which one uses with seeming familiarity and nice control are really little-understood things capable of

[1] Muncie, Indiana; the fictional name used by Robert S. and Helen M. Lynd in *Middletown* and *Middletown in Transition*, their two famous studies (1929 and 1937) of a typical middle-sized American community.

rising up and smiting one. The local press . . . became
. . . a conscious and unconscious suppressor of unpleasant evidence. Hopeful statements by local bankers and industrialists . . . tended to make the front page, while
shrinkages in plant forces and related unhappy news commanded small space on inside pages or were omitted entirely."

Optimism at any price appears to be an ineradicable
part of our national temperament. Our convictions still
stem from the days when we gave beads to the Indians in
exchange for priceless land, when we were conquering the
rich frontiers, when we were separating Mexico and Spain
from slices of their territory, when we defeated the Kaiser's
Germans, and during the 20's launched one of the greatest campaigns of high-pressure salesmanship in history.
Since, in the physical sphere, our past has registered an
unbroken series of victories, we look even disasters in the
face and deny them. Our defeats, being solely in the realm
of morals and ideas, linger less acutely in our conscious
minds, though they do at times fill us with uneasiness. The
slave trade, the slave society of the South, the whole fes-
tering Negro problem today (in the North as well as the
South), have lain and do lie heavily on the conscience of
the country and assuredly represent great defeats in the
sphere of morals and ideas. The War to end Wars, though
it vanquished our enemies on the field of battle, was a
debacle as far as the issues for which we fought were concerned. Yet these experiences had little effect on our tendency to euphemize and call misfortunes by other names.

When the depression came, it took us two years to acknowledge its existence and three to recognize its seriousness. The dodges and rationalizations employed to conjure away the depression, to call it by other names, and dissolve it by means of Mr. Hoover's conferences and cheery editorials in the newspapers,[2] taxed the ingenuity of the human mind. They are fully recorded in Frederick Lewis Allen's *Lords of Creation* and Gilbert Seldes' *The Years of the Locust.*

What is significant in this is not so much that America fled from the bitter truth, as that such flight was a logical result not only of our entire historical experience but of the attitudes established during the period immediately preceding, the period of the 20's. A generation so nourished was inexorably bound to retreat, once life grew harsh. It has been the fashion to regard with amusement or contempt the moral cowardice of Americans during the last years of Hoover's administration, but it was human nature, not alone the nature of Americans, that was on trial. All peoples, from the ancient Jews, Greeks, and Romans to our own, have demonstrated the same incapacity to acknowledge disaster when it first appears. If it took all of three years, from the stock market crash to the election of Roosevelt, for the country to react in some positive way to its misfortunes—three years of spiritual stagna-

---

[2] The anti-depression hocus-pocus in the newspapers reached its climax when on the opening of the professional baseball season in the spring of 1931, the *New York Herald Tribune* wistfully regarded the crowds attending opening day as a sign that business would soon improve, "since baseball has always been a good barometer of trade."

tion—the time-passage was by no means extreme, considering the intensity of the boom and the violence of the depression. James Rorty [3] may have been disturbed by the apathy of 95 per cent of the people at the time, their willingness to sink into a state of morbid helplessness, but if this was a calamity, it was not a permanent one, and disappeared with the coming of the New Deal. What we see in all this is a universal behavior pattern that symbolizes the conduct of humanity under similar circumstances, different only in the exaggeration with which America, because of its physical youth and sentimental optimism, invests all its reactions to experience.

The aberrations, futilities, and fads of 1930-32 indicate the state of the public mind, waiting for the coming of a savior or the appearance of some quick and absorbing escape. In the winter of 1929-30, there was a revival of faith in the bankers and big businessmen as the repositories of wisdom and stability, as the stock market made a few short, intermittent recoveries. But its final collapse in May, 1930, weakened the confidence that the industrial barons had amassed since the beginning of the century. The impulse to hero-worship was left without an object and did not find one until the advent of Franklin D. Roosevelt.

[3] In his book *Where Life is Better*, he says, "I encountered nothing in 15,000 miles of travel that disgusted and appalled me so much as this American addiction to makebelieve. Apparently, not even empty bellies can cure it. Of all the facts I dug up, none seemed so significant or so dangerous as the overwhelming fact of our lazy, irresponsible, adolescent inability to face the truth or tell it."

In the meantime, a variety of small passions rushed into the breach. There was the miniature golf fad that raged for a whole six months in 1930. When this expired, the great hue and cry of technocracy arose, which threatened for a time to create hero-worship for a new class of saviors, the engineers and industrial managers, dressed up now as "technocrats." The technocrats were the very latest type of captains of industry, spruce and streamlined. They were the statisticians, the efficiency experts, who were presumably to create what James Burnham was to call ten years later "the managerial revolution." They proposed to rationalize our economic system, parceling out capital and labor the way grocers do canned goods, meshing production and distribution units with the neat finality of a graph. But with industry at sixes and sevens, and no machinery available for the transfer of power to the engineers, the technocrats remained paper theorists, and technocracy one of the many doldrum dreams of those unhappy years.

The chief intellectual controversy of that season was the furore over New Humanism,[4] initiated by Irving Babbitt and Paul Elmer More, a pair of academicians who performed a skillful surgical operation upon Puritanism, detached it from its formal theology, and publicized it under a new name. Where the old humanism of the Renaissance, best symbolized by Erasmus, sought to liberate all impulses of the human spirit, sensual and intellectual, the New Humanism believed in the mortification of the

[4] Signaled by the publication of *Humanism and America*, edited by Norman Foerster, in February, 1930.

flesh, a process which it euphemized as "the inner check," and pivoted on the theory that man was a dual personality with a higher or rational self and a lower or animal self. This distrust of the senses owed a good deal to Plato, and the philosophy as a whole was a kind of eclectic fusion of Plato, with his love of the intellect, and Calvin, with his flagellating scorn of the body. The movement passed into high gear as a reaction against the fleshpots of the 20's, and came to wide public notice in time to dramatize the depression. The New Humanists were urging a tightening-of-the-belt policy of the spirit at the very moment that economic deflation was beginning to mortify the national flesh.

Though Babbitt and More had been arguing their case for years, it is significant that they did not receive a widespread hearing until 1930. That a close relationship existed between the stock market crash and the emergence of long obscure movements of aggressive change in morals and conduct, like New Humanism, appears evident. The forces that integrated into the same web phenomena as outwardly diverse as New Humanism, technocracy, and miniature golf, may not be visible to the naked eye, but these symptoms of the impulses to change and escape were products of the same profound national experience and were details in the same mosaic.

New Humanism remained popular about as long as miniature golf. It was a cheerless program at best, and suffered from the pointedly cheerless styles of Babbitt and More. Moreover, it compelled men to accept the ascetic life as a permanent condition. Though in a crisis men may be willing to endure hard times, they will do so only on the promise of good times to come. That promise may be fulfilled in the world to come, as Christ indicated, or it may be fulfilled in this, as political leaders have sworn since politics began, but the promise must be made. New Humanism made no such promise; hence it flared only at a moment when, after the ten-year spree of the boom, asceticism and the purely intellectual life seemed attractive, and then simmered away into an item on the agenda of graduate courses in criticism and philosophy. But it serves as an illuminating symbol of how a country in a state of growing collapse will pay heed even to movements that go against the very grain of its nature.

The predictions [5] and peccadilloes of the time were equally illuminating. On February 16, 1930, Henry Ford, the mechanical genius of the mass-production age, made two of his characteristic prophecies: that the Machine Age was about to become the greatest creator of jobs in history, and that Prohibition would be increasingly enforced and alcohol would soon become an industrial commodity only. On February 9, Senator Edwards called on New Jersey Democrats to end Hague rule. On March 2, Governor Franklin D. Roosevelt of New York made a plea for Home Rule [6] as the nation's salvation. On March 8, President

---

[5] These were collected in a book by Edward Angly, amusingly entitled *Oh Yeah*.

[6] The theory that states and municipalities should solve their own problems without calling on the Federal government for help.

Hoover reported a gain in employment and asserted that the crisis was past. Republican newspapers were claiming that "pessimism about unemployment . . . was being generated for political effect . . . and that Hoover's leadership was brilliant and effective." On July 1, the President stated that the depression was being relieved by construction. Pierre Laval became Premier of France early in 1931, an event generally approved by the American press on the grounds that "M. Laval brings an unusually winning personality to his new job." By April 3, the depression had become so fixed a part of the daily landscape that New York rabbis were already predicting a new Moses who would be along soon to end it. King Alfonso of Spain abdicated on April 16, and the experts were saying that "the present Spanish situation will be clarified with exceptional rapidity and success." In September, England went off the gold standard, an event which had serious financial repercussions in America. But on November 2, an editorial in the *New York Herald Tribune* stated: "The end of last week gave many signs of marking a turn in the economic tide, justifying President Hoover's optimistic statement of Friday."

The Nazis won some victories in the provincial legislatures early in November, prompting this choice American editorial comment: "In one way the Nazi arrival in power is to be welcomed, for a period in office with its attendant responsibilities seems now the only way in which the Hitler bubble can be pricked."

On January 17, 1932, Mark Sullivan, the columnist,

was saying that an open quarrel between Al Smith and Franklin D. Roosevelt would eliminate both from the race for the Democratic nomination. On July 1, at the very moment that Roosevelt was being nominated after an open quarrel with Smith, Hoover was signing a bill cutting $160,000,000 from the Federal budget and asserting that more Federal saving was needed to combat the depression. In the same month John Dewey uttered the definitive comment on the two party platforms and the campaign to follow:

"Here we are in the midst of the greatest crisis since the Civil War and the only thing the two national parties seem to want to debate is booze."

And as late as 1932 the leaders of the American Federation of Labor were opposing unemployment insurance on the grounds that it was un-American.

What is amazing in all this is not that men are unable to gauge the future, but that people continue to place faith in experts who misgauge it so unfailingly. The assumption that success in the material sense is synonymous with wisdom is common to every society, democratic or otherwise. Thirty years of Henry Ford and his unique performances in the field of prophecy have placed no damper on American belief in the prescience of its leaders. Nor is there much reason to think that the unbroken record of wrong guesses made by the experts in the second World War has in any way reduced the exquisite gullibility of our people.

Naturally enough, that gullibility was most intense during the three years now under consideration. The impulse to grasp at any straw was equaled only by the impulse to cling in desperation to old habits. Part of the country believed confusedly with President Hoover that the surest way to save the country was to imitate the techniques of the Puritan pioneers: reduce costs, tighten belts, close all the windows, bolt the shutters, and generally make oneself as small and inconspicuous a target as possible for the slings and arrows of misfortune. Politically, this took the form of cutting the budget, holding frequent conferences with the leaders of commerce and labor, issuing periodic statements that prosperity was just around the corner, declaring moratoria on foreign debts, praying, suggesting to factory owners that they not lower wages, and trusting that the system would get back on an even keel of its own volition. This program was attractive to a great many people because it involved them in the least possible effort and encouraged them to keep moving in familiar, hence more or less comfortable grooves.

As clamorous, though not as numerous, on the other side, were those who were confusedly convinced that more radical means were required. These included persons as oddly assorted as the technocrats, the Communists, the Southern Agrarians, the small-town primitives who regarded Wall Street as the fountainhead of all evil, the advocates of a vast program of public works, the partisans of industrial unionism, and an amorphous mass who had no specific ideas or allegiances but who were certain that something had to be done. Huddled in between were an indeterminate number of people who simply suffered and, engulfed in a misery the nature of which they did not understand, waited for the Gods or the Fates or Chance or Somebody to get the national economy moving again.

II

In the meanwhile, the country saw more movies, listened more frequently to the radio, and did a great deal of reading.

The movies supplied every conceivable type of entertainment, a great deal of it based on novels and plays. The period from 1930 to 1932 was one of the most distinguished of the decade on the screen. There were the war pictures: *Hell's Angels, All Quiet on the Western Front, Journey's End,* and *A Farewell to Arms;* sophisticated comedies like *Private Lives* and *The Animal Kingdom;* serious dramas on the order of *Anna Christie* and *Strange Interlude.* There were extravaganzas like Cecil B. deMille's *The Sign of the Cross,* and a considerable crop of gangster movies, of which the most prominent were *The Big House, Public Enemy,* and *Little Caesar.* Tarzan made his début in the talkies as did Frankenstein's monster and Mae West (in *Night after Night*). Will Rogers was playing in *A Connecticut Yankee* and the three Barrymores in *Rasputin and the Empress. Arrowsmith* was on display, as was Charlie Chaplin in *City Lights.* There were a good many sentimental films on the order of *The Champ* and a few socially conscious ones like *I Am a Fugitive from a Chain Gang*. The movies offered something for almost every mood, a thematic variety made all the more refreshing by the novelty of the talkies, improving now with nearly every film.

The radio programs of the depression years were somewhat less varied in content and appeal. The famous comedians of the 30's, Bob Hope, Jack Benny, Fred Allen, Edgar Bergen, Burns and Allen, were not yet in evidence, nor were the better-known news analysts. Bing Crosby was still to come, as were the technical experimenters and playwrights, Corwin, Oboler, and Orson Welles. Major Bowes and his Amateur Hour were still in the offing, as were the noted political orators. President Hoover was making numerous radio appearances, few of them magnetic. The Variety Program was being developed by Rudy Vallee, the most popular crooner of the early 30's. The favorite soap opera was Myrt and Marge, the favorite comic program, Amos and Andy (which had started in 1929). The first world-wide news broadcast was heard in 1930, the first radio forum in 1932. But on the whole, the great period of the radio was still ahead.

What the country was reading was a rich indicator of how it felt and the texture of the world in which it thought itself to be living. Apart from the usual barrage of light romances and "escape" literature—which never lose their popularity and never cease being endlessly produced—certain tendencies that were later in the 30's to burgeon into dynamic life made their appearance. The decade's interest in historical fiction became manifest with the appearance in 1930 of Kenneth Roberts' *Arundel*, supplemented in the area of historical biography by the almost simultaneous publication of John Corbin's *The Unknown Washington*. The 30's witnessed a strong curiosity on the part of Americans about their past, a curiosity that produced a tremendous cascade of historical novels, culminating, in size at least, in *Gone with the Wind*, and historical biographies of which Lloyd Lewis's *Sherman*, Douglas Southall Freeman's *Lee*, and Marquis James's *Jackson* were the most striking examples.

The reason for this was fairly plain. A decade that witnessed the capitalist system shaking from self-delivered blows, that lived through the abandonment of traditions as old as the country itself, that saw its relations to the outside world growingly determined by the spread of fascism, was driven by the very momentum of these experiences to an examination of itself and its national roots. That is why the historical novel was not merely a drug to carry the reader out of an unbearable present; it was in the profounder sense an instrument of rediscovering national self-belief which, as a result of the economic collapse, had become dangerously weakened. In a thousand tales of the Revolution and the Civil War, the idea that America had endured crises even worse than the depression was drummed home. Successful exploits were recounted again and again; an affirmation of what the country had once done was the almost unvarying theme. All this was, of course, calculated to restore public morale and induce the people to take courage for the future from the triumphs of the past.

Arundel was a case in point. It described the campaign of Benedict Arnold against Quebec, during the early months of the Revolutionary War, in detail so colorful and on a canvas so magnified that it stimulated the reader's sense of patriotism. The fact that the campaign collapsed in no way diminished the valor of the American soldier, nor did it deflate pride over the heroic deeds of our colonial forbears. But this was not mere fatuous jingoism. The strategic errors, the motley nature of the American army, the egotism and corruption that went on behind the scenes, were unrestrainedly exposed. If the final residue of the novel was admiration, it was an adult admiration, founded on an adult view of the events of the story. The Pollyanna era in American history and historical fiction was distinctly over, and no chronicle of early America was henceforth to be governed by flagwaving of the old kind. The 30's shook what saccharinity remained from pre-World War I days out of American literature, and nowhere more thoroughly than from the historical novel. It was, for example, quite inconceivable for such historical novels as were written prior to 1914 to have had as heroines women as self-seeking and unprincipled as Scarlett O'Hara. Certainly the characters of Kenneth Roberts, whether sophisticated Tories like Oliver Wiswell or naïve egotists like Major

Rogers, are free of that false romanticism which seeks to make human nature in books better than it is in life.[7] This process of maturation was distinctly the product of the times. If the first World War disillusioned the American people with political shibboleths, the depression shook their faith in economic ones. These successive disillusionments had a tremendous effect on the outlook of writers vis-à-vis their readers; it made them, for a long time to come, disaffected with sweetness and light and more inclined to examine everything skeptically, as, since the days of Socrates, most civilized men have examined their experiences.

Simultaneously with the fresh awakening of interest in American history came a revival of concern for the American Indian.[8] Oliver La Farge's *Laughing Boy*, which was a notable literary event in 1930, headed a considerable stream of literature sympathetic to the Indian, culminating toward the end of the decade in Howard Fast's *The Last Frontier*. This belated desire to do justice to our pre-Mayflower residents was a symptom of the lacerations which the country was enduring. Misery is an irresistible common denominator. Like other catastrophes, the depression thrust its assorted victims into a common pool. Those who lost

[7] Though Mr. Roberts' recent book, *Lydia Bailey*, has a heroine who is certainly too good for this sinful world. His heroes, however, continue to be credible.

[8] As far back as the 1880's, Helen Hunt Jackson had been protesting the injustices done the Indian in noted books like A *Century of Dishonor* (1881) and *Ramona* (1889). Later writers, like Mary Austin and John G. Neihardt, also wrote sympathetically of the Indian.

their money or their jobs began seeking company, and vicarious forms of escape. The movies supplied them with drug dreams of better times. The slick magazines behaved as though the world had come to a dead stop in the summer of 1929, and nothing had occurred since. Over the radio could be heard the long "my baby and me" song cycle designed to prove that love was the cure for everything. And literature was discovering the American Indian, the worker, the regionalist, and the young couple adrift in hard times.

Laughing Boy projected the conflict between Indians and whites in a manner wholly uncomplimentary to the whites. It was a lively story, and appeared at a time when the public was ready to pay off old debts and repair ancient injustices. The Noble Savage tradition of the eighteenth century experienced a brief rebirth. Now that the whites were suffering, their historical orientation began to change, and the Indian, far from remaining an ignorant and dispensable savage, became simply a fellow victim of the misfortune that attends all life. The novel, by suggesting how difficult it is for an Indian trained in white ways to fuse the two civilizations, was pleading the cause of cultural pluralism. At first glance it would seem that quite another thesis was being propagated: the idea of racialism and the incompatibility of different peoples. But La Farge was arguing not that Indians and whites cannot co-exist in the same country without irreconcilable conflict, but that such co-existence was possible only on a basis of mutual respect and tolerance. As with the Negroes and whites, the issue was not whether intermarriage or cultural interfusion could be successful, but whether each culture could work out its own folkways and destiny without interference from the other. This is the doctrine of cultural pluralism, as indigenous as any principle in the democratic pattern. This, ultimately, was the nuclear tenet of *Laughing Boy*, and the main historical reason for its impact in 1930 and 1931, when democracy was undergoing one of its most searching re-examinations.

III

At the same time, though from a wholly different orientation, the context of American society was being minutely inspected in *The 42nd Parallel*, the first volume in John Dos Passos' *U.S.A.*, a trilogy designed to seize nothing less than the whole rhythm of American life. For this colossal undertaking, revolutionary implementation was necessary, and Dos Passos invented lavishly to advance his design. First, he created the newsreel technique. This device, bristling with headlines from the events of the day and thumbnail biographies of leading historical personages, moved about to suit the changing incidents of the story. Then came the ingenious Camera Eye which assembled a multitude of details in the same pattern. The Camera Eye on the subway in *The 42nd Parallel*, for example, hooked together in the same sequence snatches of conversation from a variety of passengers to create an effect of the complex and multitudinous skein of living and talking going on simultaneously everywhere. Armed with these fresh tools, Dos Passos began working his way through the entanglements of the American scene.

It has often been said that the characters in Dos Passos are less important than the things they do, and decidedly less important than the ultimate protagonist of the Dos Passos novel, society itself. This society has some very distinctive features and reflects with precision the author's view of civilization in America. Though this view was founded in Dos Passos' experiences in the first World War and formulated during the post-war disillusionment of the 20's, it did not fully emerge until 1930, and hence did not leave its mark upon the American public until after the depression had begun. The light in which we see that society is immensely unfavorable. It is the familiar picture of the world as a jungle, though in Dos Passos, unfamiliarly drawn. The characters begin life as decent people, then are corrupted by the competitive universe in which they find themselves. The men either lose their ideals, socialist or otherwise, and turn into weaklings, like Mac, or sell their souls for money, like the memorable J. Ward Moorehouse. The women grow hard and calloused or exist in a vague state of resistance, which is equivalent to impotence. The Rousseauism of Dos Passos is never more marked than in *The 42nd Parallel*. His personages are all good at birth and become corrupted by contact with an evil society. The revolutionary implication in all this is perfectly apparent. Dos Passos does not like the capitalist system, a conviction that he exposed and documented further in *1919* and *The Big Money*, the two later volumes of *U.S.A.*

But the revolutionary note remains implied, and never becomes overt. It is there in the background, plain enough but not obtrusive. By a kind of historical coincidence, it reflected the prevailing public frame of mind between the crash and the first inauguration of Franklin D. Roosevelt: a state of vague dissatisfaction with capitalism, tinged with faint overtones of revolution. These overtones were, of course, played upon vigorously by the forces in the country with a conscious revolutionary program, forces led chiefly by the Communists. But despite the ripeness of the situation, which led to the most extravagant left-wing hopes, revolution took very little hold in the American mind. Hence bewilderment, rather than a passion for specific change, remained the dominant national emotion. To this bewilderment, with its revolutionary potential, *The 42nd Parallel* provided an ideal literary expression.

On a smaller scale, and in a variety of minor keys, other writers were playing with the same discordant theme. In *The Sheltered Life*, Ellen Glasgow was continuing her delicate study of the disintegration of the old South that was so pronounced in *They Stooped to Folly*, and accenting once again her favorite moral doctrine that fortitude was what people needed above all else to endure and survive difficult times. In a period when very few persons had any clear idea of what was happening or where the country was going, advice rooted in keeping a stiff upper lip was about as acceptable as any.

Farther south, in Alabama, T. S. Stribling was beginning his trilogy, displaying the confusion that resulted from the impact of a brutal and moneygrubbing industrialism upon a decaying plantation aristocracy.[9] In the first volume, *The Forge*, and in the second, *The Store*, Colonel Milti-ades Vaiden goes from one class to another without con-spicuous success in either, but during his passage dredges up all the ugly problems of lynching and miscegenation. Stribling is not to be compared with Faulkner or even Ellen Glasgow as a technician in the novel; yet he was against many aspects of life in the South, and hence was involved not merely in the great critical re-examination of the South on the part of Southerners that began to ac-quire momentum around 1930 with the publication of the Agrarian Manifesto; but also in the whole wave of critical rebellion that engulfed the country after the crash.

It was also the time when Willa Cather was carrying to a climax in *Shadows on the Rock* her retreat from the harsh world into the cool and aesthetic security of Catholi-cism. In this sweetened, muted story of eighteenth century Quebec, the Church is the final anchorage, the spiritual not the temporal Church, the Church *sub specie aeterni-tatis*. It was a retreat much like that of Cardinal Newman nearly a hundred years before, from a society of the boom that seemed (as did the society of the Industrial Revolu-tion in England) swollen with material gain and the gross pursuit of money. It was a retreat as scrupulously aesthetic

[9] This was also to be one of Faulkner's main themes in the 30's, and the subject of Lillian Hellman's well-known plays, *The Little Foxes* (1939), and *Another Part of the Forest* (1946).

as that of T. S. Eliot into Anglo-Royalism and Anglo-Catholicism.

It was, at its source, grounded in the same impulse that moved Ernest Hemingway to flee bourgeois America and seek death molded into an art form in the Spanish bull ring. His Spanish bullfighting manual, *Death in the After-noon*, which appeared in 1932, was an exquisite expression of nihilism made arresting and beautiful. Since civilization, to Hemingway, was predatory, the only logical behavior for the sensible artist was to study the most destructive activities in which men indulged, and give them literary form. Hence in *A Farewell to Arms* he made a close-up appraisal of war; in *The Sun Also Rises* and *Death in the Afternoon* he did the same for alcoholism, sexual impotence, and bull fighting. In *Green Hills of Africa* he was to descant on the pleasures of big game hunting, and in *To Have and Have Not* he was to draw a characteristic vignette of smugglers and rum-runners off the Florida Keys engaged in their bloody and dangerous work.

Offhand, no two writers seem farther apart than Willa Cather and Hemingway. Certainly Catholicism and nihilism have nothing in common. But however different the refuges they sought, their search began with the impulse to escape from a middle-class America which they could not spiritually endure. Assuredly, the desire to withdraw from an unsatisfactory universe, which found its simplest literary outlet in *Anthony Adverse*, the best seller of 1933, was evident in its most complex literary forms, in the ancient Catholicism of Miss Cather's Quebec and the aesthetic intricacies of Hemingway's bull ring in Pamplona.

And how hungrily the bewildered and suffering public of 1932 took to its heart *The Good Earth*, which recounted misfortune and misery at the other end of the world! Its popularity lay not alone in the fact that it was almost the first book to unlock for the West the interior of China (there had been plenty of melodramatic novels about Shanghai). Nor did it lie entirely in the derivatively Biblical style that Miss Buck assumed, which lent her story the simple, earthy air of the epic. It lay most deeply perhaps in the impact of life upon Wang Lung, the hero, who begins the story as a poor, hard-working peasant about to take a wife and ends very rich, very polygamous, and not nearly so happy as at the beginning. Wealth to Wang Lung is a source of discord, spiritual and domestic. It complicates his existence by injecting into it involved and, to him, insoluble problems which he had never known in the days of his industrious poverty. This attitude toward riches, which lies at the core of *The Good Earth*, could not have appeared at a more timely psychological moment, at a moment of the great draining away of national income to a depressing low, when the public was searching frantically for rationalizations to make poverty and unemployment more tolerable. The life of Wang Lung offered one such rationalization: in some ways, it appeared to say, people are better off when they are poor.

Within the same psychological area, and in the same year, another of John Steinbeck's early books, *Pastures of Heaven*, put in a modest appearance. Like his first, it was in the tradition of whimsical sentiment, its short stories dealing with half-wits, bohemian philosophers seeking refuge from society, amiably amoral Mexican girls, and tormented children of paradise, living in a lovely California valley called the "pastures of heaven." It made a slightly greater indentation upon the public mind than *Cup of Gold* because it was better written, and contained the memorable figure of Tularecito, the half-witted, six-year-old boy with enormous physical strength and a genius for drawing animals. But it was just another of the numerous books that defended primitivism against civilization,[10] and gave no hint that Steinbeck was to become the representative writer of the decade.

While the great mass of people were floundering about in the early years of the depression, reading with one eye the growing critiques of American society and with the other the flood of ivory tower literature, ranging from the slick emulsions of *The Saturday Evening Post* to the artful whimsicality of Steinbeck, they were waiting for something to happen; and they felt that what they were waiting for had happened when they elected Franklin D. Roosevelt to the presidency in November, 1932, and inaugurated (without knowing it at the time) the Roosevelt era.

But that era is not to be fully understood without first examining the aggressive activities of two of the leading groups dramatizing the last phase of President Hoover's administration.

[10] A recurring literary theme which, in the second and third decades of the century, had found dramatic expression in the writings and life of D. H. Lawrence.

3: ASSORTED UTOPIAS

THE first of the groups were the Marxists. Inspired by the example of Russia, they struggled to give shape to the loose formlessness of the depression and lead the country as rapidly as possible to the Communist Utopia. In the process, they aroused storms of partisan sentiment about themselves, and helped aggravate feelings already high against the Soviet Union.

In January and February of 1930, the attention of the American public was diverted from its troubles at home by stories of Soviet persecution of the Church. On February 16 the headlines announced that there was much indignation in France, England, and Vatican City, and on March 16 protest meetings in New York against the alleged Soviet policy "attracted throngs." On February 16, 1931, the British were wrangling over charges of brutality in Soviet labor camps. The *coup de grâce* was delivered six days later when Czarist exiles decided to boycott Soviet caviar.

The first of the numerous Communist Party demonstrations against unemployment and starvation took place at City Hall on March 2. It was broken up by Mayor Walker's police, and five of the leaders were imprisoned without bail. On July 1 a policeman killed a Communist demonstrator in a Harlem parade. On July 6 things had come to such a pass that the Soviet newspaper *Pravda* made one of the strategic errors of the decade by asserting that America was ripe for revolution, and urged a new Communist drive in the United States. The Communists proceeded on this theory until the Seventh World Congress of the Third International, in 1935, when the United Front policy was born under the expanding menace of fascism. But until then, demonstrations, strikes, agitation, vociferous protests, became the order of the day and succeeded one another with accelerated frequency. The last stages of capitalism seemed indeed to have arrived, what with staggering unemployment figures, huge stoppages in industry, and vast disillusionment with the *status quo*. The Communists knew what they wanted to do: organize the nationwide discontent, canalize the energy of the masses, and lead the workers and impoverished farmers in a revolution to achieve the same general aims as the Revolution of 1917. With *Pravda* urging them on and a sense of manifest destiny hovering overhead, they were, from 1930 to the coming of the New Deal, one of the most articulate political groups in the country.

Developing events gave them plenty of grist for their mill. Poverty had been accumulating so rapidly during 1930 that on December 7 it was officially announced in New York that begging on the city streets had become a menace. July 19, 1931, saw hungry Oklahomans marching on their grocery stores, demanding food, and race riots induced by hard times breaking out in Alabama. Bread lines, charity distributions, dispossessions and foreclosures on a growing scale, and a multitude of spontaneous uprisings, were climaxed in the summer of 1932 by the famous Bonus March on Washington which President Hoover broke up through the use of United States Army troops.

These disturbances at home were accompanied by equal disturbances abroad. In October, 1930, another of the official campaigns against the Versailles Treaty was launched in Germany as the French began withdrawing from the Rhineland into the security (sic) of the Maginot Line, then in the early stages of construction. With the Nazis gaining in local and provincial elections, this campaign was echoed in Mussolini's Italy and the Rothermere press in England. Early in 1931, King Alfonso was overthrown and the stage set for the Spanish Civil War five years later. In July, the government of Chiang Kai-Shek announced the levying of taxes on the illegal opium traffic to finance another of his interminable and unsuccessful campaigns against the Chinese Communists. On September 20 the stage was primed for the second World War with the Japanese invasion of Manchuria.

The spring and summer of 1932 were largely taken up with the kidnaping of the Lindbergh baby, but this did not wholly obscure the uprisings in Bombay in May, during which British troops killed thirty natives. One country after another deserted the Gold Standard during '31 and '32, and the economies of the industrialized nations went through a series of spastic convulsions. There were many

people during that period who felt certain that capitalism
was tottering and that the revolutionary era inaugurated by
the Bolsheviks, in 1917, was about to enter a second phase.
None were more sure than the Communists.

That they did not succeed is now ancient history. The
United States, though suffering, was not disposed to revolution. Poorer countries were enduring, in the same years,
a series of internal disturbances leading, in Germany, to
the disaster of Hitlerism; in France, to the ultimate collapse of the Third Republic. There were days in 1931 and
1932 when mutterings of revolution were audible in the
sociological seismographs of the United States. But the
mutterings died away. Though the national income
dropped precipitously, it was still a sum most countries
would have regarded as adequate in prosperous times.
There was desperation, but not enough for a socialist upheaval.

But though the Communists did not achieve their
principal aim, they achieved certain lesser ones. They
helped mobilize sentiment in favor of collective security
(until the signing of the Nazi-Soviet Pact). To a good
many young people floundering during the depression, as
Louis Adamic pointed out in *My America,* they provided
intellectual direction and a documented promise of a better world to come. They fought for the rights of national
minorities, the Negroes in particular, and, by dramatizing
unemployment, served as an irritant to the conscience of
the nation. Not least of all, through the instrumentation
of proletarian criticism and the proletarian novel, they were

a major influence in the literature of the 30's.

The proletarian writing of the decade was launched in February, 1930, with the appearance of Michael Gold's *Jews Without Money*. This lively and frenetic autobiography of a boy's wretched life in an East Side slum was moving through the sheer weight of the suffering it described. It piled one appalling scene upon another, and wound up on the last page invoking the glories of socialism, which, by implication, would one day rescue the East Sides of America from their misery. As a portrait of life in the lower depths, *Jews Without Money* had a certain historical interest, though its communicative plane was purely emotional.

Of far greater importance in the development of proletarian literature was *The Autobiography of Lincoln Steffens* which appeared in 1931. It was the fashion, as Frederick Lewis Allen observed in *Since Yesterday*, for young people to read Steffens, see the apocalyptic light, and proceed straight to Moscow. Steffens had gone to the Soviet Union in 1919 and returned with his famous utterance, "I have seen the future and it works," which was the most stirring American encomium for Russia until the epic of Stalingrad produced a sheaf of new ones. The theory of the book was purely Marxist, applied to capitalism in the United States. As a reporter and later as a political economist of amateur standing, Steffens noted the corruption of the big political machines in the big cities, observed the tie-up between the machines and big business, and arrived at the ultimate conclusion that business and the business element were the principal sources of moral and political infection in the life of the country. This was a paraphrase of Lenin's thesis that the state apparatus of any society is controlled by its ruling class—feudal, capitalist, or proletarian, as the case may be. What made the Steffens version so persuasive was that he was as natively American as he could possibly be, that his observations and interviews and research were candid and indisputably authentic, and that he reached his revolutionary conclusions within an American frame. He was indeed one of the few indigenous radicals produced in America during the present century. Jack London was another, Randolph Bourne a third.

There is something awe-inspiring about a book that sees the light of day at the climactic moment. In its own way, it is a spectacle as dramatic as that of a historical situation and a historical personage swimming into each other's orbit and merging at precisely the strategic time. This is true of a picaresque tale like *Anthony Adverse*; it is doubly true of a book of ideas, and among books of ideas few have realized themselves in the public eye as completely as the Steffens autobiography. It chose the year 1931 for its birth; no birthdate was ever chosen more felicitously. By that year, many people were beginning to recognize that the depression had arrived, perhaps for a long stay. By that year the vague and inchoate unrest that the collapse had aroused in the American mind had begun to ferment, and what would emerge from the fermentation no one but the Communists was quite prepared to say. By 1931, too, hard times for the young had really been going on for four years, for jobs had begun to be scarce since the employment decline of 1927. The dismal prospect of graduating from school into a society that offered no work, of remaining economically stagnant for an indefinite time, was the indispensable prerequisite for the acceptance of the Steffens argument, which had by far its greatest vogue among young people in their twenties. To them, it offered a clear explanation of what was wrong in language they recognized as their own, and suggested a solution which burst upon them with a blinding and apocalyptic light. They began reading Marx and Engels, reconstructing the activities of Lenin, studying the history of the Soviet Union, joining the Communist Party, working in virtually all the organizations to the left of center, and in these ways filled for a number of years the economic and psychological vacuum into which circumstances had thrust them. For them, the *New Masses* became the center of truth, Granville Hicks the St. Paul of literary criticism, Robert Forsythe the most stimulating of satirists, Clifford Odets the most brilliant of playwrights, and Grace Lumpkin, William Rollins, Jack Conroy, Josephine Herbst, Fielding Burke, and, for a time later in the decade, Richard Wright,[1] the most significant of American novelists.

The shortcomings of proletarian literature were plain enough. Alfred Kazin in his *On Native Grounds* analyzes them in encyclopedic detail. The worst of these faults was

---

[1] By far the most talented of the group.

the transformation of workers *per se* into epic heroes and employers into unredeemable villains; nothing more black and white was to be found outside the theology of Calvin, and nothing more hostile to art and the psychology of portraiture. The rest of the proletarian formula, the automatic struggle between workers and bosses, the murder of a striker or two to provide emotional symbolism, and the beating of drums at the end to signalize the rising of the proletariat and the triumph of "progressive humanity," was laid on with a humorless trowel and in a spirit of religious dogmatism. Even as late as 1943 a novel like Ruth McKenney's *Jake Home* was executing the same wooden gyrations; this time the climax pivoted around the hero leading a crowd of demonstrators through a wall of hostile police (or Cossacks, as they were referred to colloquially in the proletarian novels), to triumph in Union Square.

Less well remembered are the measurable virtues of the proletarian school, and its vivid contributions to the literature of the 30's. Curiously enough, though radical writing was based on a formidable denunciation of capitalist society and, in this sense, was of a piece with the antibourgeois fiction of Lewis, Dos Passos, and Ring Lardner, it was grounded also in a philosophy of hope and salvation, and hence helped restore an affirmative note to American letters that had been missing since the genteel days of William Dean Howells. Whether this restoration was grounded in truth or error remains arguable. But the restoration took place, and left its mark. Perhaps its most striking single influence was its effect upon the emerging Steinbeck of the later 30's, who in *The Grapes of Wrath* was to take over the proletarian formula, revolution and all, and catalyze it into one of the epics of the twentieth century.

However absurd the proletarian dogma that social and political virtue resided exclusively in the proletariat, the left-wing writers helped focus the attention of their middle-class readers (one of the unavoidable ironies of the situation was that the readers of proletarian literature were largely drawn from the middle classes) upon the conditions of life among laborers and tenant farmers. Books dealing with the proletariat had appeared long before. Elizabeth Stuart Phelps, in *The Silent Partner* (1871), described factory workers in New England. At the turn of the century, Jack London began his numerous fictional protests against labor conditions. D. H. Lawrence's *Sons and Lovers* (1909), remains to this day one of the best psychological novels about coal miners in the language, and Upton Sinclair had been a one-man press agent for the workers since *The Jungle* appeared in 1906. Other works, like *Comrade Yetta* (1913), by Albert Edwards (Arthur Bullard), and Ernest Poole's *The Harbor* (1915) chronicled other phases of proletarian life. But the movement, which indeed goes back at least as far as Dickens, did not become organized and militantly self-conscious until the depression, when mass unemployment swelled to dangerous proportions and the upheaval that started with the Russian Revolution seemed to the literary proletarians about to drive America into the arms of the working class.

The flood of novels dealing with factory workers and their rural equivalents produced little that remains of interest today, but it did fetch onto the literary stage nearly every variety of trade and craft in the American economy. Tom Tippett's *Horse Shoe Bottoms* and Edward Dahlberg's *Bottom Dogs* described the coal mines; Thomas Bell's *Out of This Furnace* the steel mills; Albert Maltz's *The Underground Stream* the automobile factories of Detroit; Steinbeck's *In Dubious Battle* the fruit orchards of California; Grace Lumpkin's *To Make My Bread* the textile mills of the South; Leane Zugsmith's *A Time to Remember* the department stores; Pietro Di Donato's *Christ in Concrete* the bricklayers; and so on in an extensive list. There were novels like Tom Kromer's *Waiting for Nothing*, dealing with workers professionally dispossessed from all work, and novels like Jack Conroy's *A World to Win*, dealing with young men in the process of attaching themselves emotionally to the proletariat without as yet being economically involved. And there were any number of books concerned with middle-class heroes who lost their proletarian sympathies, as with the college professor in Miss Zugsmith's *The Summer Soldier*, or who acquired them as did the young playwright in John Hyde Preston's *The Liberals*. Regardless of what else the proletarians may or may not have legated to posterity, they enlarged the thematic range of fiction and in this way left a permanent imprint on the century, an imprint that seems likely to survive their individual reputations.

Of that vast and fluctuating group, only Bell, Maltz,

and Steinbeck remained active in the 40's.[2] Maltz is the only one of the three to use the Communist Party line as a conscious instrument in his novels, a burden which in a writer of a shade less integrity and skill would be wholly fatal. But Maltz manages to survive. His Princey in *The Underground Stream* is a robust and sympathetic character, largely because Marxism to him is not a formula but a way of life, and the struggle between him and Greb, the employers' agent, is a struggle between two human beings rather than, as in the average proletarian novel, between two mouthpieces of opposing class views. Maltz's Germans in *The Cross and the Arrow*, published in the autumn of 1944, while the Allied armies were at the frontiers of the Third Reich, are personalized with equal intensity, though they fail rather painfully to make the reader believe that they are peculiarly German and live in Germany rather than almost anywhere else. The drama of their varying relationships with Nazism cuts under theories and develops despite them. Sometimes Maltz's novels and short stories [3] absorb communism into their bloodstream, sometimes they exist beneath its weight. He is an illustration of how talent, if sufficiently vital, can survive any thesis superimposed upon it.

Thomas Bell is also concerned with workers, but their political views end with trade-unionism and anti-fascism.

[2] And, of course, Richard Wright, who was never strictly a proletarian writer. His *Uncle Tom's Children*, *Native Son*, and *Black Boy* dealt not with workers and bosses, but with the sufferings and oppressions of Negroes.

[3] *Man on a Road*, the story of a miner dying of silicosis, though heavily written, is the most notable of these.

He, even more than Maltz, has a talent for making his characters live and for getting them to talk idiomatically and convincingly. Though his novels are nearly always small-proportioned and on a minor scale, they are cameoed with a skill that had by no means reached its limit. Where Maltz is primarily interested in the economic and political problems of his characters, Bell is as much interested in their private lives. *All Brides Are Beautiful* describes with a tenderness that borders on sentimentality the early married life of a young couple during the depression; though the things that happen to them as a result of unemployment and their own emotional immaturity are familiar, they are described with surprising freshness. In *Out of this Furnace*, a few years later, Bell stepped out of the small canvas in which he had hitherto functioned so well to write a long, two-generation novel about Slovak workers in a Pennsylvania steel town. Himself of Slovak origin, he defines the speech and the psychological nuances of his immigrant characters with a rare sense of intimacy, but the novel is rambling and in the end sinks under its own weight. He returned the next time to his original framework, and wrote, as a consequence, his crispest and most successful book about the private life of the proletariat. *Till I Come Back to You* (1943) is an effective short novel that deals with one crucial day in the life of Miley Brooks, a machinist. In that one day Miley enlists in the army because he hates fascism, says good-by to his friends and enemies, comes to an understanding with his sweetheart, and articulates the mood of organized workers everywhere in the country with dramatic simplicity, all within the miniature structure in which Bell is so effective a craftsman. That proletarian literature as a movement has had a fermenting influence upon him is hardly open to doubt.

The other writers who came within the proletarian tide have today all but vanished. Conroy, Rollins and Grace Lumpkin have disappeared without a trace. Leane Zugsmith added a book of sensitive short stories, *Home Is Where You Hang Your Childhood*, to her two socially conscious novels, then withdrew into silence. With the exception of Ruth McKenney,[4] proletarian literature acquired no new recruits in the 40's, and her *Jake Home*, an almost primitively sectarian pseudo-epic, added no luster to the historical reputation of the movement. The disappearance of most of its creative writers was complemented by the withdrawal of its leading critic, Granville Hicks, in the autumn of 1939 on the occasion of the Nazi-Soviet Pact, leaving behind him as a kind of critical testament of the proletariat an interpretation of American literature called *The Great Tradition*, published in 1933.[5] The book employed Marxian dialectics with ruthless literalism, approved or condemned American writers since the Civil War to the degree in which they did or did not sympathize with the plight of "the toiling masses," and labored devotedly to find genius in the ranks of the writers within the proletarian fold. Its tone was doctrinaire, its arguments

[4] Best known for her humorous sketches in *My Sister Eileen*, which had nothing to do with proletarian literature.

[5] This was preceded by V. F. Calverton's *Liberation of American Literature*, in 1932, another influential Marxian interpretation of American letters.

pretentious, its conclusions naïve and dogmatic, its critical value mainly that of a museum piece, surviving as a suggestive and important reminder of a significant movement in our national life. The vigor with which literary proletarianism flared through the angry decade of depression and war was equaled at last by its transience.

II

Side by side with the Marxism of the northern cities, flourishing in the same situation and starting from the same premise, there appeared at the beginning of the 30's the second of the anti-capitalist movements of the decade, the movement called Southern Agrarianism.[6] If the Marxists wished to give power to the masses, the Agrarians meant to give it to an educated aristocracy ruling over an eighteenth century economy. Where the Marxists foresaw an ever-growing concentration of industrial activity in units that were to increase in size, the Agrarians strove to break up the large productive units into groups of small ones, and, through decentralization, return to the society of Jefferson's time, when the great bulk of the people owned their own land. The Agrarians, consequently, looked as strenuously at the past as the Marxists did to the future.

[6] The Agrarian Manifesto, *I'll Take My Stand,* was published in 1930. The more prominent of the contributors were Allen Tate, John Crowe Ransom, Robert Penn Warren, and Donald Davidson, all of whom had been members of the Fugitives, the little group located at Vanderbilt University who published, 1922 to 1925, a magazine of poetry called *The Fugitive.* It was of this publication that H. L. Mencken observed equivocally: "It constitutes at present the entire literature of Tennessee."

Where the Marxists drew their inspiration from the socialist thinkers of the nineteenth century, the Agrarians went
back to Plato and his philosopher-kings vigorously trained
to rule the state, to Carlyle and the superman formulators
of modern times, to Chesterton and Belloc and their strong
religious orthodoxy.

The Agrarians had no more use for the indolent members of the plantation society of the ante-bellum South
than Carlyle had for the idle, fox-hunting aristocracy of
eighteenth century England. They were for intellectual
discipline in the strictest sense of the phrase, for the rule
of the mentally fittest. Their ideas, indeed, involved a star-
tling combination of economic democracy and political oligarchy, property and economic independence for the mass
of people at the bottom of an agricultural society, and at
the top the trained, well-tempered intellectual élite. They
never acquired a mass following, as did the Marxists, for
they sought to turn the clock of history—of Southern history at least—back to a specific era in the past instead of
embracing a definable future. It is axiomatic that the future is a far more potent political weapon than the past;
nobody really wants to return to the past, however pleasingly it may be displayed and however much it may provide a release for the imagination in literature or art. In
physical actuality, it is the future alone that is a marketable commodity, since it can be kneaded to the contours
of every variety of wishful thinking and has committed no
discernible errors. The Agrarians were, in an *a priori* sense,
limiting the attractiveness of their movement to an intel-

lectual few by their glorification of a past forever over, as well as by the ruthless purity of their insistence on mental discipline.

These ideas determined the literature produced by the Agrarians during the 1930's. The poetry and criticism of Allen Tate and John Crowe Ransom are the products of writers fanatically wedded to intellectual asceticism. They distrust sloppiness and looseness of form, romantic sentiment, fancy when divorced from logic. A poem without a sustaining and carefully worked image or idea they regard as poor stuff. Hence they attack Shakespeare because he is at times ragged and full of loose ends, because his emotion often outruns the willingness of his intellect to control it; and they admire John Donne because his metaphysical imagery is worked out with ruthless precision. The fact that Donne is frequently obscure and his meanings often tortuous does not mute their argument. It is not sense and clarity they are after so much as the muscular exercise of logic, which they regard as the sign of the superior mind. They are thus willing to sacrifice the end to the means, and in this way are further distinguished from the Marxists, who are quite willing to sacrifice any means to a particularized end. It is not the conclusions that the Agrarians reach which are important but the critical technique, the technique of literal intellectualism, by which this judgment is arrived at.

The ideas of Ransom, Tate, and the other Agrarians extend to every sphere of experience. In politics they are in the literal sense reactionary (Tate called one of his books

Reactionary Essays on Poetry and Ideas), seeking a return to an oligarchic system based on a division of classes. In poetry they yearn for the asceticism of a cult devoted to complexity of image and based upon an appeal to the superior few. For the travails of the South, they prescribed a return to the one-mule, thirty-acre farm, supervised by a sort of plantation aristocracy brought up to date by injections of culture. For the country as a whole, sinking into the depression, they frankly demanded the overthrow of industrialism and for the rule by money, the substitution of the rule by brains. Just as the technocrats had their élite in the engineers, as the Marxists had theirs in the working class, the Agrarians pinned their hopes on the intellectuals, and with this magic formula pursued their grim course through the decade with a consuming and Messianic fervor that grew stronger as it grew more lonely.

As it grew more lonely and became more isolated from the main current of the times, it became more harsh-tempered, more obscurantist in ideas, and began to assimilate a number of critics not originally Agrarian into its aesthetic ranks. One of these, Kenneth Burke, was perhaps the most persistent innovator of new jargon. In a characteristic passage on Keats, he writes as follows:

"We are here set to analyze the *Ode on a Grecian Urn* as a viaticum that leads, by a series of transformations, into the oracle, 'Beauty is truth, truth beauty.' We shall analyze the Ode 'dramatistically,' in terms of symbolic action."

Since it is possible for the educated man of average mind to understand Keats in direct terms, it became imperative for the intellectualists to create a new and rarefied area of experience and terminology not communicable to the average reader. Obscurantism here, as everywhere, is rooted in snobbism and in what Thorstein Veblen called conspicuous consumption, the tendency of a class to distinguish itself from other classes by external ornament. This external ornament may take the form of clean fingernails, as it did with the middle class of the nineteenth century distinguishing itself from the nail-grimed proletariat, or the form of a new intellectual language understood only by the initiated few. All this is done with a great deal of brilliant ingenuity, Burke's criticism, indeed, having the quality of a kind of beautiful verbal lacework. Another member of the obscurantist school, Yvor Winters, pursues similar ideas with a hard, dogmatic temper which, though impressive in its ferocity, arouses only sympathy for the writers he attacks. His *Maule's Curse* is appropriately subtitled *Seven Studies in the History of American Obscurantism*, and, because of its thorny and knotted diction, is much harder to read than the obscurantist authors it discusses.

The new jargon invented for criticism by the Agrarians and their confreres was the opening gun in the battle of semantics, the science which tended to lay most of the troubles of society at the door of language. If people, argued its spokesmen, only understood the implications and sense of the words they used, the world would be a far happier place and indeed, "the very future of mankind may depend upon a rectification of word-habits." One of the better known semanticists, S. I. Hayakawa, in his *Language in Action*, believes that words are the dominating influence in our lives:

"Whether he realizes it or not, however, Mr. Smith is affected every hour of his life not only by the words he hears and uses, *but also by his unconscious assumptions about language*. These unconscious assumptions determine the way he takes words—which in turn determines the way he acts, whether wisely or foolishly. Words and the way he takes them determine his beliefs, his prejudices, his ideals, his aspirations—they constitute the moral and intellectual atmosphere in which he lives, in short, his semantic environment. If he is constantly absorbing false and lying words, or if his unconscious assumptions about language happen to be, as most of our notions are that have not been exposed to scientific influence, naïve, superstitious, or primitive, he may be constantly breathing a poisoned air without knowing it."

No one would dispute the statement that people misuse words and thereby sometimes get into trouble, but to lay to this all the miseries of mankind is to engage in a kind of intellectual cultism. In this case the cult is language, and the chief act of worship is to cause the universe to revolve around it. But, despite its absurdities and exaggerations, semantics performed the obviously useful service of making its public more conscious of words and their social significance. In the long view, this too can be ascribed to the labors on behalf of intellectual purity begun by the Agrarians in the early 30's.

The two principal theories of civilization which acquired their American definition at the beginning of the angry decade began back-to-back. Proletarians and Agrarians accepted the same premise, the growing iniquities of capitalism, and then proceeded to march briskly in opposite directions, one providing for the urban working classes, the other for the rural hinterland; one proclaiming the dictatorship of the mass, the other the oligarchy of the few; one embracing the attraction of a socialist future, the other wedding itself to the blandishments of the eighteenth century with its population of propertied independents. The Marxists abhorred aesthetics and imposed the tyranny of the social thesis upon the novel. The agrarians embraced aesthetics and imposed the tyranny of pure logic and pure form upon poetry.

They were two of the most vociferous groups in the years between the collapse of the stock market and the appearance of the New Deal, a period when their joint premise about the monstrousness of industrial capitalism seemed to them to be growing into a self-evident truth.

Until, in 1933, a new President appeared, bringing with him a revival of confidence in the existing social system, and hence a slackening in the necessity to search for new Utopias.

4: MESSIAH, ANNO 1933

O N NEW YEAR'S DAY, 1933, the *New York Herald Tribune* (spearheading the press generally) finally gave up the struggle against admitting the existence of the depression.

"The world . . . is beginning to feel that the old clichés are wearing very thin indeed," it said editorially; "men and women everywhere seem to be testing their own ideas, considering new possibilities . . ."

What these new possibilities were was not yet clear. What was clear, as clear as an avalanche, was that by March 3, one day before the inauguration of Mr. Hoover's successor, 5,504 banks, with total deposits of $3,432,000,-000, had closed their doors. It was also clear that the depression was growing worse instead of better, that nobody seemed to have anything useful to say about ways and means of turning the tide, that the presidential campaign the previous fall had centered with epic irrelevance more on the issue of Prohibition than anything else, that the grim phenomenon of the unemployed husband was becoming the latest sociological reality, and that for the first time in American history, city schoolteachers, with assured jobs and fixed incomes, were being regarded with envy by the rest of the population.

The vote of the previous November that had given Roosevelt forty-two of the forty-eight states was a blind gesture of despair. Except that he was against Prohibition, defended a balanced budget (!), and asserted in a vague way that he was against "tradition" if it stood in the way of social and economic reconstruction, the Democratic candidate stood for glittering generalities and behaved in the conventional fashion of most politicians seeking office. The country voted for him as a protest against Hoover, then slid back into apathy. Yet a stage producer could not have managed the events of that winter more theatrically. At the beginning of February, 1933, the country's banks began shutting down. On February 15 the whole course of history was altered by one frantic movement of a woman's hand. Roosevelt was shot at in Miami by a half-mad anarchist who missed his target because a woman in the crowd seized his arm and deflected his aim. Mayor Cermak of Chicago died instead and only the space of a few inches kept John N. Garner from becoming President of the United States. One sensational event succeeded another until by Inauguration Day the nation, economically stagnant, emotionally exhausted, eagerly awaited the new President.

History is filled with instances of men who begin life as liberals and wind up as conservatives. Edmund Burke is perhaps the most illustrious of these, Napoleon the most famous, Laval and Mussolini the most odious. Rarer is the

man who begins his career as a traditionalist and concludes as a progressive. There was little in Roosevelt's
background to suggest the kind of President he was to be.
He was a wealthy country gentleman who had gone to
Groton and Harvard without the faintest deviation from
conventionality. His revolt against Tammany Hall as a
state legislator in Albany was more an expression of rural
disaffection with that den of iniquity, the big city, than a
sign of reformist zeal. Nothing in his career as a New
York lawyer or Assistant Secretary of the Navy, and little
during his stay in New York State's Governor's Mansion,
indicated any measurable departure from the accepted cus-
toms of these offices. His last declarations as governor were
in defense of States' rights, and he campaigned for the
presidency partly as a disciple of the balanced budget. He
did not hesitate to woo the support of Frank Hague, Ed
Kelly, and Boss Crump, to dicker with William Randolph Hearst, to accept Garner, a conservative Southern
Democrat, as his running mate. The elegant and worldly
gentleman from Hyde Park was no stranger to the boys
in the back room. No one suspected that he was to be the
vessel through which American economic life would over-
take the political; that in four years he would institute over-
due reforms which England had had for forty years; that
he would steal the Communist thunder by instigating evolutionary changes which, for once, would be rapid; that he
would repair the damage the depression had done to the
capitalist state rapidly enough to enable it to withstand
the shocks of an onrushing world war—that, in a word, he

would be a Messiah—Messiah, anno 1933—who for one blazing season would unite all the warring elements in the country.

II

The spiritual paralysis that gripped the country in the months before Roosevelt's inauguration was ultimately symbolized in the early winter of 1933 by the appearance of a book which was destined to break nearly all twentieth century sales records, that was indicative of the public passion for the long historical novel which gripped the 30's, and created a legendary name, the name of Anthony Adverse. He was the perfect picaresque hero with the usual ingredients skillfully arranged to produce the maximum suspense: he was born under mysterious circumstances which just hinted at the prospect of his having noble blood; he wandered romantically through a variety of places on three continents; he won and lost large sums of money; he conquered all obstacles. Enchanting women of varying colors made love to him, and he to them—all in the grand manner, with sweeping gestures in the best cloak-and-sword tradition. What could be sillier, more fantastically remote from reality, and yet more satisfying?

The success of the novel was, of course, another illustration of the old theory that wretched circumstances breed a desire for escape. The Americans were wretched enough; three years of the depression had filled their cup of misery to overflowing, and bred a sufficiently strong passion for nostrums and anodynes. But not just *any* nostrums and anodynes. They had to be skillfully blended, or they wouldn't do. After fifteen years of Hemingway, Fitzgerald, and Dos Passos, the reading tastes of the country had grown more sophisticated. Where Harold Bell Wright, Gene Stratton Porter, and books like *The Trail of the Lonesome Pine, Pollyanna,* and *Ben Hur* had suited public taste before the first World War, their naïvete and lush sentiment were now no longer digestible. It was no longer possible to glorify the process by which a dude Easterner became hardened to the Wild West as in *The Virginian* and *When a Man's a Man.* Sermons tacked to the ends of chapters and moral bromides postscripting books were distinctly out of fashion. The little men and women of Louisa May Alcott, the devout shepherds of John Fox, the Couéist heroines like the girl of the Limberlost, had become anachronisms. The painted sunsets of Zane Grey were beginning to give ground to the hard fiber of *The Ox-Bow Incident.* And even historical novels with religious themes, like *Quo Vadis,* were now armored with at least a thin shell of Roman sophistication, as in *The Robe.* The core of these popular literary narcotics had not changed, but their surface appearance had grown more veneered and intricate.

Anthony Adverse was a supreme example of this surface maturation. It translated the conventional romance of the old-line novels into the framework of the new psychiatry, and Freud now strode darkly and mesmerically through the interstices of Anthony's adventures. Sex was present but in a new and fashionable form, laced with a good deal of local color, indeed a kaleidoscope of local color. Native beauties, white and brown, were painted into the story with rapid strokes, taken from the landscapes of North Africa and Italy, the West Indian islands and the colonies lately emancipated from England. The landscape itself, jeweled with every exotic attraction the author could cull from his own travels and the travels of others, flowed lambently before the reader's eye, pleasingly lush, and aromatic with the frondage and vegetation of a dozen tropical places. The novel was suffused with a feeling for water and air, with sunlight hot and shifting, and the other natural elements that can be harnessed by writers as skillfully as by scientists. An intimacy of place, of sense impression, exuded from the book like steam from the pipes of a steam bath, befogging the mind and soothing the nerves all in the same hypnotic motion. It drew its ingredients from a number of fields, geography and psychology predominating, so that the final blend was complex and satisfactory. There was little resemblance between *Anthony Adverse* and serious literature, but its particular elements were fused with greater finesse than many a work closer to life.

The intricate form of escape which the adventures of Hervey Allen's hero provided the harassed American public was complemented in another sphere by the small-scale pathos and whimsy of Robert Nathan. *One More Spring* also saw the light of day in 1933, and proceeded to siphon the depression into a small and idyllic retreat that dulled its sting. The hungry little people, taking refuge in Central Park from unemployment and the miseries of a self-de-

structive world, provided the reader with that peculiar combination of reality and a feeling of superiority to it so difficult to compound in literature with aesthetic pretensions.
Nathan is a devotee of aesthetics, of the *roman démeublé*
that Willa Cather publicized, of the miniature cameolike
form. He weighs his words on a thistledown scale, and his
novels are as light as fluff. He managed to encase even the
depression in the framework of a wistful fairy tale, in which
his Central Park waifs are gently entombed. *One More
Spring* demonstrated how neatly its author fitted the definition of the minor novelist, a writer with a superior technique operating within a narrow horizon. Nathan is the
master of a single mood, a mood of exquisite whimsy, to
which his style is admirably suited. Beyond it, he does not
venture, and even when he chose the depression as a
theme, he alchemized it under the pressure of his temperament into the kind of literary sublimation to which the
public was prepared to respond in 1933.

More obvious in its appeal and popularity during the
first Roosevelt season was that artfully titled piece of non-
fictional goods, *Life Begins at Forty.* The 30's were particularly rich in social narcotics, *Wake Up and Live, How
to Win Friends and Influence People, How to Live Within
Your Income, How to Make the Most of Your Life, Live
Alone and Like It,* and *How to Live Without a Woman,*
being among the most widely publicized, a sufficient index
to the weakened confidence of the nation, which created
for salves and palliatives, literary and otherwise, an enormous market. These were accompanied by a great number

of books popularizing religion and psychology. As the world of the early 30's grew more confused, the books of Emmett Fox and Harry Emerson Fosdick became immensely popular. Fosdick's *As I See Religion, The Power to See It Through*, and *The Secret of Victorious Living* sold in the thousands, as did Fox's *Power Through Constructive Thinking* and *The Sermon on the Mount*. In the closely allied field of psychology, Henry C. Link was reducing the abstractions of the new science to the language of the average man, and providing him, in *The New Psychology of Selling and Advertising, The Return to Religion*, and *The Rediscovery of Man*, with easy lessons in self-assurance and spiritual props in periods of stress.

Professor Pitkin's opus, *Life Begins at Forty*, though not within the professional fields of religion or psychology, addressed its public with equal assurance. Forty was, of course, the right age, the minimum age, one might say, for the readers of a book designed to comfort the victims of the crash. Since most people affected by the debacle of October, 1929, were middle-aged, and presumably lacked the psychological resiliency which, by reputation, is a monopoly of youth, messages of hope for the future, assurances that life for them was just beginning, must have seemed like manna from the Almighty. The Pitkin promise was to people in their forties what the Townsend Plan was soon to be to those in their sixties: a kind of euphoria which Coué in his fondest dreams never thought of inducing.

The disorientation of all the adult age groups in

American society became a prime factor not merely in the emergence and success of certain types of books but in the extraordinary popularity of Roosevelt, providing the ammunition for the landslides of '32 and '36. The young longed for jobs, the middle-aged for the revival of business, the old for pensions and security. While Roosevelt plucked votes from all three in about equal numbers, Pitkin appealed to the second group with a skill no less effective. He recounted the famous men of history whose careers began in middle age, argued that the forties are a period of intellectual maturity and wisdom, and claimed that life at its fullest can be enjoyed chiefly in middle age. He accented the conventional virtues of the middling years, lightly pulled every stop that led in the direction of flattery and self-satisfaction, and wrapped his message in phrased packages neatly crisscrossed with multicolored rhetorical twine.

Not all the literary events of 1933 followed the escapist or Elysian pattern hitherto described. The intensity of the depression had loosened a good many standing inhibitions. For one thing, literary censorship suffered two hard blows in the same year, the first coming with the lifting of the ban on George Moore's *A Story-Teller's Holiday,* the second with the far more significant decision by Federal Judge Woolsey in December, rescinding the ban on James Joyce's *Ulysses.* Moore's autobiography is a rather dated anti-Victorian shocker belonging to the far-off 90's of Oscar Wilde, and what seems surprising is that it was ever banned at all. *Ulysses,* of course, was another story.

Its enemies were obviously attacking a major target in it. Having succeeded in the first place in keeping Dublin, the city so wonderfully narrated in the novel, from publishing it, they managed for more than a decade to drive it underground in the rest of the English-speaking world. Shortly before the assault on *Ulysses* began, the Volstead Act was passed, placing a similar prohibition on liquor. Liquor and literature (the Joycean form of it, at any rate), lingered in the *demi-monde* during the administrations of Harding, Coolidge, and Hoover, and became respectable again, as do so many things during profound psychological upheavals, with the appearance of Roosevelt. Beer and *Ulysses* were officially sanctioned in the same month, December, 1933. And despite local flurries, such as the Boston ban on *Strange Fruit*, the Comstockians have not been the same since.

III

Another sign of the new era was the growing interest in the affairs of Latin America, one of the early evidences of that wider interest in foreign affairs which was to mark the decade. Three countries in particular commanded popular attention. Cuba, after long years of oppression under Machado, came to a boil first, when revolutionary elements headed by Colonel Batista rose to overthrow the tyrant. Unsavory episodes followed, in which our State Department, through Ambassadors Caffery and Welles, sought to intervene in favor of American sugar interests. But the ferment was too strong, the impulse toward the Good Neighbor Policy too powerful, for this kind of intervention to succeed. Batista rose to the presidency, and Cuba embarked upon a democratic course. This was to prove almost as short-lived under Batista as later under Castro.

While Cuba was moving in the direction of civil liberty, Brazil was moving with equal rapidity toward dictatorship. Vargas, elected president in 1930, had bided his time until the state apparatus was firmly in his hands, then seized power as a dictator in a sudden *coup*. The oppressiveness of his régime increased steadily until by 1935 nearly all the opposition leaders were in jail or underground, and the country was groaning under as efficient a tyranny as any seen in South America. The anti-fascist pressures of the second World War began forcing Vargas into a slow retreat from the extremes of his dictatorship, and finally into arranging a free election (after fifteen years) in which he was not a candidate.

As for Mexico, the third of the Latin-American states that took hold of the American imagination during the 30's, its history was associated indissolubly with the administration of Lazaro Cardenas, who expropriated British and American oil properties to an accompanying clamor from outraged corporations. This act, followed by moves to secularize Mexico's schools, increase the agricultural holdings of the peons, and carry out the aims of the Mexican revolution, aroused the admiration of American liberals and the fury of foreign investors. Even more than Cuba, Mexico provided the acid test of the Good Neighbor Policy, which became successfully established in the process. An agreement was reached between ourselves and the Mexicans over the purchase price to be paid the oil companies, while, by contrast, Britain, to whom, in those years, the Good Neighbor Policy was hardly to be considered in dealings with primitive or semi-colonial countries, broke off diplomatic relations with Mexico.

A spate of books on Latin America had been appearing for some years. Among these, *The Crime of Cuba* (1933) was the sixth of a series of studies of the hemisphere south of us by Carleton Beals, an aggressively liberal observer who carried on a kind of one-man literary war against the foreign interests in the countries he discussed. The vastness of Brazil was described by Peter Fleming, an Englishman, in *Brazilian Journey*. Waldo Frank, whose novels purveyed a unique brand of romantic mysticism, had made a grand tour of South America and brought to it the appurtenances of his poetic, frequently apoplectic prose in *America Hispana* (1931). As for Mexico, it commanded the curiosity of dozens of travelers, from colorful figures like Anita Brenner to articulate economists like Stuart Chase; from trim devotees of the golden mean in reportage like Hudson Strode, to sympathizers with the Indians in the forgotten villages like John Steinbeck. The whole experience, literary and political, for our country, was a step outside the hard chrysalis of isolation into which the nation had withdrawn as an aftermath of the first World War.

Another step was taken in November, 1933, with the beginning of diplomatic relations with the Soviet Union.

One of the early policies of the new administration was the hacking away at established prejudices, and the expansion of the country's relationships with the outside world. All sorts of things began to circulate freely after Roosevelt's first inauguration: liquor and literature, notions about government responsibility for the unemployed, Liberty Leagues having nothing to do with liberty, Christian Fronts having nothing to do with Christianity, and, by no means last in importance, ideas about Russia. The average American, fifteen years after the Bolshevik Revolution, had two fairly set notions about the Russians: they were either bloodstained, bomb-throwing Communists with long beards and fierce eyes, threatening civilization from the editorial pages of the Hearst press, or they were Czarist aristocrats in elegant cabarets, watching natives in high boots dancing the *kazatzka* and making languid love to ladies called Natasha (Hollywood was the chief dispenser of this view of Russian history). That anybody Russian bore any resemblance to a recognizable human being was quite outside our fixed images on the subject.

Not that the arrival of Maxim Litvinov, in November, to sign the diplomatic papers destroyed these illusions overnight. What it did was to accelerate the long process of reversal and recognition which was in the end to set up still a third notion about the Soviets: that they were people pretty much like ourselves, who wore civilized clothes, took vacations, had children, and worried about war. This conception was buffeted by numerous shocks and countershocks. The policy of the United Front formulated by the

Third International, in 1935, softened many a prejudice against the Kremlin. The trials of 1937 and the Nazi-Soviet pact of 1939 spurred opinion in the opposite direction, though by the late summer of 1941, the heroic resistance of the Russian people to the German invasion was to swing the pendulum back again. Though not at first apparent, though often submerged in the years that followed, the American-Soviet relationship begun in 1933 was to be one of our most powerful safety lines during the crisis of the second World War.

While the country was stirring from its long inertia, and taking fresh interest in the affairs of the world, literature was poised for a new advance. For three years, the Communists had been increasingly active, and proletarian fiction was about to start on its spectacular course. Housed on 14th Street, the Theater Union, with its espousal of left-wing drama,[1] was getting under way. James T. Farrell was on the verge of being heard from for the first time, Thomas Wolfe for the second, and John Dos Passos virtually for the last, at least in his great manner. Sinclair Lewis's career as a serious satirist was over, though no one was aware of it yet. The book lists of '33 were dominated by *Anthony Adverse*, the soothing ointment of Professor Pitkin, and less intricate literary headache powders, ranging from *Mutiny on the Bounty* to Richard Halliburton's *The Flying Carpet*.

[1] *Stevedore*, a play dealing with class conflict on the docks of New Orleans, and *The Black Pit*, dramatizing the struggle of the coal miners, were its most notable productions.

5: ART, BUSINESS, AND THE
BLUE EAGLE

O F ALL MEN, the artist has been perhaps the most insecure. When not subsidized by an aristocracy with aesthetic interests as during the Renaissance, or supported by a centralized state as in the Soviet Union, he has generally been permitted to scrabble or starve without interference. Not that those two systems of patronage failed to exact a certain price. The princes of the Renaissance demanded sycophantic dedications; the Soviet Union has at intervals required political propaganda from its writers and painters. At other times, in other countries, creative culture, among the professions, has had the lowest price tag. A young lawyer or doctor or tradesman could look forward to a far earlier financial success than the beginning artist, with the result that few people ever trained themselves consciously for careers as writers, as people consciously prepare for medicine or engineering. So for every Shaw who cheerfully pitches into literature from the start (and earns a farthing during his first ten years as a writer), there are dozens of Shakespeares who begin as actors, Maughams who start as doctors, Gauguins who begin as stockbrokers, Sherwood Andersons who start as business-men, and Hemingways who begin as newspaper corre-spondents. One might add that the artist usually is worse off in an economy ruled by an unregulated spirit of "free enterprise" and "free competition" than in almost any other kind, because his commodity, when sold in the open market, has a less obvious value than that of nearly every other craft.

If it were possible during the depression for anyone to suffer more than the average man, it was the average artist, and of all the hungry eyes turned toward Washington dur-ing the Hundred Days,[1] his was perhaps the hungriest. He had no lobby, moreover, and even if he had, it is doubtful whether it would have received much attention; there were few precedents in America for intimate communication between politics and the arts. So the banks were whipped into shape first, then agriculture through the AAA,[2] labor through the Wagner Act, unemployed youth through the CCC,[3] unemployed white-collar workers through the CWA,[4] business through the NRA[5] and, finally, Wall Street through the Securities and Exchange Act. Then, after everybody else had been taken care of, the Roosevelt Ad-ministration, still improvising at top speed, creating inno-vations from month to month, at last came around to the

[1] As the turbulent early months of President Roosevelt's first term in office came to be called.

[2] Agricultural Adjustment Act.

[3] Civilian Conservation Corps.

[4] Civil Works Administration.

[5] National Industrial Recovery Act.

man with the least negotiable commodity. The WPA,[6] so far as the artist was concerned, remains to this day a small landmark in American civilization, in that it established, on a broad scale, a link between government and the creative arts, and indicated the former's concern, if not actual responsibility, for that profession which, even more than commerce, comprised in temperament the instinctive rugged individualists.

The experiment was not only something new in American life; it was something new in the history of art. Instead of writing dedications and running special errands for wealthy patrons, or drawing posters and drafting leaflets to win the kulaks over to the revolution, the artist applying for a WPA job had only to fill out a questionnaire and testify that he needed it. Once on the government payroll, he did pretty much as he aesthetically pleased. If he drew murals on rural post offices, it wasn't necessary that he portray Franklin D. Roosevelt in a heroic attitude. If assigned to prepare a state guide book in a subdivision of the Federal Writers' Project, he wasn't required to insert essays on the virtues of democracy. If he became an actor with the Federal Theater, he did not have to glorify Washington in plays about the Revolution or Andrew Carnegie in documentaries about the steel industry or the pooh-bahs and sacred cows of any American generation. He remained, in short, a free man; and though paid, his integrity as an artist was not part of the purchase price. What this new method in dealing with the economic relations of the crea-

[6] Works Progress Administration.

tive arts did for the self-respect of the individual artist cannot be measured on graphs. It pulled him out of Stygian darkness, gave him something useful and important to do at a time when usefulness and productivity seemed as outmoded in American life as the buffalo, and galvanized his profession.

Though the WPA hardly produced any single work of art likely to survive through eternity,[7] it did contribute to the culture of the country, if culture is measured in terms of a fruitful and creative daily life. The Federal Theater virtually created the documentary play, which brought to the stage the methods John Dos Passos had brought to literature when he introduced the Newsreel and Camera Eye techniques in *The 42nd Parallel*, and that the documentary film, chiefly in the hands of Pare Lorentz, was soon to bring to the screen. The most famous of the documentary plays, *Triple-A Plowed Under, One-Third of a Nation* (on housing), and *The Living Newspaper*, were a link between the consciously proletarian drama begun by the Theater Union, in 1933, with *Stevedore* and the official trade-union theater represented by that light-hearted satirical revue *Pins and Needles*, produced by the International Ladies' Garment Workers Union. When not molding new forms, the WPA

---

[7] Though Richard Wright's *Uncle Tom's Children*, which won a prize offered by *Story* magazine for the best story by a writer on the Federal Writers' Project, was an outstanding literary work. The same can be said of Pare Lorentz's script for *The River*, the famous documentary which he produced not for the WPA, but for another government agency, the Farm Security Administration.

Theater was putting on at nominal admission fees performances of classical plays in most of the larger cities, making it financially possible for thousands of people to attend the theater for the first time. Marlowe's *Dr. Faustus*, among the more famous of these productions, may not have fallen upon the American public with anything like atomic concussiveness, but that it was an enriching experience, and to some a unique one, is beyond dispute. There was boondoggling and waste motion in the regional theater projects, as in virtually every public or private enterprise, but the projects contributed as perceptibly to American culture as the CCC camps did to the preservation of American forests and wild life.

What the actors of the WPA did, the writers, musicians, and painters did in almost equal measure. They had nothing as new as the documentary play to show for their efforts, but they too extended the aesthetic franchises to great numbers of people to whom oils and symphonies were as foreign as the Left Bank. To this day, many a rural library and post office is easier on the eyes for the frescoes put upon it by some obscure Federal artist. The municipal WPA symphony orchestras, like the radio, functioned as a link between music, hitherto expensively packaged, and the people. The writers turned out a voluminous stream of literature, headed by the famous guide books to various states, almanacs and accounts of special folkways. A good deal of valuable and original historical research went into them, and though some were superficial and other marred with errors, the lot of them constituted a permanent ad-

dition to popular culture. The painters produced no Leo-
nardos; the orchestra conductors were not Toscaninis; as
far as is known, the writers' projects did not unearth any
Hemingways; yet, short of the highest level of excellence
and genius, they left a scroll of respectable achievements
behind them.

The WPA in general and its artists' divisions in particular were under growing attack almost from the start.
Though the loudest clamor was raised by Southern Democrats and New England Republicans, who argued that the
WPA was a step toward socialism, the deepest source of
opposition lay rooted in the profound distrust of culture
with a capital C that was a legacy of the frontier. There
are a greater number of unflattering epithets for the creative artist in American English than in almost any other
civilized language; he is regarded as somehow unmanly,
called a long-hair, sissy, panty-waist, is looked at with suspicion or contempt. It was said of top sergeants in the first
World War that they automatically assigned painters and
concert pianists to latrine duty, and though conditions improved in the second World War,[8] the hostility towards
artistic expression remained strong. To wide sections of a
population one generation removed from the last frontier,
two generations from the Wild West, and only three from
the covered wagon, the idea of supporting down-at-the
heel actors and writers with public funds was utterly re-

---

[8] Concert pianists like Eugene List and Jacques Abram became sergeants
themselves, and the first played for the Big Three at Potsdam. Both returned
to civilian life in 1946, their techniques unimpaired.

pulsive. The country had been pioneered and conquered by stamina, physical courage, hard labor, and other virtues and attributes far removed from the febrile sensitivity popularly associated with the aesthetic temperament. The rural taxpayer who saw his money used to subsidize that temperament was filled with resentment.[9] It was his accumulated hostility supported by the opposition of the conservative press, articulated by the anger and derision of the anti-New Deal congressmen, which undermined in a large measure the foundations of the WPA. When economic conditions began to improve in the spasmodic way characteristic of the first two Roosevelt Administrations, the project lost its original reason for existence, and was liquidated. With its liquidation ended the third of the great historical experiments in the economic relationship between the artist and society.

II

The experiment was born in 1934, a year in which the fantasies of a fantastic time seemed woven more thickly than usual. It was, for example, the year of the great Sam Insull chase. Theodore Dreiser had written the prelimi-

---

[9] This resentment suggests how radical sentiment shifted in the 30's from the country to the city. Figures like Henry George in New York and John Peter Altgeld in Chicago had had their following, but in the main the progressive movements of the nineteenth century, like Populism, had been agrarian in origin. With the New Deal, the big cities, which were the home of the trade unions and the new radical political parties, became the centers of experiment and reform, while the farmers and the rural areas remained staunchly conservative and Republican.

nary script of the affair in *The Titan* two decades before; Insull's career as a Chicago utility magnate and patron of the arts closely followed that of Frank Cowperwood, Dreiser's legendary tycoon. When his empire collapsed, in 1933, under a combination of personal malfeasance and hard times, as Cowperwood's had collapsed under somewhat similar circumstances, Insull fled to Europe one jump ahead of government agents with warrants for his arrest. Dreiser's story ended with his hero fleeing to safety in Europe, and Insull, a man of no mean imagination, continued it into an even more exciting sequel. Armed with astonishingly naïve courage and affecting an air of ingenuous innocence, he moved briskly from one country to another, leaving each only a day or so before his pursuers managed to secure edicts of extradition against him. By February 1 he had arrived in Greece, and seemed about to leave Europe altogether for another continent when he made his great gesture, a gesture from the age of Dumas. He had beating upon him the concentrated gaze of nearly the whole newspaper-reading public of the United States, including the tens of thousands of people whom he had defrauded, when he offered the government of Turkey a bribe of fifteen million dollars to grant him asylum from his pursuers. No matter that the offer was refused; no matter that Insull was eventually hauled back to Chicago and a court of justice, and a sentimental trial in the best American "poor old man in the dock" manner. The trail of his nimble flight across Europe with his would-be jailers often staying at the same hotel without being able to lay a hand upon him, the cool bravado of his epic bribe in which the methods he had used in business were simply extended to an international scale, the pattern of the chase in the grand style which seemed to be under the directorship of an invisible René Clair, had a historical as well as a topical significance. It was the last chapter in the saga of the robber barons, which had begun after the Civil War with the careers of Rockefeller and Vanderbilt and had now come to a uniquely melodramatic and personalized end with the downfall of Samuel Insull. With the coming of the Securities and Exchange Act and the other ethical restraints upon wild speculation formulated by the New Deal, the era of the malefactors of great wealth in the flamboyant sense became a thing of the past.

A second extraordinary incident of that extraordinary year was the invasion of politics by the old literary war horse Upton Sinclair. Nothing could have been more sweetly logical than for the author of *The Jungle*, *Co-op*, and *King Coal* to run for the governorship of California on a platform of communal economics which, since it ran to size, was appropriately called EPIC.[10] Having hammered away since 1906 in his pamphleteering novels at the evils of the profit system, Sinclair assumed a public stance perfectly in keeping with his art. He was doing, indeed, what Plato in *The Republic* had argued was the duty of every educated and thinking citizen, to participate in politics; or if he proved unwilling—as most educated and thinking

[10] End Poverty in California.

Athenians would have, gazing at the mire of the political arena—the state should pass laws compelling him to do so. Sinclair's program called for the government in Sacramento to operate the factories and farms made idle in the depression by staffing them with the unemployed made idle in the same disaster. Since this was a practical application of the New Deal theory that the government was responsible for giving people useful jobs if private enterprise could not, the Democratic party sponsored Sinclair as its official candidate, though it may have felt some queasiness at his failure to indicate, as Roosevelt had done, that all this was to be temporary, and contingent upon the restoration of private trade. The essence of EPIC had been worked out germinally in *Co-op*, and there was nothing in Sinclair's public statements not to be found in his numerous books, each dealing as it did with one or another basic industry, each resting upon an intimate, close-range study of the operations of the industry on a day-to-day basis over a period of months.

The excitement generated in the campaign acquired the proportions of a tempest. The charges soon to be a part of the Republican attacks upon Roosevelt were first formulated and tried out on Sinclair: that he was a Red, a bloody revolutionary seeking to overthrow the Constitution, an impractical visionary, a man who wrote books (as though this disqualified him from being an efficient public servant), a monster who would destroy everything in California from the movies to the climate. Since the Republican party in California was under the control of Herbert

Hoover and Hiram Johnson and had no liberal wing, no holds were barred, and the result was one of the most vilifying, bare-knuckle fights in the political history of the Far West. Heading the outcry against Sinclair were the film producers, who set up shop as the propaganda branch of the Republican party. They began by issuing a joint threat that if the EPIC ticket were elected, they would move the film industry from Hollywood to another section of the country. When the unlikelihood of this became plain, they produced a series of shorts and newsreels which showed streams of vagrants from other states pouring into California at Sinclair's invitation, and presented speeches by prominent Hollywood personalities, warning against the new threat to what became one of the slogans of the 30's, "the American way of life." The aged, who had come to California in large numbers to spend their declining years and who subsisted on pensions and trust funds, were showered with statements that victory for the Democratic candidate would undermine the credit and banking system upon which they depended. Appeals to every stratum of the population, invocation of the Founding Fathers, every implement of political warfare, were drafted into the crusade to save the state. Sinclair's allies, aside from a small number of articulate liberals, were the amorphous mass of people who had not yet been freed from the smothering weight of the depression, but even many of these, despite misfortune, still retained their faith in the old slogans. Sinclair was more vulnerable as a candidate than Roosevelt in the years to come because he had committed himself spe-

CARL A. RUDISILL LIBRARY
LENOIR RHYNE COLLEGE

cifically in print. When Roosevelt was accused of being a
Communist, it was hard to sell this notion about the Hyde
Park country gentleman to the general public. But Sinclair
had attacked capitalism in one novel after another; it
wasn't necessary to quote him out of context to prove that
he was a Socialist, and socialism, even after four years of
the depression, had not begun to attract Americans as it
had the French and British. The process of metamorphos-
ing Sinclair into a monster was pretty complete by election
day, and he was defeated by a wide, though by no means
humiliating, margin.

With the defeat, ended one of the more remarkable
adventures of the decade, after which the era's greatest fictional pamphleteer withdrew to the narrower task of thundering from the wings. Or so one expected. Who could
guess that the stresses and strains of EPIC probably
marked the last great effort of his career? For instead of
proceeding on the course that had produced the books
which, however childish and psychologically simple as novels, were among the notable pamphlets of the century, Sinclair passed into a becalmed old age. The Lanny Budd
novels that began appearing in the later 30's, while no less
numerous and ramified than the earlier works, were nothing more than leisurely historical memoirs of the public
life of the Western world since 1910. Though melodramatic enough in the sense that every celebrity from Hitler
to Isadora Duncan appears in bas-relief, they are without
fire and without that zeal which Sinclair had inherited from
Zola to expose social and economic injustice. They stand

in about the same relationship to *The Jungle* and *Boston* [11]
as Dr. A. J. Cronin's agreeably surfaced chronicle, *The
Citadel*, stands to those great novels of medicine and medical men, *Arrowsmith* and *Of Human Bondage*. The ma-
terials are all there, but the spirit lags. Without losing any
of his mechanical facility and staggering energy, Sinclair
has lost his crusading ardor, which was his single *raison
d'être* as a creative journalist, using fiction as an instrument of journalism. Stripped of his passion for reform, he
is only a readable novelist whose best days seem past.

The other public events of 1934 fitted into a cyclical
pattern which was in some ways to keep recurring until
Pearl Harbor. On January 1, Father Coughlin was continuing his radio career by warning of plots against the
New Deal, which, one may add hastily, was not one of the
elements in the pattern that was ever again to recur. On
February 4, Japan was sending another of its innumerable
envoys to the United States "intent on peace." On March
1, Richard Whitney, chairman of the New York Stock Exchange, attacked the Securities and Exchange Act as a
threat to trade, an ironic utterance in view of Mr. Whitney's subsequent imprisonment on a charge of embezzling
one of his clients' funds. On March 2, by way of climax-
ing the year of the great Insull scandal, the Book-of-the-
Month Club selected Matthew Josephson's *The Robber
Barons* as its choice for the month. On March 4, marking
the end of Roosevelt's first year in office, the Republicans

---

[11] One of Sinclair's best and most convincing novels, dealing with the
Sacco-Vanzetti case.

celebrated the anniversary by assailing the President on the grounds that "he had retarded recovery, deceived the country," and generally brought things to a pretty pass. March also witnessed the last chapter of the career of John Dillinger, in his own way a kind of robber baron, too; or, perhaps better yet, the last of the rugged individualists, the epithet applied by Robert Sherwood a year later to his prototype in *The Petrified Forest.* For a few spectacular weeks, Insull and Dillinger were chasing one another furiously through the headlines, and when the financier subsided meekly in the arms of Federal agents and the gangster subsided fiercely under the bullets of Federal agents, the day of the willful hero had clearly drawn to a close. Henceforth there were to be no conspicuous exceptions to the iron hold of events, economic and political, upon the destiny of the individual; free will was to operate only within the framework of the collective will of powerful nations (whether predatory or peaceful) and hardly at all within the experience of the individual. One profound difference between the 20's and the 30's lay precisely here: the individual thought he had some elbow-room during the first, but felt himself increasingly squeezed during the second, which is why in 1924 the young drunks in F. Scott Fitzgerald have the choice of drinking or not drinking at the outset, whereas by 1934 James T. Farrell's Studs Lonigan has very little choice of going or not going to the dogs, and by 1939 the Joads are so buffeted by outside circumstances beyond their control that individual action on their part counts for nothing, and their only hope, as Casy and

Steinbeck both assure us, is through collective action, the last contemporary refuge of free will.

The first manifestations of this collective will came from the ranks of labor, in the spring of 1934. There was a taxi strike in New York City in February, walkouts in a few steel and cotton mills in June, a Minneapolis trucking strike in August. And in August, too, the Hudson Motor Union announced its withdrawal from the A. F. of L. The import of this last little item was not plain at the time, but it proved to be the first move in the direction of the unionization of the automobile industry under the aegis of the United Automobile Workers and the C.I.O. Lauren Gilfillan, a young college graduate, spent a few weeks in a ramshackle company coal town outside Pittsburgh and wrote *I Went to Pit College*, which flared for a season as one of the early indications of public interest in the proletariat that was to illuminate the decade.

Working the other side of the fence at the same time, the native fascists—some crackpot, some quite respectable—were girding for the kind of action which they hoped would lead to what Lawrence Dennis, their leading theorist, called "the coming Fascist Revolution in America." The California Silver Shirts had already purchased their first argent uniforms, and Victor McLaglen was reputed to be outfitting his private Hollywood constabulary in a manner appropriate to what might be their strong-arm rôle. It was still a little early for Huey Long who, though making himself heard from the floor of the Senate, had not yet organized his "Share-the-Wealth" movement, which in its day was to be by all odds the most dangerous of the home-grown fascist crop; but Father Coughlin was by the end of the year already turning over in his mind blueprints for the National Union for Social Justice, and discerning readers of the public press could see small signs pointing to the ultimate formation of the German-American Bund. An ex-preacher in Kansas, Gerald Winrod, could be heard in the backwoods, ranting against the Jews, and, with little difficulty, anyone interested could secure all sorts of pamphleted material, presenting a case against every minority group in the country. There were strikebreaking bureaus in every large city which supplied thugs at so much per head to break picket lines, and many of the large corporations had agencies to spy upon their workers and report any trace of union activity. The records of the La Follette Civil Liberties Committee, which the Senate was soon to set up to investigate these matters, unfold one of the black tales in American industrial life, a tale to which those unions dominated by racketeering and undemocratic labor leaders (some of whom were eventually sent to jail for their crimes) were to contribute a conspicuous page.

All the while, in other parts of the world, the terrors of the second World War were being foreshadowed by a series of ominous and bloody events. In the north of Spain, a revolt of the Asturian miners was being ruthlessly suppressed through the importation of Moorish troops from Africa. Hitler was carrying out his "blood purge" against a cadre of former associates. Dollfuss, after slaughtering the socialist working class of Vienna, in February, was himself murdered by the Nazis in July. In October, King Alexander of Yugoslavia and Foreign Minister Barthou of France were assassinated by Croatian terrorists in the pay of Mussolini, and in December, Kirov, a close associate of Stalin, met a similar fate on a street in Leningrad. Meanwhile, in the Chaco jungles far to the south, the unpublicized but sanguinary war between Bolivia and Paraguay was dragging on without headlines and seemingly without end.

Counterstroking these tendencies toward destruction was the great event of the year in the United States, the NRA, which, under the sign of the Blue Eagle, sought to settle in a peaceful way once and for all the tensions between capital and labor within the framework of capitalism. By summoning employers and employees in each industry to set up mutually agreeable codes regulating prices, wages and cutthroat competition, the government was recognizing labor as a partner equal to management in the economic life of the country. The structure of NRA bore certain physical similarities to Mussolini's corporate state, a circumstance that led John T. Flynn [12] to believe that the New Deal was really preparing the way for fascism. Political theorists, of whom Friedrich A. Hayek [13] was the most conspicuous, were later to attack every kind of central government planning as leading to dictatorship.

But a policy must ultimately be judged in terms of

[12] In his book, *As We Go Marching*.
[13] In his widely publicized *The Road to Serfdom*.

the intention of its formulator. The policy of invoking States' rights, for example, may sometimes be a means of protecting the people against the encroachments of a rapacious federalism, as it was when Jefferson invoked it against Hamilton. Or it may be a reactionary slogan to maintain an oppression of the people against a liberalizing federalism, as it is in the hands of some Southern senators when they filibuster, for example, against the elimination of the poll tax. Mussolini used his corporative devices first to destroy labor and then to harness management to his own private ends. Roosevelt used them to help free labor from what he felt was its inferior position in American economy, and to encourage voluntary co-operation between employer and employee, with the government not as the tyrant but as the moderator. Since these ideas had been common practice in England for a generation or more, there was nothing startlingly new about them. The seminars and round-table discussions of the NRA, in theory at least, were the very essence of that humanist view of things which believes that all problems can be rationally and peacefully settled if the will to be rational is stimulated. The NRA was administered by General Hugh Johnson, a military martinet with somewhat aggressive manners and a bellicose disposition, and it was ultimately invalidated by the Supreme Court; but, while in existence, it sought to encourage that will and to create a climate in which it might prosper.

III

The last months of 1934 witnessed not only the subsidence of the NRA, but the emergence in the literary world of three novels which were to leave a small but distinctive impress upon the times. The first of these, written by Ruth Suckow, was a quiet, rather dull book called *The Folks*, which found in the small town neither the cultureless mediocrities of Sinclair Lewis nor the sexually maladjusted, spiritually frustrated creatures of Sherwood Anderson and Edgar Lee Masters. Miss Suckow's locale is Iowa; and her characters, the Fergusons, who live in the smallish town of Belmond, are perfectly ordinary people engulfed in a middle-class gray. Though they flourish in the Bible Belt, they have few of the characteristics of H. L. Mencken's "booboisie." Pa Ferguson works in the bank, is thrifty and good-natured. Ma Ferguson, one cut above Pa in taste and manners, is generous and good-natured. Two of the four children are undistinguished, marry mediocre persons, and settle down to contented mediocrity. A third rebels, goes to New York, and lives a free Bohemian life. A fourth marries the average home-town girl, and sinks into dull routine, though he keeps longing for better things. The sociology of the book prefaces Thornton Wilder's *Our Town*, which put upon the stage, in 1938, the same kind of people and the same kind of town.

The Folks was one of the few novels of the 30's which had no trace of Freud or Marx. It lacked social significance

in the usual sense, and permitted not the smallest impinge-
ment of the outside world upon its characters, whose private lives and emotional problems oscillate in an absolute vacuum. At the other extreme, it skirted away from the gelati-
nous qualities of regional literature. Though Belmond,
Iowa, was present, it was present unobtrusively. Its inhabitants did not drawl or speak in dialect. The Fergusons had
relatives on a near by farm, but even the farmers had no exaggerated folkways that lent themselves to synthetic exploi-
tation in either literature or technicolor. This was not the
Iowa of Phil Stong with its state fairs, tender romances,
and splashes of local color. The characters were plain folks
without being at all folksy. Its uneventful realism and
scrupulous insistence on avoiding any sort of melodrama
or generating any kind of false suspense were the novel's
principal virtues and caused it to occupy in a small way,
in the fiction of the 30's, a place analogous to that held by
Middletown in Transition in the sociological annals of the
same time.

Appearing simultaneously with *The Folks* was *The
Foundry*, by Albert Halper, a writer absorbed not in the
small town but in the young persons who live in shabby
one-room apartments off Union Square, the rootless intellectuals, the workers in foundries and mail order houses,
the very people whose lives were being transformed by
the Federal Writers' Project, the NRA, and the Wagner
Labor Relations Act. His first novel, *Union Square*, had enjoyed a somewhat exaggerated success, considering its tendency to break down the residents of 14th Street into rather

well-worn types, and to lay on its effects with a heavy emphasis that left nothing to the imagination. The tone of the novel was strident, its style mannered, the story overwritten, and, despite occasional strokes of brilliance, clearly the work of a man who was straining too hard but had hit happily upon a theme which was of considerable topical interest. With the appearance of *The Foundry*, most of these errors had been brought under control. The workers and bosses in a Chicago foundry, manufacturing printing plates, are swept up into an intricately woven design. The rhythm of the machines under whose pounding and tempo they labor is orchestrated through a variety of percussive devices, and the whole novel is written with an air of heartiness and gusto often associated with what has come to be known as "an affirmative view of life." Here, indeed, was that rare kind of proletarian novel which avoided proletarian formulas. It avoided soapbox oratory, political and economic theses, and every kind of doctrinaire tone. Primarily concerned with its characters as human beings, it managed to suggest the closed versus the open shop debate, the tensions between workers and employers, paternal capitalism aimed at crushing unionization, the problem of technological unemployment and its attendant sabotage of labor-saving machines, without at any time obscuring its steady focus on the personalities and emotional lives of the people involved in these issues. There are no clear-cut victories for either side in the foundry, and no absolute defeats; in a small and concentrated way, Halper defines what life is like within the fabric of industrialized America.

The novel contains some memorable and brilliant scenes: the appearance of the machine nicknamed "The Big Smasher" and its subsequent fate; the playing of the *Printing House Blues* and how it came to be composed by August, the foundry's shipping clerk; the suicide of Jack Duffy and how his corpse was silent witness to the last of the great operations of the foundry before the depression closed it down.

But the book has its irritating mannerisms, too, one of the worst being the tendency to pun:

"The press boys, sniffing the debacle, pressed him [the banker] for another statement, but all the great man did was to press his jaws together firmly. Surely Pintel Markowitz, in his little hole-in-the-wall store around the corner on South State Street, could have done just as good a job of pressing, for was he not an expert tailor?"

Nor is everything in the book indispensable. The love affair between Miss Weber and the Attorney General serves little purpose, the criminal career of young Frankie and the philandering of his sister are equally superfluous. But the novel represented an advance over *Union Square*,[14] and the relationship between it and the America of the NRA, the America already beginning to record the bitter lessons of the speculative boom and the thundering crash, is evident.

[14] *The Foundry* appears, in retrospect to have been the supreme effort of its author's career. *The Chute*, which reached an expectant public in 1937, was a sad disappointment; it was a carbon copy of *The Foundry* in every essential. Like every literary carbon copy, the print was blurred, the characters familiar in the wrong way, the effect as a whole less emphatic.

The last of the three important novels to appear in the crowded final months of 1934 was *Appointment in Samarra*. Its author, John O'Hara, displayed a concern equally pronounced about still a third section of American society, the frequenters of the cocktail lounges, country clubs, and Park Avenue apartments. He grew up as a writer under the influence of F. Scott Fitzgerald, and inherited from that sensitive craftsman of the 20's his sharp, somewhat nervous stroking and an absorption in the lives of a certain upper-class stratum of people in their early thirties who graduated from fashionable eastern universities, belonged to the country club set, and were rapidly going to the devil sexually and alcoholically. *Appointment in Samarra* studied them against the background of a small Pennsylvania town. *Butterfield 8*, published three years later, scrutinized them in the metropolitan setting of New York City. For some time afterward, O'Hara concentrated on the short story, a form which he practiced with increasing skill without altering his choice of subject or shifting his lines of inquiry.

Of his published work, *Appointment in Samarra* remains the most illuminating and characteristic, and like all his others, is a sharp, pitiless study of human beings in the process of destroying themselves. Julian English, his wife, and his friends, in their small, stratified Pennsylvania town are in a state of inner corrosion; the story opens just an instant before the corrosion seeps to the surface and becomes visible. What ails them grows increasingly plain: they are suffering from a deep-rooted insecurity which robs

them of emotional balance in moments of crisis, moves
them to hate one another and themselves under the coat-
ing of conventional loves and attachments, shreds their
nerves, drives them to drink and through drink to maudlin
sexual adventures, and finally to suicide of one kind or another without anyone to mourn their departure. The source
of their insecurity O'Hara does not indicate. Was it the
nihilist impact of the first World War? Or the nerve-jags
of the 20's, aggravated by the Volstead Act and the boom?
Or the instability of their individual childhoods, which the
author, in the case of Julian, obliquely suggests? Or simply
the accident of temperament without reference to society
or the facts of American life? We are not told. We are
left instead with an appalling sense of how thin are the
ties that hold Julian and his intimates together, how narrow is their margin of emotional safety, how profound their
alienation from their own selves and from one another.
From the start, they have the stamp of death on them. Beyond all else, O'Hara is a sort of literary neurologist, a
hypersensitive recorder of each nerve twitch, each mind
tic. His characters pass through abruptly alternating moods.
"I feel good." "I feel like hell." Not terribly articulate
themselves, O'Hara is articulate for them, and his brush-
work is splendid. He lays out Gibbsville, Pennsylvania,
with quick strokes, sketching in the country club aristocracy, the bootleggers, the Catholics, the Jews (to whom
his characters refer with vicious contempt), and the middle
class. They are all inspected with a heartless and chilling
clarity; indeed, a kind of chill issues from this whole prob-

ing style which repels us in the very act of illumination.

The Pal Joey sketches that appeared later, and nearly all the short stories, give forth the same chill, the same odor of doom. Pal Joey is an unsavory night club entertainer who preys upon others financially and emotionally. The short stories record in a style compounded of steel filaments characters whose fortunes are slanting downward, the angle of the downward slant being caught with mathematical precision. The husband in *Are We Leaving Tomorrow?* who sits in a Florida hotel drinking endlessly, discouraging respectable acquaintances by deliberately telling obscene stories, hovered over by an anxious wife, is a typical portrait. Here, too, we do not learn what ails him or how he got into his present psychotic state, but its symptoms and his conduct are described with heartless accuracy. The old man in *Through Wood and Dale*, who accidentally enters a young lady's room while she is undressed, and thereby loses his reputation, illustrates again the writer's interest in disaster which, if it fails to arrive by itself, will be jogged into being by his contrivance.

There is in all this a bitterness which F. Scott Fitzgerald, even in his lowest moments, never quite reached. Fitzgerald, at least, has an Amory Blaine who at the end of *This Side of Paradise* can look to the future with a hopeful gleam, and twenty odd years later a Monroe Stahr, the movie tycoon in the unfinished *The Last Tycoon*, who seems to have some chance of emerging right side up. O'Hara's people are cursed from the start. Fitzgerald's suffer from the political shock of the first World War and its depressing aftermath. O'Hara's suffer from a double shock, the political one of 1919 and the economic one of 1929. If the creations of Fitzgerald have enough room and breath to come up for air occasionally, those of his most skillful disciple have neither room nor strength. They flounder and smother in the swamp of the age, and their author only stands on the edge and watches them with pitiless and disillusioned eyes.

6: CHICAGO, YOKNAPATAWPHA COUNTY, AND POINTS SOUTH

THE stagnation into which America passed during the early 30's showed up more plainly in some places than in others, and there were literary chroniclers on hand to study its effects on the people who lived there. Depravity in the deep South found an Erskine Caldwell, the corruption of country club society a John O'Hara; the miseries of the Dust Bowl an Edwin Lanham [1] and a John Steinbeck; the slums of New York a Sidney Kingsley.[2] Writers all over America, proletarian and sophisticate, employing the old methods of fiction or the new stream of consciousness, were hacking away at the successive waves of wreckage beached by the crises since 1914.

If a line were to be drawn from Chicago down to the Gulf of Mexico, it would begin with one of the decade's great ruins and end with another. From every point of view except that of violence and dissolution, it is a far cry from Studs Lonigan to the Snopeses, Sartorises, Sutpens, and

---

[1] Whose *The Stricklands*, despite structural flaws, was a fine account of life among the tenant farmers of Oklahoma stricken by drought, dust, and depression.

[2] Whose well-knit play *Dead End* ran for nearly two years on Broadway.

Joe Christmases of William Faulkner, but violence and dissolution bind the Catholic boy from the lower middle-class Chicago neighborhood to the hag-ridden Protestants of Faulkner's mythical Yoknapatawpha County more tightly than could ties of religion or place. Both are landmarks in the American wasteland, major images of that social decay which overtook the slums of the big cities and the perishing villages of the deep South in the same time sequence.

As writers, Farrell and Faulkner lend themselves to certain illuminating contrasts. The one is of interest to us because of his principal character, the other because of himself. Studs Lonigan is likely to survive in American fiction, but Farrell's second hero, Danny O'Neill, and his third, Bernard Clare, are stenciled and dull. The figures in Faulkner have no vivid individuality, but scenes involving them are projected with such blazing imagination, such rhapsodic intensity, as to make other Southern novelists, with the exception of Thomas Wolfe, seem pale by contrast. With the passing years, it grows increasingly evident that Farrell's later work will linger in the permanent shadow of the Lonigan trilogy, whereas Faulkner's creative sense seemed inexhaustible. There are things in his later novel, *The Hamlet,* quite equal in originality to the great passages of *Absalom, Absalom!, Light in August,* or *The Sound and the Fury.* One never doubts that the city Farrell describes is really Chicago, scenically as well as sociologically, but Faulkner's Mississippi is so veiled in sensuous rhetoric, so filled with an intense aesthetic consciousness,

that one is hard put to say whether it is a country of reality
or of the author's imagination. The ultimate contrast, however, lies in the difference of narrative method. Farrell's is
purely monolithic, with everything channeled through the
eyes of his lone male protagonist. Faulkner favors the cir-
cular process of surveying a single event, or a small handful of events, from various angles, each articulated by a
different character placed at different points in the same
circle, or several narrators spinning their own circles at different radii from the event located at the center. This
process is far more complex than Farrell's, lends itself to
ramifications outside the range of *Studs Lonigan*, and is
marked by that greater looseness of structure to which
Faulkner, by temperament, is inclined. Yet the two, despite
the strong contrasts that mark off so many areas of their
fiction, are one in their preoccupation with tragedy.

II

Half the tragedy of Studs Lonigan is due to the shortcomings of his environment, half to the weaknesses of his
character, a ratio that at a stroke solves most of the structural problems of the trilogy, since it decides how much
time and energy is to be spent on his surroundings, how
much on himself in relation to them. This is a ratio that
Farrell learned from his tutelary master, Dreiser, and one
has only to glance at *An American Tragedy* to note how
much Clyde Griffiths and his story have contributed to the
shaping of Studs. Clyde is, in almost every respect, the

prototype of Studs: weak, sensual, gregarious, driven to do wicked things without himself becoming wicked—evil being an attribute of society, never of the individual. The tale of Studs is more firmly knit and in some ways more convincing than that of Clyde because Dreiser permits his environmental formula to run away with him in a way that Farrell is careful to avoid. The last three hundred pages of *An American Tragedy* demonstrate in painstaking detail the crooked police investigation and the fraudulent trial which lead to Clyde's execution for a crime which he did, after all, commit, and, hence, in the demonstration of which no fraud was at all necessary. These three hundred pages throw the whole novel out of balance, for during them Clyde drops more or less out of sight, and the writer devotes himself to proving the wickedness of society, a homily better suited to the pulpit than to the novel. Nor are they essential, since the reader is prepared to believe without exhaustive argument that police frame-ups sometimes occur. Farrell avoids this tendency to ride theses too hard—a tendency endemic in Dreiser—by keeping his hero firmly in the center of things, and viewing the decisive events through his eyes. Numerous attacks are launched against society and its institutions, but these are never splintered off from the main story and treated by themselves. Interest in Studs and interest in his Chicago are nicely equated, and this equating process invests the Lonigan novels with that firmness of structure which is a familiar attribute of memorable fiction.

It is also a process that begins on the first page with

fourteen-year-old Studs in the bathroom, smoking one of his first cigarettes on the day of his graduation from parochial school. The monologue that runs through his mind, with his sister intermittently pounding on the door telling him to hurry up, is one of the most dramatic and illuminating of its kind, for it lights up not alone the impressionable and still plastic character of the boy, but his family, his school, his church, his gang of friends—the chief elements of the society into which he was born. Studs' bad habits are visible, like brown spots on an apple that has grown a little wormy, but he is a likable youngster, energetic and marked with a certain perceptiveness. Two pitfalls in projecting him as a literary figure are neatly side-stepped, a circumstance to a very large degree responsible for the success of the story. The Lonigans are not an impoverished family living in a slum house, which would provide the author with an easy explanation of all the disasters overtaking his hero, and let the weight of economic determinism burden his tale. This easy explanation was the great handicap of the proletarian novel, and which, in the end, brought it down. The Lonigans are not badly off, and they belong to the respectable lower middle class. Nor are they a depraved family of alcoholics and wife-beaters, to whom Studs' bad end might be ascribed in as *a priori* a manner as to their hypothetical poverty and slum-dwelling. Mr. Lonigan is a hard-working, earnest painting contractor who drinks very little, treats his wife with respect, and tries to set a good example for his son. Mrs. Lonigan is a conventionally good woman. To have a fictional Irish family

that on the one hand does not drink and quarrel or, on the
other, is not wildly imaginative and full of fey fancies, is
in itself to be regarded as a triumph of realism.

Parental failure in Studs' case lies not in the stereo-
types of poverty or bad habits, but in the lack of understanding of the young by the old, aggravated by the gap
between parents still close to the Old Sod and their Amer-
ican-born children. Studs' parents want him to live a rigidly
conventional life, fear and obey the priest, and avoid the
pool room. His mother anxiously waits for Studs to have
the Call; his father wants him to prepare for a junior part-
nership in his business. Of the temptations of sex and the
allurements of sand-lot baseball, of the pleasures of gang
comradeship and the rebellions against conventional society through which all adolescents pass, they have not the
remotest conception, and this ignorance—which Farrell
skillfully documents—is a principal factor in the ultimate
disintegration of Studs.

Here is a typical family scene at the Lonigan family
table:

"The old man carved the meat. . . . He asked Studs
why he was late for dinner. He said Studs was always late
for dinner. Everybody else got to the bathroom early
enough, so that they could be at the table when dinner was
announced. He said that he spent good money for food,
and that Studs' mother slaved over a hot stove so that they
could have a decent meal. He and the mother both had
some right to demand gratitude and respect for this. Studs
said that he didn't see nothing wrong in having stopped

to wash his hands; and his father, starting into rag-chewing, put Studs in a mood of opposition, made him feel that he was in the right, made him believe that he had delayed only to wash his hands, and that his father was being inconsiderate and un-understanding. . . . Frances said that she wished the Sunday quarreling could be stopped. She was tired of sitting down to a Sunday dinner and being forced to listen to this interminable ragging. Old man Lonigan said that there wouldn't be no quarreling if everybody did what was right. He said that he was boss of the household, and that as long as he remained boss of the household there were certain rules that would be observed and one was that everybody must be at the table on time. It got Studs sore. The old man was always pulling that stuff."

Having carefully planned the initial premises of his novel, Farrell proceeds to tick off the main experiences of his hero with a vigor that remains unflagging through three long volumes. The city itself is described with a fierce and effective naturalism, and enacts in its own way as sharp a rôle in the story as Dublin does in *Ulysses* and Paris in *The Ambassadors.* Chicago's crowded sidewalks, lake-fronted parks, the abrasive rattling of its els, its violent changes of season, are all stimulating.

"The July night leaked heat all over Fifty-eighth Street, and the fitful death of the sun shed softening colors that spread gauzelike and glamorous over the street, stilling those harshnesses and commercial uglinesses that were emphasized by the brighter revelations of day. About the street there seemed to be a supervening beauty of reflected life. The dust, the scraps of paper, the piled-up store windows, the first electric light sizzling into brightness. Sammie Schmaltz, the paper man, yelling his final-box-score editions, a boy's broken hoop left forgotten against the elevated girder, the people hurrying out of the elevated station and others walking lazily about, all bespoke the life of a community, the tang and sorrow and joy of a people that lived, worked, suffered, procreated, aspired, filled out their little days, and died."

Studs' life in the city oscillates between the pool room and the church, between his genteel but uninspiring home and the rooms of his raffish friends where liquor sprees and "gang shags" are the order of the day. He is not, however, torn between the forces of good and evil, for the forces of good, at any rate, are no longer institutionalized, as they were in nineteenth century fiction. The Church, for example, is no longer the center of absolute truth, and appears, indeed, in strongly anti-clerical terms. The droning platitudes of the parochial school principal on Studs' graduation day are recorded with mordant accuracy. The scene, with its ominous overtones, in which Studs becomes initiated into the Order of Christopher, is reminiscent of the episodes at the Jesuit retreat which affect Stephen Dedalus so strongly in A *Portrait of the Artist as a Young Man.* Farrell is obviously steeped in Joyce, and though his heroes have none of the sensitive and poetic imagination of Dedalus, their religious experiences are filled with the same mixture of boredom and horrified fascination.

One gets, throughout, a vague sense of the oppressiveness and hostility of Studs' environment, but there is no conscious villainy on anyone's part. Indeed, everyone—teachers, parents, priests—means well. Even his friends, though depraved, have an air of innocence. But lack of understanding, the pressures of a ruthlessly competitive society, the apathies and weaknesses of his own character, gradually bring Studs down. And in some ways the greatest achievement of the book is that even after it becomes apparent that Studs is skidding irresistibly downhill, we continue reading with undiminished interest. Throughout, he and his problems and experiences are belligerently alive.

But with the death of Studs, something vital passes out of Farrell's writing. Scarcely evident in *A World I Never Made*, this dwindling vitality comes to view in *No Star Is Lost*, and is most pronounced in *My Days of Anger* and *Bernard Clare*. In these novels, Farrell takes hold of a new idea, diametrically the reverse of the one that animated *Studs Lonigan*. Where Studs is defeated by life, Danny O'Neill triumphs over it. This turnabout should have sufficed to lend freshness to the volumes dealing with Danny, but it does not. Farrell's method remains the same, as do his stage properties: the Irish, Chicago, the decor, the sociology, the family relationships. If anything, Danny's external circumstances are less favorable than Studs'. But why Danny succeeds where Studs fails is never made clear; in any case, the failure of Studs remains convincing while Danny's triumph is heavily contrived. The explanation perhaps lies in the fact that Studs and his surroundings are equally real, whereas only Danny's surroundings are real.

As a boy, he is only a recording mechanism for the laments of his relatives, ranging from his sister Margaret, entangled in a long and hopeless affair, to his uncle Al O'Flaherty, the traveling shoe salesman, who mouths all the platitudes of the Rotarian mind and is easily the best drawn character in the series. As a young man, Danny is less an individualized human being than a type of perpetually distempered, arrogant college student who longs for the literary life, and is sensitive in a manufactured way. He exhausts himself psychologically very early in *My Days of Anger*, the last and dullest of the O'Neill volumes, and even his hostile surroundings are laid on with wearying repetition. When, at the end, he emancipates himself from the stupefying world of Farrell's Chicago Irish and leaves for New York to take up a career as a writer, his triumph emerges from nothing compulsive either in his milieu or himself. It is a perfectly arbitrary act, willed by the author.

In New York, he turns up at the start of Farrell's next series under the name of Bernard Clare, but he is still the prototype of the sullenly angry, self-puffing young man, without nuance, and, in the hands of his author at any rate, apparently incapable of psychological growth. His experiences, like Danny's, remain more interesting than himself, and we weary of his perpetual conceit long before the book closes. The failure lies not in the limitations of naturalism as a method, which some critics have claimed, but in the narrowness and inflexibility of Farrell's imagination. Where Studs was a fluid complex of conflicting impulses, the later heroes are undifferentiated as children, caricatured as young

men, and at all times too heavily stamped with their author's design.

In recent years, Farrell has diverted part of his energies into literary criticism and polemics, most of it as angry
and one-tracked as his recent fiction. A *Note on Marxism*
documented at great length his break with the Communist
party, and while some of it was a shrewd analysis of the
dangers and sterilities of the literal application of Marxism
to literature, it consigned the author to a kind of permanent involvement in the factionalisms of left-wing politics.
His own position, that of an anti-Stalinist Marxist, he has
pursued with doggedness and energy, but with little profit
to his creative work. Thousands of words have flowed from
his polemical pen about the sins of the Communists, and
the evils of the capitalist system. He has carried on a one-
man vendetta against Archibald MacLeish for accusing
American writers of breeding a pacifist spirit in the people
between wars; and in *The League of Frightened Philis-
tines* attacked all sorts of prominent persons who he felt
were reactionary or who had retreated to safe middle-class
conventions at the first sign of danger. Some of his invective was quite memorable, as when he dubbed Mortimer
J. Adler (the neo-medievalist at the University of Chicago,
who has been instructing the country on how to read, how
to think about war and peace,[3] etcetera), a provincial
Torquemada. Most of it, however, had been repetitious. If
he has excoriated Hollywood once for producing a cheap

---

[3] These are the themes of his two able and trenchantly written books,
How to Read a Book and *How to Think about War and Peace.*

opiate culture, he has done so a dozen times. His apologias for Joyce and Dreiser have been too numerous to classify. His accounts of the dilemma of the honest writer under capitalism have been multitudinous. In a word, his criticism has become as tedious as his fiction. At times, the ventures of a writer into polemics has nourished his creative muse. Shelley is a supreme illustration of this. For the most part, as in Farrell's case, such ventures have been wasteful and stifling. If they have advanced criticism, they have hampered genius.

Studs Lonigan, however, remains a monument of the fiction of the 30's, and all of Farrell's subsequent dead-ends can do nothing to weaken the permanence of his reputation based on that one trilogy alone.

III

No such single landmark emerges from the writing of Faulkner. His genius is diffuse and blurred, and runs to the memorable episode rather than the integrated book. Yet even in the clouded intervals between successful episodes, one can hear the humming and vibrating of his imagination at work, an imagination which, however uneven and undisciplined, is one of the powerful creative centers of contemporary American literature.

Few writers have aroused so much hostility, few have stimulated so many varying theories to explain their work. The commonest error with regard to Faulkner lay in the identification of his horrors with his whole writing self, as though he were mainly interested in purveying literary accounts of sodomy, miscegenation, murder, rape, and four or five different degrees of imbecility decked out like so many *hors d'œuvres* for the appetite of a public already conditioned to sensationalism by the tabloid press. These subjects stand in about the same relationship to Faulkner's real aim as the violence in Chaucer and Shakespeare (of which there is a great deal) stands to theirs, or the smut in Rabelais, Baudelaire, and Joyce to theirs. Nor can it be argued that Faulkner's horrors, when not laid on thickly, are redundant. There is great variety, even in his idiots. Benjie Compson of *The Sound and the Fury* is as different from Ike Snopes of *The Hamlet* as two people with the same subnormal IQ can be. With a single exception, Faulkner's interest in abnormality is imaginative, not literal; he is concerned with giving the reader some insight into human nature, rather than providing him with synthetic thrills. The single exception is *Sanctuary*, which Faulkner frankly announced as a potboiler written for money, as accurate a comment as any author has made about his own work. Certainly the vicarious sexual experiences of the impotent Popeye, *Sanctuary's* central figure, are exhausted at the first reading, and do not contribute to the building-up of an aesthetic pattern which in all the other novels is larger and more complex than the melodramatic incidents.

Another frequent complaint against Faulkner is the obscurantism of his style and narrative method. He assuredly places a greater strain on the attention than any of his American contemporaries, and reminds one of Henry

James of the late period, the James who wrote *The Golden Bowl*, the most difficult of his novels, which suggests in structure the most difficult of Faulkner's novels, *Absalom, Absalom!* It is not only that Faulkner's sentences are long and unrelentingly elliptical:

". . . talking in that grim haggard amazed voice until at last listening would renege and hearing-sense self-confound and the long-dead object of her impotent yet indomitable frustration would appear, as though by out-raged recapitulation evoked, quiet inattentive and harm-less, out of the biding and dreamy and victorious dust."

Or that he likes to hook unrelated words together and form new compounds (in the manner of Joyce):

". . . the two separate Quentins now talking to one another in the long silence of notpeople, in notlan-guage . . ."

Or that his characters become sunk in deep, semi-conscious reveries whose meanderings are hard to follow:

"Itself circumambient and enclosed by its effluvium of hell, its aura of unregeneration, it mused (mused, thought, seemed to possess sentience, as if, though dispos-sessed of the peace—who was impervious anyhow to fatigue—which she declined to give it . . ."

It is also that he is unwilling to tell a story straight, that he seems to have accepted as an almost professional canon the selection of a technique in any given novel which follows the longest way round to its objective. Sometimes this technique takes the form of a series of circles unwinding around a central point, as in *Absalom, Absalom!*; sometimes the form of a great number of rapid staccato shifts from one character to another, as in *As I Lay Dying*. On occasions, *The Hamlet* being the most conspicuous, the pattern will be a series of loosely related scenes centering about a specific place; on other occasions, as in *The Sound and the Fury*, it will consist of closely woven interior monologues by members of the same family. The purpose of all this complexity is nearly always to survey events through as fine a mesh as possible, indeed, never to let an incident go until it has been filtered through the psychological apparatus of as many persons as space permits. At times the mesh becomes too fine and the reader, while getting the individual event, misses the larger perspective of which it is a part—a fault which makes *As I Lay Dying* much more of a glittering piece of virtuosity than a soundly executed novel. Or, again, one feels that the style is too formidable for the theme, and not worth all the effort—a feeling left most strongly by *The Wild Palms*.

Except in his very happiest moments, a disharmony exists between Faulkner's methods and subjects, and the relationship between them is more often centrifugal than not. In this sense, the resemblance between Faulkner and Henry James becomes even more striking. In James, too, the style is complex, and used as a mesh to strain not so much events as certain rarefied states of consciousness down to their molecular components. And in James, too, the style distracts more often than not. Perhaps only in

The Ambassadors and *The Wings of the Dove* is the welding of style and theme complete, a harmony achieved by Faulkner in *The Sound and the Fury*, pivoting on Benjie's amazing monologue, and *Light in August*, held together by the compelling and dramatic figure of Joe Christmas. Yet it cannot reasonably be denied that his methods are often in the way. What requires affirmation is that he is hardly ever obscure and complex for the sake of obscurity and complexity, or for the sake of exhibitionism. His methods have an aesthetic purpose, and though this purpose is not often perfectly achieved, it is always there.

The critical explanations of Faulkner are as many-sided as the man himself. Apart from those who naïvely dismiss him as a purveyor of horrors armed with a pretentious style, his critics range from Maxwell Geismar, who sees his work dominated by a fear and hatred of women and Negroes,[4] to Malcolm Cowley, who finds his relationship to the South like that of Hawthorne to New England, and describes him as "an epic or bardic poet in prose, a creator of myths that he weaves together into a legend of the South." Warren Beck discovers in him more sympathy and compassion for his characters than most readers do, and Conrad Aiken is intensely appreciative of his formidable style. George Marion O'Donnell and others have made extensive analyses of the social layout of his novels, of how sets of characters represent different strata of the population. Thus the Sartorises are symbols of the old aristocracy, the Sutpens of the men of no family back-

---

[4] In his chapter on Faulkner in *Writers in Crisis*.

ground who helped settle the South before the Civil War, the Snopeses of the mountain people who descend silently and rapaciously upon the villages and hamlets to become the vanguard of the new commercialized middle class. The elements of truth in all these theories are enough to indicate the difficulties of finding any one exclusive key to Faulkner. Mr. Cowley remains Faulkner's most perceptive critic precisely because he recognizes the antitheses and ramifications of his work, the frontier humor, the feeling for Southern landscape and weather, the significance of his original narrative methods—although what phrases like "a creator of myths" and "legend of the South" mean specifically, is not wholly clear.

The fact is that Faulkner evades exact interpretation rather more than most writers. His imagination takes off too frequently at too many unexpected angles. Moreover, his attitudes are never fixed. Just when the reader is sure that Faulkner has at last stabilized a sentiment, the sentiment is liquidated in another scene or another novel. His two demons, according to Mr. Geismar—Negroes and women—illustrate this fluidity especially well. Many of his women are, to be sure, empty and rather mindless sexual vessels. Since Faulkner's imagination always inflates its objects, women of this type, like Lena Grove, Temple Drake, Eula Varner, Judith Sutpen, Narcissa Benbow, are stamped most vigorously upon the reader's mind. But he has other women who are not empty or mindless at all. Miss Jenny, the elderly aunt in *Sartoris*, is a charming and intelligent lady, surprisingly normal indeed to appear in the work of

a man popularly associated with barbarisms and abnormali-
ties. Caddie Compson, the sister in *The Sound and the
Fury*, is young and sexually attractive, but she is capable
of very deep feeling on a non-sexual plane. Her attachment
to her idiot brother Benjie, the tenderness of her sentiments toward her brother Quentin, the fierceness of her
love for her daughter, round out a personality with several
emotional sides and of very considerable interest. The same
is true, to a lesser degree, of Charlotte Rittenhouse in *The
Wild Palms*, and of Mrs. Armstid in *The Hamlet*, whose
dogged loyalty to her monomaniac husband is one of the
climaxes in that episodic novel.

As for Negroes, Mr. Geismar's belief that Faulkner
blames them for the ruin of the South and the eventual de-
generation of the Western world, carries one tendency in
Faulkner to a conclusion which, however satisfyingly complete, is somewhat exaggerated. The disasters in *Absalom,
Absalom!* and *Light in August* may be due to miscegenation, but those in *Sartoris* and *The Sound and the Fury*
have nothing to do with the race problem at all. That he
once held the Negro in contempt is evident. In *Sartoris*,
he draws the following comparison between the Negro and
the mule: "Misunderstood even by that creature, the nigger who drives him [the mule], whose impulses and mental processes most closely resemble his . . ." But it does
not require direct observations of this kind to demonstrate
Faulkner's feelings in the matter; they are apparent enough
in his account of the Negro in the 20's and 30's. But
these feelings are only on occasion those of hatred and

fear. Just as frequently, they are a mixture of disdain and indifference. Of the last two novels of the 30's, *The Wild Palms* makes no mention at all of the Negro, and *The Hamlet* has only one neutral reference, the insignificant case of the colored man who helps the fabulous horse-trader in the book harness and unharness the animals being sold and exchanged. This seems hardly the attitude of a writer who believes that the white man's civilization is being threatened by the Negro.

Yet there can be no doubt that at one time in Faulkner's career the problem of miscegenation haunted him with pathological intensity. It did not concern him during the early novels, which appeared in the late 1920's, nor during his most recent work. It was an exclusive preoccupation, however, of what can be called his middle period, when the furious story, *Light in August,* and that most involved and difficult of the novels, *Absalom, Absalom!,* were written. The racialism of Faulkner's treatment of the problem is absolute. The tragedy of the central figure of each novel, Joe Christmas and Charles Bon, begins when each discovers that he has Negro blood. In each case it is the white part of the man that is outraged. In each case the character seeks revenge upon the white world which he quite rightly blames for his dilemma. Joe Christmas has an affair with a white woman whom he eventually murders. Charles makes love to his white half-sister, thus bringing about not merely his own death but the destruction of the white Sutpens. The Negro strain remains passive throughout, both within the protagonist and in the society outside. The whites, like Henry Bon, are horrified, but the Negroes have no reactions at all. They are purely *lumpen* elements. The race problem exists not for them, but for their violators. Faulkner obviously has a certain kind of profound guilt feeling about race relations. Southern whites, in begetting children with Negroes, are committing a crime not against the Negroes but against themselves. This is not the callous attitude of the Southerner who believes it all right for white men to have their fling with Negro women without thinking any more about it. Faulkner's is the attitude of the fastidious Southerner whose feeling of racial superiority is so ingrained that injustices against the colored people will arouse no desire to right the wrongs done them, but only a desire to punish the whites for their sins against themselves. The sin is not a moral one, as between equal human beings, but a racial one, as between a superior and inferior people. That Faulkner thus represents the feelings of many an educated and dignified Southerner is perfectly plain. This is not the South of the lynch mob and the Ku Klux Klan, nor is it, on the other hand, the South which advocates within the democratic tradition of the United States the equality of all its citizens. But the involved feelings of guilt, shame, morbidity, anguish, and their corollaries, that cling to race relations, Faulkner reflects with great acuteness. In this sense, he is not only an imaginative and original novelist, but a primary source for understanding the South of our time.

IV

Relevant in this connection is the work of another significant Southern writer of the 30's, Erskine Caldwell, whose terrain, Georgia, he explores as strictly on the level of action as Faulkner does Mississippi on the level of consciousness.

Where plot to Faulkner is a fixed point around which swarm masses of feeling, plot to Caldwell is a fluid process that arouses more or less fixed and unchanging reactions. A good deal happens in *Tobacco Road*, but the characters are the same at the end as at the beginning. His short stories, some of which are magnificently dramatic, controlled, and socially significant in the best rather than the stereotyped sense of that phrase, reflect with particular sharpness the formula of incidents in a state of rapid movement revolving around characters whose emotions are static and predetermined. The events of *Saturday Afternoon*, perhaps the best story of a lynching in American literature, proceed at a blazing tempo; yet Tom, the flyspecked butcher, to whom the killing of the ginger-colored Negro who tends his cotton too well means no more than going fishing on a dull day, has a perfectly stratified personality which the reader knows will never change. The main event is heightened by subsidiary events, such as the drug store boy selling cokes to the white men as they grunt and sweat during the lynching. That other hair-raising story, *Kneel to the Rising Sun*, deals with Caldwell's stock characters: the half-cowed white sharecropper, the vicious boss farmer, the "uppity" Negro, who go through the same motions with regard to one another here as in nearly all the tales, as though they were traditional figures in a classical ballet. Except in the stories dealing solely with Negroes, like *Big Buck*, it is never Caldwell's characters but always the things that happen to them which are important. In his own way, he is as much an extraordinary manipulator of action as Faulkner is of intense and, at times, psychotic feeling.

Faulkner's back country whites are haunted by visions of a lost past or, as with the Snopeses, of a mercenary future. Caldwell's live within the framework of their sensual, brutalized present. Where Faulkner's supreme dimension is time, Caldwell's is space, and the whole quality of their art lies distinguished in these separate dimensions. Plot, being essentially a matter of space, becomes of necessity Caldwell's sphere of operations, and though his characters are seldom nuanced and the range of his emotions remains pretty narrow, he handles incident and action and spatial movement with a skill that holds the reader to attention, even the reader who may balk at his view of the South.

Yet the very exigencies and narrownesses of space landlock Caldwell's writing, and make it, despite its clearer and firmer outlines, more limited and less important than Faulkner's. It demonstrates that a mastery of plot linked to a cargo of social significance is not enough to establish a great reputation. Though Caldwell impresses his readers, he does not haunt them in the sense of lingering in their imaginations or compelling them to read him a second time. He makes fewer errors of commission than Faulkner, yet is not so great a writer. He is a more progressive social figure than Faulkner, who cares little about injustice, yet does not cut as wide a swath in the literature of the 30's. He has been a much more commercially successful writer than Faulkner precisely because plot is the most marketable of literary commodities, yet it seems likely that Faulkner's work will be the more remembered a century hence.

In his own time, nevertheless, Caldwell has been a useful and prolific writer, has served, along with so many of his contemporaries, as an irritant of the public conscience, has produced a number of short stories that seem likely to survive, and has done as much as anyone to keep curiosity, concern, and partisan passion about the South at a boiling point. In this last respect, at any rate, he has been quite the equal of Faulkner.

v

As always, nothing attracts both public interest and the interest of writers and artists as partisan passion. For the first time since the Civil War, the South had become, with the advent of the New Deal and its general quickening of social consciousness, the regional center of national attention. Before the depression, the South was regarded as a compound of exaggeratedly chivalrous men fuming over the lost war, cuddly girls with cute accents, and quaint darkies, concepts which the popular magazines, the movies about plantation life, and the Congressional speeches of

Southern senators, sedulously cultivated. But the advent of Roosevelt, the growth of the first organized campaigns for Negro rights since Lincoln, the annual legislative battles over the abolition of the poll tax, the rise of the Fair Employment Practices Commission, the national prominence of cases like that of the Scottsboro boys, rapidly transformed the South into a problem so inflamed that few could discuss it with perspective. Those who believed the South to be the most backward area of the country, who saw in it the home of the Ku Klux Klan, lynching, white racialism, bigotry and poverty odiously mixed, refused to see that the South was also the home of liberal senators like Pepper, Barkley, and Hill, governors like Ellis Arnall, institutions like the University of North Carolina, and movements like the Southern Conference for Human Welfare, and that among writers, most of the bitterest critics of the less wholesome aspects of Southern life were themselves Southern. Those who believed that the South was simply the victim of Yankee and Communist propaganda, felt that the South had produced the finest civilization in American history, that the Negroes were happy children who should be left undisturbed in their primitive paradise, and that while public figures like Bilbo were perhaps to be deplored, they were overshadowed by sound conservative statesmen like Senators Byrd, George, and Connally. There was seldom a middle ground between these two extremes, seldom a realization that the struggle between decency and indecency was as strong in the South as, say, in Farrell's Chicago, that the South could produce a Huey

Long and at the same time be the scene of the New Deal's greatest physical achievement, the TVA, and that, above all, in the thick of these violent alarums, it could beget a body of writers as significant as Wolfe, Caldwell, Faulkner, and Ellen Glasgow.

In a historical sense Ellen Glasgow was unique among her regional colleagues in that her career represented that middle ground which so few observers of the South appreciated, and that Faulkner on one hand, and Caldwell on the other, never appreciated at all. To her, the South was like every place else in the world. A character in *The Sheltered Life*, observes: "It is all nonsense to talk as if Southerners were a special breed, all wanting the same things and thinking after the same pattern." Though her novels are full of stresses and strains, they are under her firm control, and she lived through two world wars and a worldwide depression without losing her sense of direction or aesthetic balance. She is a phenomenal illustration of the unity art can impose on the multiplicity of life. In her case this was made possible by her dealing with only that area of life which she could reasonably encompass. This turned out to be a much smaller area than Faulkner and Wolfe tackled, and they are both conspicuous illustrations of writers who strove to conquer the multiplicity of life. They are, of course, greater writers than Miss Glasgow, though not so clear of outline or so free of loose ends or as pure of style as she.

The three stages of her career have the even development and ripe dimensions characteristic much more of the

Victorians than of our contemporaries. She begins before the first World War as a civilized rebel against the decayed traditions of the ante-bellum South, against the false chivalry and absurd stiff-necked idealism of the plantation gentry, and her early novels describe a succession of young heroines who, in various ways, seek to liberate their emotional life from the old-fashioned dictates of their parents. These stories are simply plotted and follow rather obvious psychological lines. The war and the distempered years that came in its wake had a very great sharpening effect upon her conceptions, for the novels of her second, or what may be called her great period, are more complicated and mature. The old as well as the young are now regarded with sympathy, especially figures like General Archbald in *The Sheltered Life*, who, while outwardly conforming, remain skeptical in their minds (where the principal drama of the Glasgow novel so often takes place). The currents at work increase in number, the relationship between the characters grows more complex, the writer's view of her society expands and becomes more perceptive. Her art reaches a climax in *They Stooped to Folly* and *The Sheltered Life*, where the variety of types and the sensitive quality of the thoughts running through the consciousness of the principal characters are among the fine achievements of American literature. Another novel of the great period, only a cut below these two, is *The Romantic Comedians*, which treats the conventional story of the old man who marries a young woman with freshness and discretion.

It is in *Barren Ground*, however, perhaps Miss Glasgow's most widely read and, in some quarters, most widely praised novel, that the signs of the approaching third period of her career are to be most clearly seen. Dorinda Oakley, the central figure of *Barren Ground*, has been held up as the epitome of everything admirable in a woman. Yet a colder, more self-righteous heroine never walked outside the pages of Victorian fiction. After the shock of an unhappy love affair, she freezes up emotionally and transfers her affections from human beings to the land. When she marries, she refuses to live with her husband, treats him as a hired farmhand, and devotes herself with fanatical success to the creation of productive soil out of swampland.

"As she grew older, it seemed to her that men as husbands and lovers were scarcely less inadequate than love. Only men as heroes, dedicated to the service of an ideal, were worthy, she felt, of the injudicious sentiments women lavished upon them. At twenty, seeking happiness, she had been more unhappy, she told herself, than other women; but at fifty she knew that she was far happier. The difference was that at twenty her happiness had depended upon love, and at fifty it depended upon nothing but herself and the land. To the land she had given her mind and heart with the abandonment that she had found disastrous in any human relation."

No one can quarrel with the logic of her life; women suffering from psychological and sexual shocks do behave as Dorinda does. She rationalizes her sexual inhibitions into marks of superiority, and becomes callous in her relations with others. Though she remains to the end a splendidly useful member of the community, she remains also an arresting symbol of how twisted a person can become under the impact of a bruising experience.

Miss Glasgow's intention in all this is to demonstrate the values of fortitude, the ethical concept which is to dominate her last period. As she observes in the preface to *Barren Ground,*

". . . Dorinda, though she had been close to me for ten years before I began her story, is universal. She exists wherever a human being has learned to live without joy, where the spirit of fortitude has triumphed over the sense of futility."

Dorinda does not go down under misfortune; she rises above it, and if defeated on one battlefield (human relationships) she transfers her energies and triumphs to another (the soil). This is Miss Glasgow's conception not only of Dorinda; it is also her dream of the South, which, defeated on the battlefield of the Civil War, must discard its outworn conventions and start afresh on another, the struggle for economic reconstruction and a more honest emotional life. Hence, the author's sympathy for Dorinda must be taken not simply in terms of the woman as an individual but in terms of the South to which Miss Glasgow is so profoundly attached.

In her third period, her focus, like that of Galsworthy after the first World War, shifted from the young to the

old. The novels that followed *The Sheltered Life*, the novels of the last period, grow increasingly disapproving of
youthful unrest, and tend to glorify formidable old nineteenth century grandmothers like the one in *Vein of Iron*,
who represents those qualities that enabled the South to
survive despite all historical disasters. The phrase "vein of
iron" becomes the key phrase of her work in the middle
and late 30's, and, whereas earlier she had felt exquisitely
for the doubts of the aged and the protests of the young,
her advice to both now, battered as they are by the depression, is to grit their teeth and bear it. This phenomenon of
the aging writer who goes back to the conservative traditions which he had spent a lifetime attacking, is curiously
widespread. It affected Galsworthy at about the time that
he began writing *A Modern Comedy*; it marked the novels
of Sinclair Lewis after *Ann Vickers*; it was the principal
feature of the last works of Ellen Glasgow ending with
In This Our Life.

She stands out in retrospect as the last of the serious
writers of our time whose personal life, literary career, and
native region, were harmoniously related; in which the
personality of the artist, through a period of long development and unhampered opportunity, came to a full realization. In the American scene of the twentieth century,
only Willa Cather, whose style is as finely woven as Miss
Glasgow's, but whose themes were not so exclusively and
homogenously bound up with a given regional culture,
compares with her in the rounded dimensions of a long
and fruitful life. Neither belongs to the front rank of her

age; yet without them the literature of our time would have borne a different face.

Certainly the literature of the South would have had a radically different aspect without Miss Glasgow. Writing from the vantage point of Richmond, which is so appropriately referred to in her novels as Queensborough, she provides a link between the old and the new South which is not to be found elsewhere. Virginia is the heart of the upper South, wealthier and more cultured than her neighbors, and, hence, could create the most encouraging conditions for the writer who would examine the South with the least degree of anarchic passion, with the most sober and clear-eyed judgment. In this geographic sense, Ellen Glasgow was more happily placed than Caldwell or Faulkner, at least in the interests of her devotion to the task of fusing what she thought to be the best of the old ways and the new.

Yet she remained oddly unknown and unattended to during most of her lifetime, largely because she seemed always to sway against the popular current. Before 1914, with the country more placid than not in the late glow of American Victorianism, she was in a rebellious mood. In the prosperous and self-indulgent 20's, she was beginning to advocate fortitude. In the 30's, hers was one of the few voices to urge patience and a return to the virtues of the past at a time when the nation was in ferment and, for a while, abruptly disillusioned with the past. Yet, though always out of fashion, she pursued her craft tenaciously and practiced it with devotion. One feels that the whole of her is in her work, that no scintilla of talent or imagination in her remained unexpressed. Other writers of our time have a greater range than she, a wider vision of life. But none has served literature and his native region more faithfully or in a firmer, more luminous style.

7: THE LAYING OF THE
WIND-GRIEVED GHOSTS

THE distance from Richmond to Asheville is not very great as distances go, but as county seats of the contemporary novel about the South they are almost poles apart. The Tidewater tales of Ellen Glasgow deal with urbane, mild-mannered ladies and gentlemen who seldom raise their voices and only occasionally lose their heads. The novels of Thomas Wolfe deal with people to whom urbanity and mildness of manner are unknown, who seldom lower their voices and are forever in the process of losing their heads. Where Caldwell accents the desiccated squalor of backwoods life in Georgia, and Faulkner, deeply tragic and compassionate, is moved to a kind of brutal grief by his images of the ruins of Mississippi, Wolfe, while concerned with his native society, shakes free of it partly through his poetic flights over the vast continental sprawl of the United States, partly through his unending pursuit of love and the passionate response.

Apart from occasional portraits like the brilliant sketch of Mr. Jack near the beginning of *You Can't Go Home Again*, he is not a broad-gauge painter of society like Balzac, nor does he penetrate into the anguished marrow of the spirit through so many ramifications as Dostoevski. Yet Wolfe is the only American novelist of the period between wars whose dimensions begin to approach those of the nineteenth century giants. He loves and hates his characters simultaneously, and to about the same extent; and he has left for us a far more emotionally inclusive record of the times than any writer of the 30's with the single exception of Steinbeck. Steinbeck, in a small way in *Of Mice and Men* and in a large way in *The Grapes of Wrath*, has Wolfe's range of feeling; but though his emotional design is as involved, it is not inflated to the huge bulk of Wolfe, to the size with which both his nightmares and rose-colored dreams are kaleidoscoped. Nor is it a mere mechanical size imposed from the outside; it swells up internally from the bottommost levels of the soul.

Wolfe's four novels, the first three in particular, glorify people who have gusto and Rabelaisian vigor.

"There are some people who have the quality of richness and joy in them and they communicate it to everything they touch. It is first of all a physical quality; then it is a quality of the spirit. With such people it makes no difference if they are rich or poor: they are really always rich because they have such wealth and vital power with them that they give everything interest, dignity, and a warm color. . . .

"Those who have this quality are the young policemen sitting in shirt-sleeves in the all-night eating places, taxi drivers with black shirts, prize fighters, baseball players, and racing drivers, brave and gentle people; steel workers

sitting astride a giddy spar, locomotive engineers and brake-
men, lone hunters, trappers, most shy and secret people
who live alone, whether in the wilderness or in a city room;
in general, all people who deal with sensuous things, with
what has taste, smell, hardness, softness, color, must be
wrought or handled—the builders, the movers, the physical and active people, the creators.

"The people who do not have this quality are the
people who rustle papers, tap keys—the clerks, the stenogra-
phers, the college instructors, the people who eat lunch in
drug stores, the countless millions who have lived meagerly
in pallor and safety."

His characters are nearly always in flux, moody, tyran-
nized by feelings beyond their control, in almost every way
end-products of the great romantic tradition, contemporary variants of Werther and Manfred and cut from the
same stencil as King Lear. Like Lear, they are egomaniacs,
usually on a large scale like Oliver Gant, occasionally on a
small one like Eliza Gant. They are loudly articulate, given
to rant and rhetoric, oscillating from the Shakespearian
cursing of Oliver to the sensual outbursts of George
Webber as he watches Mrs. Jack. They are emotional an-
archists, recognizing no law except that of their own will,
and when galled, shake their fists in feverish defiance of
mankind, Nature, God, Fate, and such other primary
forces as seem at the time to be oppressing them. They
are forever crossing and backtracking across the line between reason and madness, and wax incoherent with rage
and disillusionment in great waves that rise and ebb in a
cyclical rhythm which is the basic tempo of Wolfe's writ-

ing. They arouse in the reader a most extraordinary ambivalence, fascinating and repelling him in about equal degree. Despite Wolfe's aggressive shortcomings, his prolixity and verbosity, his turgid mysticism and adolescent posturing, and the most astonishing inability since Wordsworth to distinguish between his own good and bad writing, he generates an unbroken emotional response, and arouses those feelings of pity and terror Aristotle once found so indispensable to true tragedy. But he never freed himself from a temperamental inability to project anything with original eloquence except the storms of youth. His later writing, particularly the lengthy philosophizing in *You Can't Go Home Again,* lacked both the fire and magnetism of *Look Homeward, Angel,* and lent little support to the hopes of those critics who felt that had he lived he might have acquired visions of maturity and insights into other states of mind as incandescent as those which he had into youth. In this sense, all comparisons between him and Shakespeare or between him and Dostoevski, come to an abrupt end.

II

More measurable than his place in the history of literature, is his refraction of wide areas of tension in contemporary American life. His novels record certain brutal prejudices which one must take at times to the Nazis themselves for ultimate reference. His comments on the Jews, for example, are almost wholly racist in tone. He described them in *Of Time and the River* with shuddering repulsion as a dark and alien people who fill him with dread as he faces them in his composition courses at the School for Utility Cultures, and labels them in *The Web and the Rock* as a self-conscious separatist group marked off from others by a love of luxury, rich food, and the good things in life. Elsewhere in the same novel, he refers to ". . . the suspicion of the hardened eye, the itching of the grasping palm, the machinations of the crafty Jew . . ." He is equally contemptuous toward Negroes, whom he seldom calls anything but "niggers." At best, they hardly qualify as human beings.

"Tall, lean, grinning cheerfully, full of dignity and reverence, the nigger was coming up the street the way he always did at three o'clock. He smiled and raised his hand to George with a courtly greeting. He called him 'Mister' Webber as he always did; the greeting was gracious and respectful, and soon forgotten as it is and should be in the good, kind minds of niggers and of idiots . . ."

By way of completing the cycle of discrimination, he abominates the poor whites. Eugene Gant and George Webber at various times pass through the slums of Altamont, and are filled not simply with loathing and disgust but with an almost personal hatred for the inhabitants.

"They stood there like some hopeless, loveless, wretched drudge of nature, bearing about them constantly the unbroken progressions of their loathsome fertility. In their arms they held their latest, youngest, wretched little child, swaddled in filthy rags, and staring forth at one with its blue, drowned eyes, its peaked and grimy little face, its nostrils and its upper lip gummed thickly with two ropes of snot. And in their pregnant bellies, which they proposed from their gaunt, unlovely figures like some dropsical ripeness foully fructifying in the sun, they carried the last and most revolting evidence of the germinal sequence of maternity, which thus was odiously revealed in every stage of its disgusting continuity—from sagging breast to swollen womb and thence to the grimy litter of their filth-bespattered brats that crawled and scrabbled round their foul skirts on the porch. The idiot proliferations of blind nature which these wretched rakes and hags and harridans of women so nakedly and brutally revealed as they stood there stupidly proposing their foul, swollen bellies in the merciless and shameful light of the hot sun filled Monk with such a feeling of choking and wordless fury, loathing, and disgust that every natural emotion of pity and sorrow was drowned out below the powerful flood tide of revulsion, and his antagonism to the women and their wretched children was scarcely to be distinguished from blind hatred."

His early comments regarding Jews, Negroes, and poor whites are automatic echoes of familiar Southern sentiment. When, however, he speaks scornfully of women as a sex, describes his own paranoia, and indulges in hysterical mystic outbursts, he goes outside the bounds of regional influence. Women for the most part are inferior to men, the enemies of men, the objects of his most embittered diatribes. He shudders at pregnancy, conception, and everything connected with the process of birth. The mothers of his heroes exercise a dark and evil influence upon them, in contrast with the healthy and invigorating influence of their fathers. The mother is the ensnaring web, the father the vitalizing rock, and all life consists of fleeing the one and searching for the other. When spring comes in *Look Homeward, Angel*, "the little girls trot pigtailed primly on their dutiful way to school; but the young gods loiter: they hear the reed, the oaten-stop, the running goat-hoofs in the spongy wood," as though girls are prosaic little bodies insensitive to the glories of the natural world which only boys understand. In that remarkable chapter from George Webber's boyhood, *Three O'Clock*, it is the male who is sunk in the profoundest philosophic reverie, and the female who brutishly interrupts it.

"And if there is work to do at three o'clock—if we must rouse ourselves from somnolent repose, and from the green-gold drowsy magic of our meditations—for God's sake give us something *real* to do. Give us great labors, but vouchsafe to us as well the promise of a great accomplishment, the thrill of peril, the hope of high and spirited adventure. For God's sake don't destroy the heart and hope and life and will, the brave and dreaming soul of man, with the common, dull, soul-sickening, mean transactions of these *little* things!

"Don't break our heart, our hope, our ecstasy, don't shatter irrevocably some brave adventure of the spirit, or some brooding dream, by sending us on errands which any stupid girl, or nigger wench, or soulless underling of life could just as well accomplish. Don't break man's heart, man's life, man's song, the soaring vision of his dream with—'Here, boy, trot around the corner for a loaf of bread' . . .

"And all because you are a woman, with a woman's niggard smallness about money, a woman's niggard dealing toward her servants, a woman's selfishness, her small humanity of feeling for the dumb, the suffering, and afflicted soul of man—and so will fret and fume and fidget now, all flustered and undone, to call me forth with:

" 'Here, boy!—Pshaw, now! . . .' "

The paranoic passages are almost as numerous as the anti-female. Eugene is physically different from other boys, and is burdened with an early conviction that nobody understands him.

"He inherited his father's conviction at times that the world was gathered in an immense conspiracy against him: the air about him was full of mockery and menace, the leaves whispered with treason, in a thousand secret places people were assembled to humiliate, degrade, and betray him. He would spend hours under the terrible imminence of some unknown danger: although he was guilty of nothing but his own nightmare fantasies, he would enter a class, a meeting, a gathering of students, with a cold constricted heart, awaiting exposure, sentence, and ruin, for he knew not what crime."

Wolfe's references to war are equally revealing. When America entered the war, in 1917, his young men are overwhelmed with joy, grieve if below the enlistment age, and are broken-hearted at the Armistice. In *Look Homeward, Angel*, he remarks:

"War is not death to young men; war is life. The earth had never worn raiment of such color as it did that year. The war seemed to unearth pockets of ore that had never been known in the nation: there was a vast unfolding and exposure of wealth and power. And somehow—this imperial wealth, this display of power in men and money, was blended into a lyrical music. In Eugene's mind, wealth and love and glory melted into a symphonic noise: the age of myth and miracle had come upon the world again."

And in *The Web and the Rock*:

"Yes, the sorrow. Does anyone really think that they were glad? Does anyone think they wanted the war to end? He is mistaken. They loved the war, they hung on to it, and they cherished it. They said the things with lips that lips were meant to say, but in their hearts they prayed:

" 'Dear God, please let the war continue. Don't let the war be over until we younger ones get in.'

"They can deny it now. Let them deny it if they like. This is the truth."

Sentiments such as these endeared Wolfe to the Germans, as did certain overtones and attributes of his style. They felt in his energism, the spurts of wild rhetoric, the repetitiousness, the mysticism, the constant appeal to the intuitive and emotional faculties of the reader rather than the rational, the very qualities so characteristic of the speeches of Hitler with their reliance on violent physical energy, constant repetitiousness, spurts of wild rhetoric, and constant appeal to the intuitive and constant avoidance of the rational. These stylistic affinities, added to Wolfe's expressed sentiments with regard to Jews, Negroes, and women, his glorification of war, his frequent references to the "compulsion of blood," his persecution complex and sense of alienation from the middle-class world into which he was born, and his fascinated interest in episodes of violence for their own sake,[1] made him something of a hero to the Nazis, and were in part responsible for the enthusiastic reception he received on his tour of Germany to spend the royalties accruing from the German translation of *Look Homeward, Angel.*

Yet, side by side with these impulses of hate and destruction, in a pattern almost classically ambivalent, there burgeons in Wolfe impulses of love and regeneration that are equally powerful, and that grow stronger in his later work. *God's Lonely Man,* one of Wolfe's more important sketches, contains his dual conceptions of loneliness: the loneliness that divides the individual from humanity, and the loneliness which, since it moves the souls of all men, brings them together. This second conception spurred Wolfe to identify himself with Christ and the social philosophy of the New Testament. Edward C. Aswell, in his useful notes appended to *The Hills Beyond,* states that loneliness as a dividing factor was illustrated by the first novels dealing with Eugene Gant; as a uniting force, bringing the hero into union with mankind, it governed the third and fourth books, dealing with George Webber. This

[1] *The Web and the Rock,* particularly, is filled with an interest in the violent and gruesome for their own sake. The description of the incident in which the two Andrews boys are killed, the episode of the butcher's wife and the daughter whom she flogs, the burning of the horses, the bloody fight between the dogs, the running amok and lynching of Dick Prosser, stand out in this connection.

passage from hate to love, from frustration to fruition, is one of the profounder dramas underlying the action of the novels.

Wolfe's misogynist comments on women are balanced by concurrent attitudes of affection and love. The wife of one of Eugene's early schoolmasters, Margaret Leonard, impresses him with her sweetness and understanding. When George Webber is not railing at Mrs. Jack, he is idealizing her in language so tender and passionate that she becomes the focus not simply of everything wonderful in life but of his activity as an artist as well. His contemptuous references to Jews have a way of oscillating to the other extreme, and ending in moments of identification with them. Eugene may be oppressed by the swarm of alien Semitic faces among his students, but he soon becomes intimately friendly with Abraham Jones, bearer of one of those faces. Eugene visits him at his home on the East Side, and establishes with him that close soul-communication which he was temperamentally driven to set up with everyone to whom he was attracted. George Webber's mistress is half Jewish, and is used at times as a symbol to differentiate the Jews from the "stingy, savorless, poor-living" people against whom all the sensuous instincts of the writer are in revolt.

This immutable counterpoint is always present in Wolfe, this tormented interplay of opposites, this perpetual alternation of hate and love, wickedness and good, in a condition so violent that the whole baffled passage of the human soul is illumined. He hungered for experience in all its aspects and contradictions and sought to encompass the universe in all its dimensions.

III

His style, like the emotions it deals with, is a mixture of opposites. It suffers from all the excesses of romanticism: it is repetitious beyond common measure because the writer proceeds under the spur of the blind illusion that every word which pops into his mind is of cosmic importance; his language glitters with lush images, and exotic connotations; he frequently associates ideas that have nothing in common. Omnivorousness is to be seen everywhere, not simply in the hunger for experience but even in the pursuit of learning. Wolfe read greedily and without abatement, and regurgitated his formal culture in the same feverish spasms with which he flung forth everything else. This culture, though energetically pursued, was pretty much the routine background of the English teacher, filled almost exclusively with references to the ancient Greeks and the classic English poets. Though acquired at first hand and digested with great rapidity, it appears on all occasions, appropriate or not, only fitfully under control, arranged with a taste that can most charitably be described as erratic, and given its aesthetic justification for no reason better than that it has grown inveined in the thinking of the writer, which for Wolfe was the best reason in the world. Egotism is regarded not simply as an unavoidable fact of temperament, but is exalted as a creative virtue as well.

Despite its bombast and prolixity, the endless circling over the same grooves, and the blistering staccato accents, the romantic style creates, out of this very frenzy, complex effects achieved nowhere else, and sensations that are at times unique and overwhelming. Wolfe achieves these effects and sensations as thoroughly as he mirrors, in their most extreme form, the errors which accompany them. If one were to select a single literary document in the literature of the Western world which contains most germinally these qualities of style and temperament, one would name the *Confessions* of Jean-Jacques Rousseau, whose view of the world was psychologically the same as Wolfe's. The intervening romanticists, the early Goethe, Chateaubriand, Byron, the early Pushkin, attenuate and melodramatize the attitudes most naïvely represented in Rousseau, attitudes which acquire their ultimate proliferation in America with the author of *Look Homeward, Angel*.

Critics associating themselves with the classical tradition prayed through Wolfe's lifetime that he would develop discipline and restraint, and wept that he died so soon because they found signs of self-control in the novels posthumously published. These signs were there, to be sure, but their effect was not precisely as anticipated. His last experiences brought a growing measure of maturity and wisdom to Wolfe, an awakening interest in the future of American democracy, a widening concern with mankind. But at a heavy price, a price that Wolfe of all writers could least afford to pay: a slackening impetuosity. *You Can't Go Home Again*, the fourth novel, is less satisfactory than *Look Homeward, Angel*, the first; for while it records the stages in his maturation as a human being, it registers a falling-away of that headlong spontaneous eloquence which expressed the core of his temperament. After the skillful portrait of Mr. Jack getting ready in the morning, the novel sinks into endlessly tedious pages in which George Webber unburdens himself of his somewhat naïve reflections on the evils of unemployment, and engages in jejune conversations with Foxhall Edwards, his editor, which sound suspiciously like the bull sessions of a college sophomore. He takes a trip to Germany and is filled partly with horror at observing the fear constricting the Germans under Fascism, partly with the joy of a satisfying love affair with an agreeable German lady. And, finally, the novel concludes with apostrophes to the American future in the vein of Whitman.

It was this genre of intellectuality which some critics found so hopeful in the last writings of Wolfe, but it was this very intellectuality that muffled *You Can't Go Home Again*, that made it almost as unsatisfactory a specimen of his late period as *Of Time and the River* [2] was the low

[2] This second novel was a long and extremely verbose continuation of *Look Homeward, Angel*, in which Eugene's experiences as a graduate student at Harvard, his associations with the idle rich in estates on the Hudson, and his trip to Europe added little except quantity to our understanding of the young man or his world. The book is noted chiefly for its extensive orchestration of the train ride Eugene takes from Altamont to New York, one of the famous pieces of rhetorical virtuosity in Wolfe. There was much critical truth in Franklin P. Adams' famous epigram when the novel appeared: "*Of Time and the River*, keep away from my door."

point of the early, that articulated a vein in the author which led away from the area of communication that he knew best, the area of sensuousness and passion. He was not a metaphysician or an analyst, not a first-class one like Shaw, not even a second-class one like Pope. Nor could he, without negating his own temperament, write with that chiseled perfection of line, that Sophoclean detachment, which the neo-classicists of the 30's clamored that he do. A re-reading of the novels nearly a decade after his death indicates how unnatural in the most literal sense of the word was the arbitrary and synthetic self-discipline that crops up in certain sections of *You Can't Go Home Again,* the fourth and last of his complete novels.

He is then to be taken with his faults, against which it is useless to rail since they proved irremediable. Indeed, given the pattern of the creative process as confirmed by our experience with literature, they are indispensable corollaries to the finished output of the writer of purple prose, and of all the novelists that America produced during the 20th century, Wolfe was surely the supreme master of purple prose. He was also one of the few writers of our time in whom one gets no really rounded sense of a delineated society or social background. One hardly ever thinks of him as a "Southern" writer: there is no co-ordinated view of the South in him as there is in Faulkner or Erskine Caldwell, or, in a quieter way, Ellen Glasgow. There are no characters like the Joads representing thousands of dust-bowl farmers exactly like themselves, in Wolfe. One does not get in him that feeling of a whole young hedonist generation as one does in Fitzgerald and Hemingway. Behind his stories no small towns in the genre of Sinclair Lewis, or aristocratic Bostons in the spectroscope of John P. Marquand suggest themselves. Oliver Gant seems like no other Southern man, Eliza Gant like no other Southern woman. And Eugene is much more the Byronic hero than he is a product of North Carolina born at the beginning of the century. It is true that Wolfe talks about the South frequently, analyzes it at length, and alternates between occasional sweet love lyrics in its praise and frequent profane outbursts against it. Eugene speaks bitterly of the Southerners' "barren spiritual wilderness, the hostile and murderous intrenchment against all new life . . . their cheap mythology, their legend of the charm of their manner . . . the quaint sweetness of their drawl . . . their life and its swarming superstition." And George: "Even as a child, George Webber realized that in a general way it was better to be more North than South. If you get too North . . . everything gets frozen and dried up. But if you get too South . . . it gets rotten not in a dry way . . . but in a horrible, stagnant, swampy, stenchlike, humid sort of way that is also filled with obscene whisperings and ropy laughter." Yet these observations, whether vitriolic or caressing, remain curiously far away from the essence of their target because they are seldom worked into the narrative, rarely become an inner part of the feelings and actions of Wolfe's protagonist. They remain as detached from the story as Fielding's little personal essays remain detached from the fictional context of *Tom Jones*.

When Eugene Gant comes north in *Of Time and the River*, he brings with him a whole body of fiercely emotionalized ideas which are as rooted in his own individual and monomaniac egotism as they are in the prejudices of his native region. His attitudes are refractions of the South, not reflections of it; hence, though the South is present in Wolfe, it is never seen objectively, and, in the long run, is not as distinct an issue of his consciousness as it always is with Caldwell and Faulkner. There are no carefully formulated social strata in Wolfe, no plantation aristocracy, no rising middle class, no problems of miscegenation, no historical decay. His intense, almost anarchic individualism is one of the prime elements distinguishing Wolfe's fiction from that of his contemporaries in a period so colored with literature of social significance.

IV

But if Southern society appears largely in terms of its distortions, and then only in intermittent flashes, the terrain of the human ego, which is Wolfe's major ground, is intensively explored. No American writer has written more eloquently of hunger and food, described vegetables and steaks more caressingly, stimulated the salivary glands with greater vicarious effect. On that plane of physical egotism which involves the appetite, Wolfe worked out an aesthetic sublimation as precise and intriguing as the aesthetic sublimation Hemingway wove around the act of violent death. Despite an excess of adjectives, where can one find a more visually moving account of the flowering earth in terms of fruits and vegetables than this:

". . . his Spring gardens wrought in the black wet earth below the fruit trees, flourished in huge crinkled lettuces that wrenched cleanly from the loamy soil with small black clots stuck to their crisp stocks; fat red radishes; heavy tomatoes. The rich plums lay bursted on the grass; his huge cherry trees oozed with heavy gum jewels; his apple trees bent with thick green clusters."

When Webber and Mrs. Jack go shopping on Sixth Avenue, the thick, juicy, succulent meats with which they return appear in words so splendidly onomatopoeic that they seem to exude the very colors and secretions of the objects they describe. John Burroughs used to describe fruit of various sorts with uncanny sensuousness and accuracy. But Wolfe heaps upon every kind of edible a flood of passionate rhetoric which does more than make the reader's mouth water; it brings within the range of his intimate literary experience a segment of the natural universe hitherto neglected, or when not neglected, dismissed as vulgar. Here, for example, is his description of the Gant menu:

"In the morning they rose in a house pungent with breakfast cookery, and they sat at a smoking table loaded with brains and eggs, ham, hot biscuit, fried apples seething in their gummed syrups, honey, golden butter, fried steak, scalding coffee. Or there were stacked batter-cakes, rum-colored molasses, fragrant brown sausages, a bowl of wet cherries, plums, fat juicy bacon, jam. At the mid-day meal, they ate heavily: a huge hot roast of beef, fat but-tered lima beans, tender corn smoking on the cob, thick red slabs of sliced tomatoes, rough savory spinach, hot yellow corn-bread, flaky biscuits, a deep-dish peach and apple cobbler spiced with cinnamon, tender cabbage, deep glass dishes piled with preserved fruits—cherries, pears, peaches. At night they might eat fried steak, hot squares of grits fried in egg and butter, pork chops, fish, young fried chicken."

If hunger is the first of the appetites he deals with consciously, sex is the second, but a second so blended with the intimate physiology of the female form as to be new and impressive in its own right. When Webber and Mrs. Jack return with their sirloin and trimmings, eat their succulent dinner, and prepare for love, Wolfe's prose plunges into one of its more energetic and original passages:

"Then he would lift her arms, observing the delicate silken whorls and screws of blonde hair in the arm pits. He would kiss and perhaps bite her tender shoulder haunch, and smell the pungent but not unpleasant odor, already slightly moist with passion. And this odor of an erotic female would have neither the rank stench of a coarse-bodied woman, nor some impossible and inhuman bouquet, disgusting to a healthy taste. It would be delicately vulgar: the odor of a healthy woman and a fine lady, who has not only been housed, clothed, fed, and attended with the simple best, but has been derived from ancestral loins similarly nourished, so that now the marrow of her bones, the substance of her flesh, the quality of her blood, the perspiration of her skin, the liquor of her tongue, the moulding of her limbs—all the delicate joinings and bindings of ligament and muscle, and the cementing jellies, the whole incorporate loveliness of her body—were of rare, subtler, and more golden stuff than would be found elsewhere the world over."

There is in this articulation of sex a rhapsodic quality that robs it of any trace of obscenity or titillation. Yet Gant and Webber are rather repulsive figures when in love because their sexual egotism is carnivorous and demanding; they posture and strut and fancy themselves irresistible; their behavior toward their mistresses is smirking and patronizing. Being badly spoiled young men, their amorous conduct is nearly always disagreeable. Fancying themselves literary geniuses, they regard women as instruments for their own self-realization both as men and artists, rather than as human beings to be loved for their own sakes. But the feelings that at times sweep even them away are greater than they are, and it is this overwhelming emotional tide that distinguishes Wolfe's projection of love, lends it an ultimate dignity, and rescues it from mere egotism. Though Webber curses Mrs. Jack as often as he caresses her, and though she imagines herself as much a catalytic agent for his genius as a woman deeply in love, their relationship is at once more admirable and more significant than the motives generating it.

But it is in describing the quest for companionship, for union with humanity, that Wolfe is most eloquent. This begins as a flight from loneliness.

"Naked and alone we came into exile. In her dark womb we did not know our mother's face; from the prison

of her flesh have we come into the unspeakable and incommunicable prison of this earth.

"Which of us has known his brother? Which of us has looked into his father's heart? Which of us has not remained forever prison-pent? Which of us is not forever a stranger and alone?"

For a long time this search seems hopeless:

"The sight of these closed golden houses with their warmth of life awoke in him a bitter, poignant, strangely mixed emotion of exile and return, of loneliness and security, of being forever shut out from the palpable and passionate integument of life and fellowship, and of being so close to it that he could touch it with his hand, enter it by a door, possess it with a word—a word that, somehow, he could never speak, a door that, somehow, he would never open. . . .

"We are small grope-things crying for the light and love by which we might be saved, and which, like us, is dying in the darkness a hand's breadth off from us if we could touch it. We are like blind sucks and sea-valves and the eyeless crawls that grope along the forest of the sea's great floor, and we die alone in the darkness, a second away from hope, a moment from ecstasy and fulfillment, a little half an hour from love."

Everything in his environment, the personal environment of his family especially, conspired to fill him with a sense of being different, with strong prejudices against all kinds of people and groups, and aggravated, in his case, all the emotions that drive a man away from his fellows and make him lonely. Eugene's father was too profane and eccentric; his mother too niggardly; he himself was too grotesquely tall; his older brother Ben, whom he worshiped, died too soon. The South in which he grew up was more that of Talmadge and Bilbo than of Frank Graham and Hodding Carter. The nightmares which tormented him, the doors upon which he beat that never opened, the wind-grieved ghosts that pursued him in his anguished fancies, were the demons that he wrestled with, and in his last books showed signs of vanquishing.

The journey of his own life was in some ways like that of the world since 1914, a struggle through a maze of divisions, psychoses, and antagonisms, to that ideal of unity and universal love toward which our own time is groping. *You Can't Go Home Again,* for all its weaknesses as a novel, records the first stilling of Wolfe's demons, the first expression of how the loneliness of his youth was the very factor beginning to drive him back after the long voyage through the darkness toward that union with his species which he had lost at birth.

"And the essence of all faith, it seems to me, for such a man as I, the essence of religion for people of my belief, is that man's life can be, and will be, better; that man's greatest enemies, in the forms in which they now exist— the forms we see on every hand of fear, hatred, slavery, cruelty, poverty, and need—can be conquered and destroyed."

Though he died before the outbreak of the second World War, his last exclamations as a writer indicated how his own private ghosts were being laid, and insofar as he represented, amid their distortions, the instincts and yearnings of all of us, indicated also that perhaps one day the ghosts tormenting us may be as surely and as permanently cast out.

8: TAPROOTS IN THE HISTORICAL NOVEL

THE year 1935 opened with an ominous scientific prediction that this planet, its oxygen supply being slowly exhausted, was on the way to becoming a dead world. Other events, having nothing to do with the oxygen supply, were doing their best to hasten that chilling day. Mussolini was preparing his invasion of Ethiopia, and like the promoter of a big bout, was announcing in advance the exact week of the affair. Hitler's project for the year was the return of the Saar to the Fatherland, an event voted by the Saarlanders themselves in January and consummated with fanfare from the Third Reich in March. Huey Long was starting on the last nine months of his life, building the most dangerous of the native fascist movements of the 30's, confident that his Share-the-Wealth program, with thousands of rural adherents in Louisiana, Texas, Arkansas, and Oklahoma already enrolled, would soon sweep the country. The Supreme Court, in the last of its efforts to stem the main current of the time, was outlawing the AAA and other New Deal legislation. But most people were spending their leisure following the trial of Bruno Richard Hauptmann for the murder of the

Lindbergh baby, the legal proceedings stretching through the whole year. 1929 seemed a long time ago. As Lewis Gannett described that far-off year, "Ivar Kreuger and Sam Insull were still great men in those days; Hitler was still laughed at as a militant edition of Charlie Chaplin; gold was still a god." By 1935, these illusions had passed into irretrievable limbo.

That year and 1936 were an interlude in which one could almost hear the country pause for breath between the first rush of recovery from the depression and the first of the great foreign crises that were to end in the second World War. It was an interlude in every sense. The New Deal had come to the end of its first frenzied experiments. To be sure, a group of self-styled "Jeffersonian" Democrats were conferring with the Republicans and issuing predictions of how they would defeat Roosevelt in 1936. But the bulk of the people were so plainly pleased with the Administration that curiosity about the campaign of 1936 was almost nonexistent. Concern with affairs abroad was almost equally at low ebb. The invasion of Ethiopia was regarded as an *opera bouffe* war, though it produced one of the decade's most biting cartoons.[1] The Japanese, having annexed Manchuria, were quietly digesting their conquest before leaping upon the succulent provinces of North China. As for Hitler, only an outraged few were really aroused over him. There were plenty of persons who sym-

[1] A group of Ethiopian natives are crouching under a bush, watching Italian bombers approaching overhead. One says to the others, "Duck, boys, here comes civilization!"

pathized with his efforts to get the Saar back into the Reich. There were even Jews who said they would be all for him if he weren't anti-Semitic.

One of the outraged few was Sinclair Lewis, whose *It Can't Happen Here*, to its eternal honor, was the first piece of American fiction devoted to awakening the country against the fascist danger. It was a very bad novel as novels go, poorly plotted, filled with ill-digested melodrama and unrealized characters. It was a bad novel even for the Sinclair Lewis of the 30's, who had fallen so far and so suddenly from the great satirist of the 20's. But it was on the side of the angels and did something to stir the air of those strangely passive years. It revealed how literature, even in less inspired moments, can serve a useful public function, and how writers can at times outthink politicians in the fascinating and complicated game of statesmanship.

Yet even literature seemed, on the whole, to be marking time. James Hilton was supplying most of the items on the menu, and delectable items they were, too, ranging from the sweet sadness of *Good-bye, Mr. Chips* to the sweet sadness of *Lost Horizon*. Though narcotics, they were narcotics of the smoothest blend, providing an absolute escape without the faintest semblance of a hangover. Alexander Woollcott was also much in evidence, supplying in the anecdotes of *While Rome Burns* a similar escape, if not quite so absolute. Woollcott's wit was suave and urbane, not savage like that of Mencken, Lewis, and Lardner, who dominated the 20's. He had something of the knife-like quality of Mencken but exercised his talents on smaller themes, ultimately not taking himself seriously, as the satirists of the 20's always did. If Mencken stems in a direct line from Juvenal and Swift, Woollcott is a descendant of Horace and Pope, and the qualities that have enshrined *The New Yorker* in the topical culture of our country were his in quintessence. His voice was not loud enough to be heard above the trumpetings of the first New Deal years, and it was to be drowned out when the approaching disasters in Europe were to govern the national consciousness. In the lull of 1935-1936, however, his town cries were wafted through radio loud-speakers, his books graced the best-seller lists, his barbed *bon mots* were already paving the way for his theatrical incarnation in *The Man Who Came to Dinner*.

The New Yorker, one of his natural outlets, occupied a special place in the periodical literature of the 30's. It commanded a glittering array of wits, ranging from James Thurber with his abstract and unclassifiable humor to S. J. Perelman and his screwball comedy, and including in addition to these and Woollcott, Robert Benchley and E. B. White, each practicing his own special brand of light satire. Its cartoons maintained a consistently high standard of excellence, with Thurber's animals, Helen Hokinson's clubwomen, and Peter Arno's roués standing out almost as national types. *The New Yorker* covered virtually every field of human experience, political and personal, foreign and domestic, and so homogeneous was its editorial policy, so unified its sense of style, that its contributors, whether foreign correspondents, movie reviewers, short story writers or

fashion editors, wrote with equal sophistication and reflected in varying ways the unique qualities of the magazine as a whole. It remained one of the most purely delightful and urbane cultural phenomena of the decade.

Two other items of interest bobbed up in that becalmed interlude between the great storms, one pointing
backward to the first World War, the other forward to the
second. The last returns on the war of 1914 were finally in
(with the exception of Irwin Shaw's one-act play, *Bury the
Dead*, produced in 1936) when a scorching little novel
called *Paths of Glory*, by Humphrey Cobb, appeared. It
hacked away at the cruelty and senselessness with which
lives were squandered to win even a few yards of muddy
ground, and wound up the long anti-militarist fever that
had begun fifteen years before with John Dos Passos'
Three Soldiers. Shortly afterward, the shadows of fascism
were becoming long enough to make further attacks on
the futility of the first war a little out-of-date; almost overnight, poets like Siegfried Sassoon who had made their
reputation from their recoil against trench life, novelists
like Richard Aldington who had done the same, and plays
like *What Price Glory* became outmoded in a way that
Victorianism had become with the heavy cannonading in
the fall of 1914. There were yet to be loud arguments
about Buchmanism and its program of Moral Rearmament, the Oxford Peace Movement, and isolationism with
its insistence on "No More Foreign Wars," but, in the
main, the first world conflict died as a public issue with
the outbreak of the Spanish Civil War, in the summer of

1936. *Paths of Glory* just did beat that deadline, and, as the last of its genre, had a place in history perhaps more significant than its place in fiction.

If this book was the last of something old, Vincent Sheean's *Personal History*, born at the same time, was evidently the first of something new. It anticipated the coming bid for world power by the fascist nations, and served as the first item in the flood of autobiographical foreign correspondence that was to be America's chief reading diet from 1936 on to the very end of the second World War. After Sheean, every reporter on assignment abroad felt a categorical drive to relate the inner history of his soul and fuse it with the political events he witnessed. The intensity with which foreign affairs were about to take hold of the public mind was to be measured by the fact that not a single reporter on home assignment was moved to publish his memoirs on the steps in his political education; whereas hardly a single foreign correspondent failed to be so moved. Every shade of political opinion was articulated in this new kind of autobiographical reportage, though more correspondents were to the left of center than the right. More were mildly to the left like Herbert L. Matthews and Howard K. Smith than strongly left like Sheean; or dead center like John Gunther or to the right like Henry J. Taylor, and in their dawning anti-fascism were, one might say, a year or two ahead of the rest of the country. They passed through the identical soul-searching process about America's rôle in the coming war as the country itself was to pass through with the outbreak of hostilities in 1939. The issues were fought out in print first, and that print served as an advance guard, an educational force in the working out of a national experience, of very considerable usefulness and import. And at the same time, it was fashioning in this blend of the personal memoir and the newspaper story something new under the literary sun.

This new type of non-fiction led the way in the general upsurge of non-fiction through the decade. As world affairs grew more tangled and difficult to understand, and invaded private life increasingly, new methods of making issues clear and softening their impact became imperative. Foreign correspondence, which sought specifically to clarify events abroad, was one such method. Earlier in the 30's, the inspirational book, both religious and psychological, designed to muffle the impact of the depression, was another. The spectacular growth of the digest magazines, *The Reader's Digest* particularly, was also linked with the need for quick exposition; these magazines presented in condensed form a great number of facts in a single issue, though *The Reader's Digest* served an inspirational purpose as well. The appearance in the 30's of the picture magazines, of which *Life* acquired the largest circulation, was motivated by the need for saving time and simplifying the universe. A single picture could now communicate an area of experience which formerly required a whole essay.

In other respects, all was quiet. With signs of economic recovery on every hand, the public seemed momentarily content with the usual ubiquitous crop of light romantic fiction. Margaret Ayer Barnes and Bess Streeter

Aldrich were much in evidence, as was that old stand-by
Booth Tarkington, and that newer one, Lloyd C. Douglas.
Indeed, the popularity of Mr. Douglas in the small cities
and towns was one of the phenomena of the decade, at-
tributable in no small measure to the smoothness of the
formula he had evolved. Though his style was of what
Edmund Wilson called "the 5-and-10-cent store" variety,
he managed to deal with serious subjects without causing
anyone pain.

In the Douglas drama, there are three main characters: a young man, a young woman, and a minister (or
sometimes a wise old invalid in a wheelchair). The two
young people have a misunderstanding at first, which grows
progressively more serious until, three chapters before the
end, the outlook seems hopeless. The minister comes forward, talks first to one, then to the other, then to both of
them, in his study. The talk is moral and metaphysical, but
in language that a farmer's wife brought up on the Bible
and the Sears, Roebuck catalogue can understand. The
misunderstanding is thereupon dissolved, and the young
couple depart arm-in-arm toward their unclouded future.
To bring tragedy so close that one can feel its hot breath,
and yet keep the reader from being burnt, requires a great
deal of skillful sleight-of-hand, of which Douglas has an
uncommon share. He has an even more uncommon share
of insight into his audience, the tens of thousands of people to whom uplift is an indispensable ingredient in the
sweetening of a literary pill, who can take the harsh face
of life only at a distance and must shut their eyes when

it comes too close. In all his novels, up to and including *The Robe*, Douglas has never once caused his readers to blink, an altogether ideal writer for a breathing-spell year. His *Green Light* and *White Banners*, which appeared in 1935 and 1936, traced their legitimate ancestry in a straight line back to Harold Bell Wright, the purest apostle of Moral Uplift in our popular literature during the first twenty years of the century.

While Harold Bell Wright's descendants were cultivating certain closely held American convictions, Robert E. Sherwood, in *The Petrified Forest*, was saying good-by to certain others. That absorbing, though imperfect play devoted itself to embalming the old idea of "rugged individualism," which had been the dominating principle of the country's economic life for a century. It had broken down during the depression, was ridiculed temporarily out of existence by the New Deal, and finally dismissed in the pause for stocktaking now under review. There is no longer room in the world for either Squier, the weak aesthete, or Duke, the last gangster, both of whom are fleeing to the petrified forest where, by symbolical definition, the now archaic types they represent will be turned to inanimate stone. Sherwood ends his play not on a strain of regret for the last two rugged individualists, but on a note of faith in Gabby, the young woman who, profiting from the wreckage of the old life, will shape a more resilient future. The playwright, who later became one of President Roosevelt's principal speech-drafters, obviously trimmed the play to fit the sequence of history [2] from the well-meaning rugged individualism of Hoover's day to the buoyant and optimistic New Deal with its enthusiastic faith in government regulation and collective social effort, its eagerness to profit from the errors of the past.

The theater of the 30's was, in fact, to keep pace with the social conscience of the New Deal. Indeed, in the plays of Clifford Odets, that conscience was driven to extremes. Odets was the official stage historian of the proletariat and the lower middle class, the darling of the left-wing critics, and the bright hope of the American theater during the middle 30 s. His *Awake and Sing*, a study of Bronx family life distorted by a largely unsuccessful pursuit of money, ended with calls to revolution. The play, though full of passion, was humorless and heavy as lead. It was soon followed by *Waiting for Lefty*, a thrilling little one-act play centering around a taxicab strike, which ended with another rousing call to action. In *Paradise Lost*, the evils of capitalism destroyed another lower middle-class family indistinguishable from the one in *Awake and Sing*. The same evils were responsible for the disasters overtaking the young East Side hero of *Golden Boy*, who, under the spur of slum poverty, became a prize fighter instead of a violinist. Two or three other plays, less significant, were turned out by Odets in the service of the Group Theater,

[2] A year later, in *Idiot's Delight*, Sherwood, still alert to history, began arguing the issues of the coming war. In a postscript to the play, he remarked: ". . . let me express the conviction that those who shrug and say, 'War is inevitable,' are false prophets." He then went on to urge the cause of collective security as a means of forestalling the Axis powers.

and then he abruptly left Broadway for Hollywood, where he has been engaged first as a script writer and more recently as a director, in the production of a series of films that can perhaps best be described as interesting failures. His plays were feverish products of the depression and the New Deal, but embraced aims which the President and his more orthodox followers were far from sharing.

Meanwhile, Harry Hopkins, the President's most intimate adviser, was warning farmers to leave the Dust Bowl, little dreaming that, among other things, he was paving the way for the great fictional masterpiece of the decade, *The Grapes of Wrath*. Other events, announcements, and predictions were flying about, carrying in their wake a variety of effects, some weak, some percussive. News arrived that 20,000 Hindus were killed during three earthquakes in India, a disaster so stupendous that it made no impression at all. It was announced that fabricated steel houses would soon be rolling off assembly lines, an item which would have been greeted with grim laughter during the greatest housing shortage in American history ten years later. The most percussive event, the phenomenon that had both in that time and later the widest influence and the most significant impact, was the rise of the most dangerously successful of the native fuehrers, Huey Long.

II

Uttering shrill cacophonies, he had sprung full-mouthed from the Louisiana bayous, with every attribute of tyranny and an instinct for leading the semi-literate mass. He shared with other backwoods Southern politicians a certain brassy idiom, a tendency to hammy histrionics, a kind of cotton-patch demagoguery. But he brought to the arena a dynamic energy, a ferocity of ambition, that were all his own. At first, he was regarded as a clown, an illusion that seems to cling to the early career of every fascist dictator. He made himself ridiculous more than once on the floor of the Senate. For a time, he rode along on the Roosevelt tide, then (like Father Coughlin, whose flirtation with the New Deal also turned into a fanatical hatred) became one of the Administration's most persistent gadflies. As boss of his state, during one of his odder and more exhibitionist moments he poured money into Louisiana State University, seeking to make it the intellectual and athletic Mecca of the South. But he insisted on running the show himself and wound up by having a run-in with the football coach, who, it is rumored, threw him out of the dressing-room on one occasion and made him a national laughingstock again. No one laughed, however, when his Share-the-Wealth program got under way; not the millionaires who were not quite sure they could buy him off if he did win power, not the labor unions, now mushrooming under the encouragement of the Wagner Act, who recognized in him the would-be American Hitler; not the crowds of thinking citizens who had the welfare of the republic at heart and shuddered at the prospect of this dangerous figure in the White House.

But the poor whites of the bayous and the cotton

patches, the sharecroppers and tenant farmers, the businessmen of the small towns in Arkansas and Texas, as well
as in his native Louisiana, flocked to his banner by the
thousands, and soon Huey's movement was making the
other native demagogues and their followings, the Townsend Planners, the Silver Shirts, the Ku Klux Klan, even
Father Coughlin and the National Union for Social Justice, look like small fry. His brassy voice over the radio was
now no longer absurd; it had acquired menacing overtones.
His shrewdness was now beginning to emerge through the
bombast. His most famous comment, "Fascism will come
to this country under the guise of anti-Fascism," was the
most intelligent political observation of 1935, and indicated how thoroughly he understood the times, how attuned he was to the native scene. He had conquered one
region of America; he was now ready to spread his aggressive campaign over the rest of the nation.

That he did not succeed, that he was assassinated in
September, 1935, that his movement came apart almost
at once, like Alexander the Great's empire, and home-
grown fascism thereby given its most terrible blow, was
no fault of his political opponents. They were playing in
extraordinary luck. The New Orleans doctor who, for
purely personal reasons and under the spur of feelings pri-
vately outraged, penetrated Huey's screen of bodyguards
and shot him before himself falling under a hail of avenging bullets, was giving them no conscious aid, nor had he
in mind the welfare of the country. The profound irrele-
vance of his act to considerations of politics was indeed one

of the marvels of that era. Yet the deed could not have been better timed from the political point of view, since it came before a Huey Long legend could grow deeply rooted in the minds of his followers. The bullets from the doctor's gun, together with those that missed President-elect Roosevelt in Miami less than three years before, altered the whole course of the decade, and perhaps the whole course of history as well.

The boss's organization collapsed with the death of the boss. One of his principal lieutenants, Gerald L. K. Smith, was later to become a fascist spokesman of minor dimensions but never anywhere near the size of his chief. Yet the memory of Huey Long, his impact upon the imagination, was to survive, and within ten years after his death no fewer than four serious novels were to be built around his personality.[3] The first, *Sun in Capricorn*, by Hamilton Basso, was a savage attack upon him. The second, John Dos Passos' *Number One*, projected him unsympathetically, but without savagery. The third, *A Lion is in the Streets*, by Adria Locke Langley, sentimentalized him to the point where he became at times a lovable, warmhearted man, at least in his private life. The fourth and most complex novel, written on a large scale and with great attention to nuance, was Robert Penn Warren's *All the King's Men*, which presented Huey not unsympathetically, and seemed in places to justify him on political grounds, on the theory that the strong man knows better than the

---

[3] Hamilton Basso discusses these novels and their relationship to the Huey Long legend in great detail in *Life* magazine, December 9, 1946.

people how best to achieve the people's welfare. Time has appeared to be on Huey's side. It has begun to purify his name, mute the harsh edges of the panacea he directed with so iron a hand, soften the vulgarity of his appearance, speech, and manner, and edit him into a presentable image for posterity. That he should have won the good offices of so perceptive a writer as Robert Penn Warren is not itself altogether surprising since Warren was a charter member of the Southern Agrarians, who made little effort to veil their admiration for an élite which rises to leadership by its superior talents. What is surprising—and of serious import—is how easily one can be seduced away from the democratic idea; how tyrants, even in America, with its endemic hatred of tyrants, can be glamorized during their lifetime and justified after their death.

In the months before his death, Huey still seemed to many people a political buffoon, to be taken no more seriously than Hitler, say, in 1929, when the Fuehrer-to-be was ranting in rathskellers and behaving like a madman in a Keystone comedy. It was only later, in Huey's case, that the country realized in a sudden sweat of relief how dangerous was the man behind the clown's mask, how narrow its escape.

III

If a finger can be put on the point where the extended lull that stretched through the middle 30's came to an end, it would probably come to rest on July, 1936. The pause was momentarily interrupted by the murder of Huey Long, though that extraordinary event was not fully assayed at the time, but in July two things happened which were to have a great positive influence on the thinking of the country from then until Pearl Harbor.

The first was the outbreak of the civil war in Spain. Several million words have already been expended on the pros and cons of the Franco rebellion; the military campaigns have been minutely examined, the dubious rôle of the Non-Intervention Committee analyzed, the legions of Hitler and Mussolini and how they received their combat training at the expense of the Spanish people, described at great length. Little has been said, however, of its impact on America, the passions it aroused, the splits produced among groups and sections in the country, the defeat it inflicted on the foreign policy of the Roosevelt Administration, and how, ultimately, it furthered the political education of a great many Americans. It set them to reflecting on the coming war, and served as the prelude to the final debate between isolationists and internationalists, which was to rise in volume and bitterness until that first Sunday in the last month of 1941. In its way, it was as loud a blast ushering in the second World War as the stock market collapse had been to the depression. For the first time on the continent of Europe, the armies of the fascist powers were openly and arrogantly displayed. After Spain, all the Neutrality Acts in the world passed by all the Senates, signed by all the Roosevelts, driving the last nails in the coffins of all the legally elected republican governments, could scarcely conceal the aims of the new imperialism, or deflect the chill that sank into the hearts of even those Americans with no special love for the Loyalists, at the triumph of General Franco, and the installation on the Iberian peninsula of a belligerent friend of the Axis.

As befits a period that lifted foreign correspondence into a form of literary art, the war in Spain attracted creative writers from nearly every country, some of whom, like André Malraux, came to fight with the International Brigade, while others went simply as reporters whose personal sympathies were more or less on the side of the besieged government. Among those in this second classification was one of America's most distinguished and influential novelists, a writer who had always been attracted by the smell of death, the stronger and more dramatic the better, to whose imagination the bloodshed in Spain was a high and passionate stimulant. Ernest Hemingway came to Spain on assignment as a reporter; he left with plans for a play, *The Fifth Column,* and a novel, *For Whom the Bell Tolls.* The civil war might have been made to order for him; it embodied most of the salient features of the script Hemingway had been working with for fifteen years: two sides fighting with unbridled ferocity, every known variety of cowardice and heroism, characters who were *aficionado* and characters who were not, and a backdrop of great events against which the fortunes of selected individuals could be projected in dimensions somewhat larger than life.

It was the act of dying that bound these several elements together, and made them centrally attractive to

Hemingway. He had already studied men dying in every kind of situation he could lay hands on: the Swede lying in bed waiting for the gunmen in *The Killers* to get him; Jake, in *The Sun Also Rises*, consigned to a living death by his sexual impotence, drinking himself into an actual one, while Lady Brett follows the same course along the road of sexual dissipation; Catherine Barkley in *A Farewell to Arms* dying in childbirth for no particular reason at all, against the canvas of the retreat at Caporetto in which thousands of Italian soldiers were slaughtered; Manuel, the bullfighter in *The Undefeated*, being killed by the bull; Morgan, the smuggler in *To Have and Have Not*, living a hard jungle existence in the dangerous waters off the Florida Keys, and dying bloodily in the pursuit of his profession. When Hemingway ran out of human death, he fell back on animals, took to big game hunting, and described in *Green Hills of Africa* the supreme thrill of drawing his rifle sights on a buck and despatching it with an accuracy and released tension beautiful to behold.

In Spain, however, he found men dying in a slightly different context, no longer out of mere resignation or boredom, or for purely occupational reasons or purely accidental ones. They were now dying for a political cause, for an idealism greater than their own egos. It was a new kind of dying for Hemingway, and it drew him; it inflamed his creative ardor, and inspired the longest and most grandiose of his novels. *For Whom the Bell Tolls* has little of the tight, clipped, underaccented style which made Hemingway famous. For him, indeed, it sprawls and rambles, goes off on frequent digressions, and even pries the author out of his traditional impersonality. He begins it in what appears to be a new vein. After all the cynical disillusioned heroes, Robert Jordan is a refreshing type. He has gone to fight with the Loyalists partly because his grandfather had fought for freedom in the Civil War and he wants to do the same in his time. But Hemingway whittles away at his idealism until pretty soon it begins to look a little threadbare. First, there are André Marty and the Communists who, according to Hemingway, seek to organize the Loyalist cause for their own purposes, and come in for some savage blasting outside the framework of the plot. Then the Loyalists themselves turn out to be pretty brutal, and the one massacre described at length in the novel is a massacre of the fascists by the government forces. There are even stinging comments on the Spaniards as a people. They are characterized as treacherous:

"Of course they turned on you. They turned on you often but they always turned on every one. They turned on themselves, too. If you had three together, two would unite against one, and then the two would start to betray each other. Not always, but often enough for you to take enough cases and start to draw it as a conclusion."

And as callous, too:

"He [Lister, a Loyalist leader] was a true fanatic and he had the complete Spanish lack of respect for life. . . .

"But they [the Spanish] did that on purpose and deliberately. Those who did that are the last flowering of what their education has produced. Those are the flowers of

Spanish chivalry. What a people they have been. What sons of bitches from Cortez, Pizarro, Menendez de Avila all down through Enrique Lister to Pablo. And what wonderful people. There is no finer and no worse people in the world. No kinder people and no crueler."

After a few hundred pages of this, Jordan and his idealism are a pretty sickly looking pair. He clings to it to the end, however, and gives up his life to save his comrades, but by that time our feeling is, "What a damn fool! What an admirable damn fool!"

Having battered away at the one redeeming motive that has ever animated his heroes, Hemingway succeeded in preserving the continuity of his nihilism. Death as a form of art has been his abiding theme, and made him one of the inevitable writers of the era of global wars. He encompassed the postwar 20's even more than the 30's, and now, in the atomic age, he seems more than ever destined to be nourished with a fresh supply of variations on his major theme, and to articulate in fiction the destructive forces of the century.

IV

On the surface, and at the time, there seemed little connection between the outbreak of the Spanish Civil War and the appearance in the same month of that other mushrooming phenomenon, Margaret Mitchell's *Gone with the Wind*. Yet the relationship between them and the America of the late 30's was close and deep-woven.

The astonishing growth of historical fiction was a direct result of the crises the country endured, both domestic and foreign. The greater the danger confronting a nation, the more it returns to the glories of its past for solace and inspiration. No literary form gratified this returning instinct more than the historical novels, which, almost without exception, reaffirmed faith in the American past, and, by implication, in America's capacity to outride the dangers of the present. As the first of the serious foreign crises, the war in Spain symbolized the many pressures from the outside driving the country back to its roots. Even Robert Jordan went to Spain under the spur of an impulse that goes back to the American Civil War. As the most widely read historical novel dealing with the American past, *Gone with the Wind* made clear how intimately literature responds to life, and adjusts itself to the psychological needs of its time.

In times of disaster the past serves two diametrically opposite functions: to generate morale and provide escape. It discharged both these functions with considerable success during the sequence of misfortunes that began with the Wall Street crash, grew with the depression and the mounting dangers from abroad, and came to a climax at Pearl Harbor. During those twelve years of confusion, there were those who were determined never to fight in another war, so sorely were they disillusioned by the callous imperialisms, the secret treaties, the mangled peace of the first World War. There were those who were equally determined to fight fascism everywhere and under all circumstances. The Oxford Peace Pledge, signed by students who swore never to fight in another war, and the policy of "quarantining the aggressors," flourished side by side. The New Deal and the Old Deal, government regulation and *laissez-faire*, sniped at each other among the articulate, while the great amorphous mass of people yearned, as always, simply for their daily bread and peace to enjoy it.

In this scene of excitation and longing, historical fiction evolved its special formulas, trimmed them to suit the cravings of the public, and acquired a phenomenal vogue. Sensitive to the times, as literature and the arts often are, it sought for the widest possible foothold, and was soon creating an impetus to faith for those seeking it and an attractive retreat for those in flight. In story after story of the Revolutionary War, the lowest ebbs of fortune were described with the unrestrained realism characteristic of the decade of Farrell, Faulkner, and Steinbeck, only to be followed by a triumphantly optimistic climax. The analogy with the times was plain. 1932 and 1933, these chronicles said pointedly, were not the only dreg years in American history. They were no worse than the winter at Valley Forge. We survived then, though all seemed lost. We will survive now, despite appearances, despite the devastating slump and the bearers of bad tidings.

Even Civil War extravaganzas like *Gone with the Wind* displayed the aggressive survival of the individual in the midst of a disintegrating society. It held before our eyes the dazzling process by which Scarlett O'Hara rebuilt her shattered plantation after the Civil War. This emerges with great clarity despite the fact that the psychological development of the heroine stops on page two. At that point, she is sitting on her porch between two young gallants eager to escort her to the coming dance. As she fences with them verbally, she is laying schemes in her mind to get Ashley to take her. Her egotism, sensuality, and absolute lack of ethical scruple, are nakedly plain. Nothing that happens during the next eleven hundred odd pages changes Scarlett in even small ways, despite the fact that she lives through the siege of Atlanta, several husbands, storms of private passion and public war, indeed every crisis a human being can endure in a book. At the end, she is scheming to get Rhett back again, exactly as we saw her for the first time, scheming to get Ashley, back on page two. Yet, though her personality comes to a dead stop early in the book, the kaleidoscope of history in which she is caught up goes forward with rapid and absorbing speed, and leaves with the reader the sharp impression that, in the evolutionary scheme of things, America has produced, and by implication will always produce, the human resources necessary for survival.

In providing havens for those who found the troubled world of the 30's too much with them, the historical fictionalists decked out their wares with the suggestive artfulness that literature had developed during the practice of many centuries. Costumery, local color, the titillation supplied by the appearance of "real" historical figures, the maneuvers of what the movies call the romantic interest, embroidered all but the most astringently serious stories. The past and the future can be drugs to mute the sense of the present, as none knew better than the practitioners in these time sequences. What more seductive than the sweet saga of Shangri-La, that lost horizon forever found in the mazes of wishful thinking? Or what more dulcet and nerve-soothing than the white columns and soft voices of Southern plantations, those favorite *mise-en-scènes* of the historical romancers? The therapeutic values of the historical novel are now beyond dispute. To those with headaches, it was an effective aspirin; to those with flagging spirits, it was a shot in the arm.

As with every genre, historical fiction has a set of unwritten conventions the observance of which its reading enthusiasts have come to expect. The first of these, of course, is the presence of historical personages complete in period dress and period dialect. There is something so electrifying about Washington or Lincoln alive and in motion, so paralyzing to the critical sense, that it gives even the most wooden of writers an initial advantage over the reader. No one, however sophisticated, is immune to the pleasure of associating with the great, the established great whose reputations are beyond dispute. It is a pleasure purified by time, a craving shared by the lettered and unlettered alike.

Moreover, the dyed-in-the-wool historical novel displays a pronounced enthusiasm for America. Whether it is the enthusiasm of a Hessian lieutenant (Bruce Lancaster's *Guns of Burgoyne*) who enlists in the British armies only to be converted to the American cause, or the enthusiasm of Allan Kenton (Howard Fast's *Conceived in Liberty*) who deserts from Washington's army at Valley Forge only, through suffering, to regain his allegiance; or even the enthusiasm of an Oliver Wiswell (in Kenneth Roberts' novel of the same name) for an America wisely governed by the Tories, some espousal of the national cause is requisite. The enduring contribution of historical fiction in the 30's lay precisely here: it fed the curiosity of Americans about their past, and was destined, during the process, to intensify that curiosity and thus help share in the realization of the national heritage. It flourished at a time when the confidence of the country in itself was being shaken by misfortune, and the yearning to find some new impetus to faith was strong. By helping to dam up confidence and stimulate faith, the historical novel played a part in the resurgence of the national spirit during the years immediately prior to the second World War.

The third of the paramount ingredients of the historical fiction formula is local color. A street in the London of Hogarth has to smell of the eighteenth century, as it did in *Northwest Passage*. A chronicle of the Civil War has to be not only the record of events political and military, but also has to have a careful transcription of accent, of social nuance, applied so notably in Stark Young's *So Red the Rose*. This period flavor, this sense of milieu, is perhaps the most difficult task for the historical craftsman, since it depends more on an effort of the imagination and less upon research than his other unique preoccupations. It is this feeling for past time and past place that enabled historical fiction to reveal to a troubled decade the invigorating sources of its national origin.

V

The fluidity and multifunctionalism of the genre were staggering. It served as a liaison between the serious novel and the light romance. It provided an inexhaustible supply of cinematic fuel for the films. It stimulated historical research. It became the great rival of the detective story for the attention of tired businessmen, academicians, and chorus girls in search of relaxation both soothing and spiced. It shifted from one section of the reading public to another, from one source to another, seeking inspirations and themes with an amoral abandon thoroughly in keeping with an age whose ethical convictions were being shuffled and reshuffled, and had not yet jelled.

Nor was that all. The expanding popularity of the historical novel coincided with the era of America's evolution to adult stature. The past twenty-five years have seen our country's self-emancipation from its sense of cultural inferiority to England and the growth of an aggressive and homogeneous American literature. Our national conduct in World War II was admirably grown up as compared with World War I. Though Germany was again our enemy, no longer did we attack our native Germans on racial grounds, transform sauerkraut to liberty cabbage, and legislate the teaching of German out of our schools. Even Japan, despite occasional traces of the "yellow skin" theme, came in for little countrywide abuse. Moreover, we have begun to recognize our citizenship in the world, and to appreciate the profound truth that freedom is an integral part of the moral responsibility of mankind. In this process of maturation, historical fiction played its small but definitive part. It built a number of bridges across the life span of the country, and in this way expanded the national horizon. It gathered our first impulses from the fog of time, polished them vigorously, and made them glitter. The bright image of Jefferson began to illuminate the mind of many an American, a phenomenon in which biography and drama [4] no less than the historical novel played leading rôles. To review the instinct and movement toward freedom of our forbears was not to end the "competitions, factions and debates" of the country, but it was to invest them with an underlying clarity. In the struggle to attain this clarity which pervaded the stormy 30's, even the pedestrian historical narratives were useful agents.

VI

Historical fiction attracted many skillful writers, almost by way of supporting its bid for literary as well as social permanence. Among them, every conceivable viewpoint, political and otherwise, was richly exploited—from Howard Fast and his dramatic left-wing narratives of American history at one extreme, to Kenneth Roberts and his

---

[4] Of which Sidney Kingsley's play, *The Patriots*, was a conspicuous example.

somewhat more leisurely and spacious, but equally significant, chronicles told from the right.

Roberts, with his patient and scrupulous research, uncovered unexploited and little-known areas of the past which he proceeded to fictionalize. His *Arundel*, with the early Benedict Arnold as the pivot, was the opening gun heralding the march of the historical novel through the decade. *Captain Caution* and *Rabble in Arms* continued, in a quiet way, his exploration of the remoter areas of our early history, but it was not until the success of *Northwest Passage* that Roberts became known to the country as a whole. This story of the legendary Major Rogers, his wars in the service of the British against the Indians, and his futile quest for the northwest passage was embroidered with a vast amount of local color. Even the chapters in which the scene shifts to London, which are so loosely tacked onto the principal narrative, recreate faithfully the atmosphere of the eighteenth century.

Roberts has always sought to avoid extremes. His historical perspective was most lucidly illustrated in *Oliver Wiswell*, in which he avoids portraying the British as unmitigated villains and the revolutionists as divinely inspired heroes. Oliver Wiswell anticipates Alexander Hamilton by hoping that the "better classes" will run the Revolution, a point of view that receives Roberts' reasoned sympathy.

What Kenneth Roberts does from a somewhat conservative standpoint, Howard Fast does from a somewhat radical one. Where Roberts is devoted to the physical and moral bravery of our early American heroes, Fast tends to glorify the ideals of racial and political justice. He has an aggressive intelligence, occasionally uncontrolled, often monochrome. Some of his best work is emotionally monotonous; the unrelieved account of the suffering of the army at Valley Forge is almost more than the reader can bear. Some of his worst distorts history to suit the requirements of the author's theses. John Peter Altgeld, hero of *The American*, is not quite the noble figure in history that he is in the novel. At times, in his most recent work particularly, Fast's doctrines atrophy his aesthetic sense, and lead him to pound belligerently at his reader at the expense of characterization and credibility.

Yet he has already produced three books that, in different ways, are strikingly effective. *The Last Frontier* narrated a small sequence of incidents in the life of a tribe penned up in its Oklahoma reservation, but it served to light up the whole Indian tragedy. *Conceived in Liberty* was an intense epic of Valley Forge, so ravaging to the souls who retreated there that it created in one terrible winter the military and spiritual instrument which decided the Revolutionary War. *Citizen Tom Paine*, more diffuse, insinuated the reader into the eighteenth century with a good deal of skill. Fast has kept his historical novels as free as possible from subservience to the needs of slick romance, and has steadfastly insisted upon their serious responsibilities and great social potential.

There were other celebrated historical novelists of the time who were advancing the range of their craft. Walter D. Edmonds, in *Rome Haul* and *Drums Along the Mo-*

hawk particularly, wrote vividly about events in up-state New York, as Frank O. Hough did about Westchester in *The Neutral Ground*. Neil H. Swanson embarked upon his long series of historical narratives in which his research was brought up to point-blank range like so much heavy artillery, and appeared as footnotes and bibliography within the text of the novels themselves. Hervey Allen, after the success of *Anthony Adverse*, wrote *Action at Aquila*, a spirited account of an isolated skirmish in the Civil War. Then, probing farther back into the American past, he launched, with *The Forest and the Fort* and *Bedford Village*, an extended series of volumes dealing with the same eighteenth century hero.

These writers, together with Roberts and Fast, and a host of others have carried historical fiction to the high point of its recent development in America, and made it, for the reading public of the 30's, a meaningful and important literary form.

9: THE JOADS IN CALIFORNIA

EVERY age has its representative writer, whose career follows its major interests, whose voice is its voice. In him we can see the moods, if not the actual events of his time, most clearly reflected and its strongest drives most forcefully crystallized. The two basic impulses of the 30's, toward escape and toward social consciousness, found their sharpest expression in the writing of John Steinbeck, whose work represents more faithfully than any of his contemporaries the temperament of the angry decade.

I

Of the principal events of the time reflected in the bright mirror of Steinbeck's fiction, few were more significant than the growth, political and economic, of organized labor. Most symptomatic of that growth was the sharpening of class consciousness, and with that sharpening, there appeared for the first time in our history the widespread acceptance of government regulation as a major force in the lives of the people. The depression was, of course, the igniting agent that set these phenomena into motion. Before it, the state of relative material prosperity the country had, with brief interruptions, enjoyed since the Civil War had kept the tensions between capital and labor pitched in a low key. The crash, however, drove the two apart, temporarily destroyed the faith of labor in the ability of capital to maintain employment, and shook the confidence of bankers and captains of industry in themselves so much that they spent the early months of President Roosevelt's first Administration in Washington, hat-in-hand, pleading for help. Where, in the previous decade, American labor unions had been prevailingly non-political, they became, under the spur of hard times, the encouragement of the New Deal, and the emergence of the C.I.O., more and more politically conscious, as the growth of various agencies, from John L. Lewis's Non-Partisan League to Sidney Hillman's Political Action Committee has sufficiently proved.

The laboratory in which these alterations in the social fabric are to be observed in their most strategic form is the year 1937. That was the year John D. Rockefeller, Sr., died. His obituaries quoted his best-known aphorisms, among them, "A clear conscience is worth more than a great fortune gathered by dishonorable methods." That was the year of the sitdown strikes and of the most serious business recession during Roosevelt's tenure. It was the year in which the angry voices of the 30's hurled their now familiar epithets at one another most loudly. It was the year in which *The Late George Apley* [1] was published, that brilliant study of the Boston Brahmins, by John P. Marquand who, after Steinbeck, was to be the most class-conscious writer of the decade. It was also the year after the appearance of *In Dubious Battle*, Steinbeck's first novel dealing with the new relationships of worker and employer, a book which, according to Joseph Henry Jackson, "many people have called the best strike novel ever written."

The ultimate significance of the sitdown strikes within the General Motors factories during January and February was not that they took place, or that they were a new wrinkle in strike technique, but that they were not broken by the use of private guards hired by the corporation, or the state militia, or Federal troops dispatched by the President. No previous type of strike had posed so serious a threat to the principle of private property or had seemed so clearly illegal; yet, hitherto, little hesitation had been displayed by industry and government to break strikes by force. The fact that no serious attempt was made to eject the sitdowners, that Governor Frank Murphy of Michigan (later Supreme Court Justice) resisted every suggestion to do so, that not even the most outraged members of the General Motors Board of Directors thought seriously of asking President Roosevelt to throw the strikers out, was

[1] Inspired in part by the appearance the year before of George Santayana's novel, *The Last Puritan*, which dealt with the same social group, though far more diffusely.

of the greatest historical consequence. It meant not only that organized labor had taken long strides forward toward equating its power in the national economy with that of management, but that property rights could no longer always be counted on as the decisive issue in public disputes.

Only a few years earlier, Henry Ford was reputed to have said to a committee of workers who threatened to strike if their wage demands were not met: "I can afford to shut down for a few years. Can you?" There was no strike. By 1937, however, times had changed; changed so much that there was no longer any question of a giant corporation blandly closing down and sitting on its haunches until its employees were starved into submission, or any question of the workers themselves not being able to hold out. In the shut automobile plants of Flint and Detroit, they were quite obviously able to hold out till doomsday. When General Motors capitulated after six weeks, and after General Motors, Chrysler and U. S. Steel signed contracts with their unions, it was evident to even the most fanatical devotee of Adam Smith economics that a new era was at hand. And when Henry Ford himself, that last intransigent, accepted the C.I.O., it was a final dramatic confirmation of the changing times. Nothing that happened after that, not even the "Little Steel Massacre" on Decoration Day, when ten pickets were killed by Chicago police, altered this main current of the 30's.

The business recession later that year was symptomatic in another way of the increase in class tensions, and the laceration of tempers already made trigger-sharp by the sitdown strikes and the long wrangle over the President's court-packing bill that had dragged through the spring and summer. In all the previous recessions (a word that might well serve as the supreme understatement of the day), including the huge one of 1929, few had accused Big Business of artificially manufacturing hard times by lying doggo on new investments, and closing down busy factories in part or whole. Now a clamor rose from many quarters, particularly the militant unions of the newly organized C.I.O. and persons high in the Administration, blaming the recession on Wall Street and its corporate and banking allies, and charging that it was a cold-blooded plot to discredit the economic policies of the New Deal.

The waning months of 1937 were filled with charges and countercharges. Secretary of the Interior Ickes bluntly warned the "Lords of Big Business" to submit to the New Deal. He claimed that the "60 families" were seeking economic control of the whole country, and accused Ford and the duPonts of being the principal obstacles to recovery. Robert H. Jackson, the Solicitor-General (later Supreme Court Justice), said that capital was striking in an attempt to destroy the New Deal. On the other side of the fence, ex-President Hoover urged the Administration to refrain from interfering with business, while John L. Lewis, then President of the C.I.O., angered by Roosevelt's attitude of "a plague on both your houses" during the sitdown strikes, blamed the slump on the government's "do-nothing" policy. No two groups in the country agreed on who or what was responsible; everyone was profoundly convinced of his own innocence. The air, in the meanwhile, was filled with polemical din, the tempers of capital, labor, and government, that newly intimate trio, being rather frayed in the process. None of them knew that this was to be the last year in a long time in which they were to wrangle over purely domestic issues. Hitler's seizure of Austria, in March, 1938, was to establish the dominance of foreign affairs over the national agenda until well after the end of hostilities in the second World War.

The emergence of the Federal government as an intimate participant in economic affairs was the chief instrument used by the New Deal to pry the country out of the depression, and eased the way later for its equally intimate participation in the personal lives of the citizenry during the prosecution of the war. No break with tradition, not even the third and fourth terms for President Roosevelt, was greater than this emergence. It ran counter to the popular distrust of government, to the belief in unregulated free enterprise, to the distrust of politics and politicians, that permeated our history. As Thurman Arnold observed in *The Folklore of Capitalism:*

". . . in every institutional mythology is the national Devil. Our Devil is governmental interference. Thus we firmly believe in the inherent malevolence of government which interferes with business. Here are people who are not to be trusted—they are the bureaucrats, the petty tyrants, the destroyers of a rule of law."

The reversal was so complete that during the sitdown strikes, it occurred to no one to do anything but turn to the government for mediation. The fact that Governor Murphy, and not John L. Lewis or Alfred P. Sloan, Jr. (at that time President of General Motors), was the central figure in the automobile dispute, indicated how thoroughly the government had been accepted as one of the centers not only of the political affairs of the nation but of its business operations as well. It was evident, too, that the government had come to stay, and that no serious entanglement, domestic or foreign, which was to crop up henceforth would be likely to be settled without some degree of Federal participation.

Whether this development was good or bad, advantageous or not, was another matter altogether, and raised a fierce enough argument in its own right.[2] More to the point was its inevitability: it was a part of the world trend during the twentieth century, which, in the numerous manifestations of state planning, state capitalism, state socialism, moved much more rapidly in other countries than in our own. One of Roosevelt's most notable achievements

[2] An argument equaled in fierceness only by that which raged over the activities of the New Deal itself. The New Deal did not keep many of the promises made by Roosevelt in the campaign of 1932. It failed to solve the peacetime problem of unemployment. It did not hesitate to maintain political alliances with corrupt city machines. Several of its legislative measures were unconstitutional. But the New Deal left a permanent legacy of good which has become an integral part of American life: the Tennessee Valley Authority, the Federal Deposit Insurance Corporation Act, the Securities and Exchange Commission, the Social Security Act, the Rural Electrification Commission. And it strove, with few interruptions, to reduce racial and religious discrimination.

was the way in which he gave this world trend idioms and contours that fitted it to the American scene and caused it to be adopted by most Americans with what, under the circumstances, was a surprisingly small amount of friction. Despite the outraged cries of those who would maintain the rugged *laissez-faire* individualism of the nineteenth century, Roosevelt defeated Alf M. Landon, in the fall of 1936, by an overwhelming majority. Four years later, Wendell Willkie, the third Republican to run for the presidency against Roosevelt, had already accepted the principle of government responsibility and only promised to discharge it more efficiently. Four years after that, Thomas E. Dewey, the fourth Republican to enter the lists, was saying the same thing, only in somewhat sharper language.

II

As class relationships grew more active during the 30's, and class consciousness more pronounced, there arose at opposite ends of the country two novelists who were to reflect these changes most perceptively. On the surface, there seemed little connection between John P. Marquand, that fastidious and immaculate chronicler of the upper stratum in Massachusetts, and John Steinbeck, the passionately indignant, sentimentally tender observer of the *paisanos*, the fruit pickers, the itinerant Okies of California. Yet, though starting from points farthest removed from one another, they were both dealing with the same subject: the class structure of American society. They were dealing with it not encyclopedically, as had Upton Sinclair, or ideologically, as had the proletarian novelists, but selectively, and with an interest in individual characters that always superseded interest in the class to which they belonged. Thus Marquand selected as his subject not the great manufacturers or bankers, but the somewhat out-of-the-way Brahmins of Boston, who represented an alliance between the old aristocracy and the new business entrepreneurs. And Steinbeck selected as his, not steel hands or miners or employees in the basic service or distribution industries, but the somewhat out-of-the-way workers in orange and peach groves, displaced and footloose laborers from other regions, and drifters and *paisanos* who belonged to what the professional economist delicately calls "unemployables." Between the two of them, Marquand from the top, Steinbeck from the bottom, the upper and lower brackets of the social structure were pretty thoroughly encompassed.

Marquand is a throwback to Edith Wharton and John Galsworthy. He writes their kind of silky-smooth, suavely ironical novel of fashionable society, and in his tone, there is nothing of the violence and heat of his time. Yet, without adding anything new to the art of fiction, he has exposed with admirable finesse the spiritual history of the Apleys, the Pulhams, and the other Massachusetts paladins who traced their ancestry to Plymouth Rock, attached their politics to the anchorages of the Republican party, and were more disturbed by the lack of polish in the New Deal than by its policies of change and reform.

"Then came the depression and that was when they all began saying 'Come the Revolution.' Personally, Jeffrey had been unable to perceive any signs of the Revolution, but a friend of his, Edward Mace, who had been a social worker in Chicago and who had written reports for various foundations which Jeffrey had never been able to read, had told Jeffrey that the New Deal had staved off violent revolution . . . One thing about the New Dealers which annoyed Jeffrey—they were always calling each other by their first names, or what was worse, by nicknames, as though they were all members of a club or of an athletic team. Edward Mace, for instance, referred to the President as 'the Skipper' and Mr. Roosevelt, not to be outdone, had stated that he was the quarterback who called the signals. This New Deal intimacy disturbed Jeffrey much more than the Revolution, which, according to Edward Mace, was going on right now, although people like Jeffrey did not know because people like Jeffrey possessed no social sense."

Like the Forsytes of Galsworthy's England, and the Newland Archers of Edith Wharton's nineteenth century New York, the Marquand characters looked upon passionate love as a dangerously antisocial state of mind and fell back in every emotional crisis upon the undisturbing women of their own sphere. The Marquand hero always has a fling at love, enjoys it no end, then succumbs to pressure from his class and comes back to the fold, there to lick his wounds until the advancing years dull the ache. With few variations, the trio of figures, the young well-born Bostonian, his equally well-born wife, and the attractive, life-loving young woman outside the Massachusetts aristocracy, go through a series of set motions, and wind up in the same fixed positions in one novel after another. Marquand invests these motions with a great deal of comic irony, and decks out his formula with enough sophistication to equip half his contemporaries practicing fiction. He is a permanent illustration of Buffon's aphorism that "the style is the man." Without original ideas, wedded to familiar formulas, he has perfected the style of high comedy practiced by George Meredith and Henry James to that point of fluent artistry where even his inferior work bears his distinctive brush strokes.

That his most recent work has been inferior is growing lamentably plain. The reason is not hard to find. Marquand has squeezed his Bostonians fairly dry, and he seems uninterested in doing anything very different. *The Late George Apley*, the first of the series, was fresh and crisp and *Wickford Point*, the second, though blurred of focus, had the magnificent sketch of a literary agent to keep it nourished. *H. M. Pulham, Esquire*, the third and perhaps the finest of the lot, carried the satirical penetration of the basic social type to its absolute interior limits. But *So Little Time*, the fourth, while remaining eminently readable, seemed a little routine, and *B. F.'s Daughter*, the fifth, though shifting the narrative focus from the well-bred young man to the well-bred young woman and feeding a little on New Deal politics and politicians, was as much a slick-surfaced commercial product as a serious piece of literary art. Marquand has gone once around the particular species of ruling class American he has chosen to study;

he is now going around a second time. The second trip is less fresh, less significant than the first. The subject has now grown a little stale, and even his style, once a finely tempered, subtle instrument, has of late begun to lose its incisiveness.

But his early novels, the novels of the 30's, are among the indispensable documents of the time. They portray one of the characteristic segments of our native aristocracy without the agitation and irascible temper with which so much of the documentation of the period is sorely burdened.

III

It took seven books and a regional disaster before the country awakened to the fact that it had found in John Steinbeck its chief literary chronicler. Between 1929, when his first novel appeared, and 1939, the year of *The Grapes of Wrath*, he was regarded by the small number of people aware of his existence as a talented but somewhat provincial writer from California who dealt mainly with local types. In 1939, however, partly because the ground had been prepared by the disasters in the Dust Bowl, partly because *The Grapes of Wrath* was so obviously a genuine American epic, he emerged from the narrow confines of his first reading public and became, with one stroke, a nationally prominent writer. One by-product of this emergence was a sudden accumulation of public interest in his earlier books. *Of Mice and Men* was turned into a play. *Tortilla Flat* became a whimsical treasure, ripened for a

Hollywood kill.[3] Readers became aware that *In Dubious Battle* was that rarest of manifestations, a proletarian novel which did not unreservedly admire the proletariat. Even the early *Pastures of Heaven* received some side-door accolades, and there was enough left in the backwash to deposit a few fragrant posies upon the tired adolescence of Steinbeck's first novel, *Cup of Gold*.

The thematic progression of these novels followed in sequence the themes absorbing the American public during the past fifteen years. At the end of the 20's, literary Bohemianism was still the prevailing fashion. This was the period of Steinbeck's first books and found its most significant expression in the saga of the *paisanos* of *Tortilla Flat*, who glorified a primitive existence and regarded property as contaminating (all of Danny's troubles in the book begin when he becomes a landlord), and classified people who worked for a living as members of an inferior species. When Bohemianism collapsed under the cumulative weight of the depression, the whimsical strain in Steinbeck was put into cold storage for a while. With the appearance of the most widely publicized of the new causes, that of organized labor, he emerged in his next incarnation as the creator of the Joads and the Salinas fruit strikers and as a confirmed and uncompromising revolutionary in the economic, if not in the political sense. The enormous public interest (following the success of *The Grapes of Wrath*)

---

[3] Although *Tortilla Flat* was sold to the movies in 1935, it was put on the shelf and was not produced until after the publication of *The Grapes of Wrath*.

in Steinbeck's labor novels, reveals how the merger of a writer and his audience can be consummated without conscious effort on the part of either.

Steinbeck's first novels made their appearance quietly enough. *Cup of Gold,* a mannered and aestheticized chronicle of Sir Henry Morgan, the famous buccaneer, was followed by *To a God Unknown,* with its equally mannered portrait of Joseph Wayne, who espoused a mystical cult of blood and soil, of primitive gods rooted in an avenging earth. Attuned though they were to the 1929-32 era, they were too imitative to emerge from the mass of similar literature that glutted the markets at the time. Nor did the short stories of that artfully titled collection, *Pastures of Heaven,* do more than reveal Steinbeck's chronic interest in half-wits and adult children that was later to flower in the figures of Lennie, the Pirate, Noah Joad, and Johnny Bear. They contained no hint of the struggles of the underprivileged. The people were poor enough, but as Steinbeck's *paisanos* are poor, amiably and cheerfully. Indeed, the idyllic climax of this whole early period comes to a head in *Tortilla Flat,* where poverty as the center of a whimsical millennium is given its final tender definition.

It is seldom that a writer is successful in two radically different veins, and can pass from one to the other and back again without appreciable loss of skill. But Steinbeck can create pure whimsy and almost equally pure revolutionary fervor in alternating sequence without seeming to strain himself at all. His moods are unpredictable. He may rage at his villains in high anger as in *The Grapes of Wrath* or chide at them as in *The Moon is Down*. He may be harsh as in *In Dubious Battle* or gentle as in *Tortilla Flat*. His attitude toward poverty swings from one extreme to another. It seems astonishing that in one book he can treat the poor as gay, carefree children of Nature, and in another as potential revolutionaries angry at the oppression grinding them down. No one doubts that the poor are manifest in both aspects; what is unique is that Steinbeck keeps them mutually exclusive and describes both with equal conviction. No treatment of the inflammable subject of poverty could be more calculated to guarantee a wider audience; for if Steinbeck is moved to treat the underprivileged in opposite ways because of the vagaries of his temperament, his readers are moved to applaud one view or its opposite, according to their respective convictions. That *The Grapes of Wrath* should have had a much more explosive effect than *Tortilla Flat* was due as much to the still-remembered miseries of the depression as to the greater literary merits of one novel over another. If it were possible to treat poverty as a sort of Rousseauistic idyll at the beginning of the 30's, it was no longer possible to do so in the later years of the decade. As the times changed, so did Steinbeck.

They changed with sudden violence. One year after the appearance of *Tortilla Flat*, Steinbeck was deep in the strikes and turmoil of *In Dubious Battle*. Within two years he was projecting the pathetic agony of *Of Mice and Men*, and preparing the way for the crescendo of conflict in *The Grapes of Wrath*. *In Dubious Battle*, a brutal story of the fruit pickers and their strike, contains no whimsicality or soft philosophizing. There is no aroma of the pastures of heaven about Mac and Jim, the two Communist strike organizers. Though Steinbeck is to be entirely on the side of the Joads in his next specific attack upon injustice, he is by no means so wholly ranged on the side of the workers here. He is critical of certain aspects of their policy, is careful to dwell upon the brittleness and hesitation of the fruit pickers at decisive moments, and suggests in his title that the battle in which they are engaged is a dubious one.

Though acutely aware of his characters' frailties, Steinbeck is affectionately disposed toward them. If there is any sustained link between his books, any transition from one temperamental state to another, it is this affection. He loves his personages with a tender and abiding love. He loves the half-wits like the Pirate of *Tortilla Flat*; he loves the Communists of *In Dubious Battle*; he even regards with compassionate understanding Colonel Lanser and Lieutenant Tonder among the German invaders of *The Moon is Down*. What arouses his anger is not so much people, as the conditions under which they are forced to live. He has a steadfast and unwavering compassion for human beings, sometimes misplaced perhaps, but always unreserved.

Compassion, in the widest and subtlest sense, reaches the flood in *The Grapes of Wrath*, one of the most profoundly moving and important books of the interval between the two World Wars. Historically, the novel has elements of Zola with his perpetual appeals to the conscience of his country, and of Godwin who, like Steinbeck here,

peppered his plots with essays predicting and apostro-
phizing revolution. But the heart of the novel does not
center around the problems and travails of the sharecroppers as an economic group, and it is certainly far removed
from the author's extraneous essays on the socialist revolution. It is rooted in the Joads as a family and as human
beings embroiled in the struggle for existence. Their struggle is no more important than themselves, and so Steinbeck, for all his comments on politics and capitalism, regards it. Grouped around the magnificent figure of Casy,
they demonstrate Steinbeck's astonishing capacity for describing people who have come within the range of his
senses. Whenever he is forced to describe people sight un-
seen, his portraits blur. He was compelled to imagine Sir
Henry Morgan, Nazi invaders, and European villagers.
These stories are, as a consequence, his least convincing.
If the Joads represent his psychological masterpiece, it is
because he has observed them most intently with his own
eyes.

What is true on the large canvas of *The Grapes of
Wrath* is equally true on the small canvas of *Of Mice and
Men*, which was published earlier. If behind the Joads
there loom all the Okies, behind George and Lennie are
etched all the itinerant ranch laborers who long for their
spot of land and the security contained therein. With his
usual acute sympathies, Steinbeck has taken hold of their
most deep-woven impulses and dreams, bringing these
lonely, rootless souls to vivid life. The mood of the novelette
is tender, the story a kind of parable shot through with love

of mankind, an enormous development over the knotted
and juvenile tenderness of *Cup of Gold,* and over the
whimsical, at times cloying love of *Tortilla Flat.*

Yet there is no sentimentality. The characters make
brief appearances and are described in bare, temperate language. The style throughout is lean and strongly underaccented, as though the craftsman were aware of the potential flabbiness and softness of his theme and sought to
hold these sentimental attributes in check by every means
at his disposal. That the performance is a *tour de force,* is
true enough, and in this sense Steinbeck has learned much
from the tales of Poe. But Steinbeck's tale, unlike those of
Poe, has human content, which rescues it at once from
mere virtuosity. One of the principal figures, to be sure, is
a half-wit, and it has been argued that the psychological
content of a story dealing with an idiot is greatly circum-
scribed in interest and value. Dostoevski refuted this in his
superb study of Prince Ippolit in *The Idiot.* And Steinbeck's Lennie is significant not so much because his idio-
cies are clearly analyzed, as because of those qualities which,
though in an enfeebled frame, bind him to the normal
world: his daydreaming, his need for friendship and the
security of a home, his passion for beauty, the loyalty and
essential amiability of his nature. These are the traits that
magnetize his relationship to George and, through George,
to us.

In structure, *Of Mice and Men* is notably superior to
The Grapes of Wrath, to which in most other ways it
stands as a yacht to a battleship. It has none of the dis-

tressingly extraneous essays on the revolution to come, none of the exaggerated symbolism of the longer work. It is, on the whole, one of the finest short novels in our literature.

How good of its kind it is can best be measured when one compares it with that later short novel by Steinbeck, *The Moon is Down.* It, too, is saturated with love and pity, a great deal of pity for the Norwegian villagers and even some for the German conquerors who enslave them. But the story rests upon two cardinal errors, and in the end founders upon them. The first is political: with few exceptions, the German officers, from the ranking colonel to the lowliest lieutenant, are not members of the Nazi party or spokesmen for the Nazi creed, an astonishing oversight on Hitler's part, and one that appeared able to exist, alas, only in the pages of fiction. The other error is psychological: in his eagerness to prove the thesis that the conquered will shatter the morale of the conquerors, Steinbeck has made his Germans peculiarly corroded with doubts and fears. The colonel from the outset is convinced that his side will lose and infects his comrades with his defeatism. The invaders contribute as much to their own destruction as do their victims. All this is a very heartening theory on paper. But the enemy were tough, hard men, not likely to crack under the pressure of moral resistance alone. To make virtually all of them disintegrate is to impose a species of wishful thinking upon the inelastic substance of reality. More than that, it grounds the story upon fallacious premises, and forces Steinbeck's humanitarian-

ism for the first time into a cul-de-sac, where it squanders
itself in misguided ways upon misguided objects.

But for all its shortcomings, *The Moon is Down* had
the timeliness of the other Steinbeck novels strung back
for a decade. It was written in the early years of the war at
a time when the relations between the Nazis and the peoples of the occupied countries were of feverish interest to
the whole world. It was received even more enthusiastically
in Europe than in America. The French underground translated and published it during the war. It was widely cir-
culated and regarded as effective propaganda against the
Germans. Steinbeck could not have chosen a theme closer
to the events of the day, or have indicated more con-
clusively his nearness to the serious curiosities of his audience. Though it does not bear comparison with *Of Mice
and Men* as a manifestation of the art of the short novel,
The Moon is Down illustrates dramatically Steinbeck's almost sensory awareness of the times, his acute perception
of how the novel can attach itself to the movements of
the age.

In the interludes between novels, Steinbeck made numerous excursions into allied arts. His *Sea of Cortez,* an
account of a quasi-scientific expedition to the Gulf of
Mexico, revealed the hold that the natural sciences, zool-
ogy and biology especially, had upon him. One of the more
arresting moments in his short stories is the scene where
a snake devours a rabbit thrust into its cage, devours it in
a series of slow, hypnotic movements that seem to hold
the author spellbound. In all the novels, a scientist of

some sort is planted. He is a doctor sometimes, as in *Tortilla Flat* and *In Dubious Battle;* or a marine biologist like Doc in *Cannery Row,* who serves as an extreme contrast to the primitivism of the major characters, whether *paisanos* or Okies. On another occasion, Steinbeck journeyed to Mexico and came back with a movie, *The Forgotten Village,* that studied the primitive peasant in another landscape.

Throughout, there is in him this passion for reducing life to its simplicities: the primitive paradise and the proletarian slum; the hard naïvete of the natives of Cannery Row and the soft-shelled wisdom of Doc; the *paisanos* lying on their backs and picking their teeth in the sun; and the undernourished Joads gazing at the terrible sight of oranges being destroyed because they can no longer be sold at a profit. In part, it was this kind of dramatic simplification that endeared him to the 30's. This, and his intensive burrowing in the lower depths of American society in a period when the successive administrations of Franklin D. Roosevelt, and the times themselves, were stirring these depths into activity, into a place in the national sun.

10: LIGHT FICTION AND HEAVY VERSE

O N OCTOBER 30, 1938, there occurred an event that might very well serve as a key to the national temper during the period between the end of the sitdown strikes and the beginning of the war. This event was a radio broadcast by the decade's *enfant terrible*, Orson Welles. The broadcast was one of those shockers which the networks usually supply for juvenile listeners in the afternoon, and occasionally dress up for the adult trade later in the evening. This one began at eight, at the very time the Charley McCarthy show, then fairly new and immensely popular, was on. The Welles script, based upon H. G. Wells's *The War of the Worlds*, described in accents of blistering realism the invasion of earth by warriors from Mars, clad in the most fearful raiment and armed with dreadful new weapons (they bore a striking resemblance to German paratroopers descending from the skies of Europe a few years later). Their main landing ground—as chance and the dictates of Martian military strategy apparently required—was the New Jersey meadows, an admirable choice, since the turf was spongy, the ground covered with high and, hence, concealing swamp weed, the terrain flat and located within eyeshot of the great prize of New York. The moment the landing was effected, the invaders fanned out in all directions, and began spreading terror through the countryside.

Most listeners began that eight o'clock with the ventriloquist's dummy, and switched to the Men from Mars during the commercial. They broke in upon a series of bloodcurdling warnings from announcers who screamed news of the danger advancing upon them with appalling speed. Within a few minutes, people all over the country began bolting out of their houses in wild flight from this planetary disaster. The telephone lines were swamped with alarms, appeals, and cries of terror. All the while, the Martians were wreaking havoc over the air waves, the Welles program ground to its close, the actors resumed their normal voices, and there was a pause for station identification. In the words of Frederick Lewis Allen:

"Even if only one person in twenty among those who heard the program took it at its face value, this credulous minority—together with the people whom they alarmed with their garbled stories of what they thought was happening—caused enough panic to serve as a remarkable case study in national hysteria."

The wits claimed the experience had demonstrated that the radio commercial had now become a menace to the national welfare. But all the wisecracks that followed did little to blunt the shock. The fact remained that, without provocation, Americans had behaved exactly as some civilian populations were to behave in the approaching war, fleeing in panic from bombs and rumors of bombs. But they at least were to have ample provocation. The truth was, though not clearly understood at the time, that the country was girding itself for war, and passing through the preliminary phases of panic and terror before settling down to the eventual state of grim endurance which comes to the combat soldier after he has become accustomed to gunfire.

The events of 1938, leading up to the Welles affair, had actively prepared the way for the general state of jumpiness. Hitler, having reintroduced conscription and remilitarized the Rhineland, was now ready for the first of his leaps upon Germany's neighbors. In March came the *Anschluss* with Austria, enforced at pistol point. Almost at once, the demands against Czechoslovakia were put forth, and the intensified phases of the Czech crisis dragged through the whole tortuous length of the summer. Domestic events were crowded from the front pages of our newspapers, and were replaced by the complex tangle of incidents and personalities involving all the capitals of Western Europe. Prime Minister Chamberlain, having done his best for the Nazis in Spain through the Non-Intervention Committee,[1] became one of the principal engineers of the Munich Agreement signed in September. By its terms, Czechoslovakia was reduced to a rump state, left without guarantees by its former allies, and ready for outright annexation the following spring. So, in exchange for a slip

[1] Which prevented England and France from aiding the Loyalists, but did nothing to prevent the Germans and Italians from aiding the Rebels.

of paper Mr. Chamberlain brought from Germany, promising "peace in our time," the Western powers handed Hitler the keys of Europe.

The daily impact of these earth-shaking events affected even those Americans who felt war was very remote. It bred an atmosphere of irritation and unrest, of foreboding and despair. It inflamed the tempers of those ranging themselves on the opposing sides of intervention and isolation, and paved the way for the great debate on foreign policy that was to dominate the years from 1939 through 1941. It created, in the last analysis, the kind of nervously impressionable state of mind that transformed even a trivial and passing radio broadcast into a match to light a conflagration. Ten years earlier, the country would have laughed at the Welles show as too absurd to be taken seriously, whether one tuned into it during the middle or not. Ten years later, in the era of the atomic bomb, an invasion from Mars would seem like just one more catastrophe to a planet that had endured horrors too numerous to classify, and was living under an atomic sword of Damocles too dreadful to contemplate.

In a smaller way, affecting a narrower range of the population, pressure from abroad was intensified by the Moscow trials, which resulted in the execution of eighteen veterans of the Bolshevik Revolution on charges of espionage on behalf of Germany and Japan. American public opinion was greatly shocked by the trials and purges and, despite the explanations offered, found them difficult to understand or condone. The debate over the rightness or wrongness of the trials waxed more furiously in the United States than in the Soviet Union, and several million reams of newsprint were devoted to the pros and cons. The pros claimed that Trotsky, the alleged ringleader, would use any means to restore himself to power, and after Russia was invaded by Hitler, they argued that the fifth column had been destroyed by the trials. The cons claimed that the victims had been either drugged or terrorized into confessing, that they were old Bolsheviks to whom treason was unthinkable, and that the whole thing was a plot by Stalin to root out the last internal opposition to his régime. The extraordinary spectacle of an American committee (headed by John Dewey) traveling to Mexico City to interview the exiled Trotsky, to determine whether legal proceedings six thousand miles away had been fair, was on view during the summer, and served as a bizarre postscript to the whole astonishing Russian affair, that in its own special way helped fray tempers and set teeth on edge, during 1938.

II

One development during this time of terrors and crises was the growth of psychiatric fiction. Back in 1934, F. Scott Fitzgerald had emerged briefly from his long silence with *Tender is the Night*, one of the first American novels in which the profession of psychiatry was a central theme. Though the story was what J. Donald Adams termed a "brilliant failure," it treated its subject with a good deal of skill. In 1937, the Book-of-the-Month Club helped assure a wide audience for another psychiatric novel, Millen Brand's *The Outward Room*, by selecting it as a book-of-the-month. The first half of this poignant and moving story, describing the young woman's escape from the asylum and her adjustment to life in the big city to which she flees, is described with both disciplined artistry in the writing and a rare perception into the heroine's unbalanced state of mind. However, the love which she finds, and the eventual cure of her neurosis, are too conveniently pat, so that the second half of the story declines in persuasiveness. Other novels of this type, less well known, appeared during the late 30's and prepared the way for the tremendous popularity of psychiatric themes, in literature and the movies, during and after the war.[2]

For the most part, however, the developing storms abroad produced for a time an almost complete black-out of serious literature at home. Between the appearance of *The Late George Apley*, in 1937, and *The Grapes of Wrath*, in 1939, virtually nothing of consequence was written, a circumstance accompanied as a matter of course by a flood of light fiction and light non-fiction. The only exception to this—and a passing and qualified one at that—was *The Yearling*, a nicely written, small-boned novel by Marjorie Kinnan Rawlings, that described with an agreeable mixture of sentiment and sentimentality the life of a growing boy in backwoods Florida.

The reading lists were saturated with books like *How*

[2] The best-known books were *The Lost Weekend* and *The Snake Pit*; the best-known movies, *Spellbound* and *The Seventh Veil*.

to Win Friends and Influence People, Alexander Woollcott's *Second Reader,* A. J. Cronin's *The Citadel,* the latest and most flaccid novels of Louis Bromfield, and the uniform fiction of those indestructible and ageless stalwarts, Kathleen Norris, Temple Bailey, Faith Baldwin, Fannie Hurst, and their host of imitators. If the historical novelists were providing balm for a crisis-ridden nation and pick-me-ups for its flagging spirit, these pillars of the women's school were only providing balm, but balm skillfully compounded, applied with a gentle and massaging motion, whose rhythm hardly broke tempo even with the coming of war.

With our light romantic lady novelists, you knew where you stood, book in, book out. The story lay cozily in the same American town, twelve to twenty-seven thousand, New England, the Middle West, Oregon, it did not matter; one managed these things with a fine universalizing hand. The hero was the town's rising young doctor—or lawyer, or engineer, or architect—but rarely dentist (dentists, for some melancholy reason, have been the stepchildren of literature; they have never acquired *ton*). Our romantic lady novelists have a passion for professionals; they scorn trade.

The hero, thirty-five, has a wife, twenty-seven, and two children, a boy, six, and a girl, four—or, to vary things, a girl, six, and a boy, four. Once, in a feverish moment, there were twins. Combinations of two boys or two girls seldom appear; they are against Nature.

In chapter one, man and wife are dancing at the

Country Club, divinely happy. In chapter two, the first cloud drifts into sight; it is their wedding anniversary and he has forgotten it—no flowers, no jewels; she has, of late, noticed a growing absent-mindedness in him, little wrinkles of worry around his eyes, and other fine touches, such as staying late at the office. Chapter three introduces the Pretty Young Thing, soon to become the third figure in what is rapidly developing into a deliciously unexpected plot. The PYT is just home from an Eastern finishing school, and has not been seen by him since she was "a gangling, freckled girl in pigtails." Now he lays eyes upon her for the first time, as it were, and in his weakened condition, what with business worries, crow's-feet, late meals, is smitten by this "chic," smart, gay apparition. They bump into each other accidentally at the railway station, incredulous recognition on his face, pleasure on hers (she has had a crush on him for years; he was always the handsomest man in town and made all the youths she knew seem callow). They lunch on the spot, and he learns that she is planning a New York career as an advertising writer or a fashion designer. These, it seems, are the only satisfying professions open to women.

Chapter four sees more wrinkles and dinners grown cold. Rumors reach the wife, but she loyally puts them aside. Chapter five describes his feelings taking shape, making it necessary for chapter six to be devoted to drawing a line between Infatuation and Love. Chapters seven and eight lead to open acknowledgments, he and the girl deciding to go off to New York together, the wife at last aware of the Serious Threat to the Home.

All this is merely a preface to the great climax, the climax of chapter nine, the scene the reader has been hungrily anticipating from the start. If a triangle includes two men, the world expects the men to meet and belabor each other with their fists. If the triangle includes two women, as here, the public demands that the women meet *vis-à-vis*. To dodge this meeting is to indulge in false advertising and be liable to prosecution by the Federal Trade Commission. But the meeting is never dodged; it's there in chapter nine, the wife and her young rival over tea, discussing What to Do with Him.

Our heroine, a cool strategist, begins with: "Now that I see you, my dear, I can understand John's attraction! You're very beautiful." They spar during the first cup of tea; by the time the second is poured, the end is already in sight. How can the infatuée resist the children when their mother brings them in, and puts things on a Whom-Does-He-Need-Most basis? One or two fierce *ripostes*, then a rapid retreat that ends in unconditional surrender, and a note the same day to bewildered Him: "It wouldn't work out. I'm off to New York tonight. This is good-by."

After the terrific percussions of chapter nine, chapter ten is all cooing pianissimo. No more office worries, late dinners, eye creases. On her birthday, bracelets AND flowers. Arms about him, one hand stroking the back of his head, she murmurs audibly: "Dear boy, how like a child he is! How I love him!" (The End.)

There it was, safe, staunch. You knew where you

stood. Even when your favorite lady author went off to Brazil or Java or somewhere else in search of local color (like new upholstery for one's old living room), you recognized, though not without a certain effort of the imagination, to be sure, familiar faces and events breath-takingly nostalgic. There were palmettos, rhumba music, gauchos, rickshas, and Gay Rio or Beautiful Batavia to throw an enchanting veil of novelty over old friends and hallowed sequences. Yet all this exoticism is only a façade for the American Colony; our hero is a mining engineer, our heroine, as ever; only the Pretty Young Thing has altered radically: she is no longer the subdeb fresh from finishing school, but the niece of the mine owner. Even so, we can feel our way to the chins-up conclusion with little ultimate difficulty. Brazil is, after all, only Oregon with tropical foliage; Java, Connecticut overrun with sugar cane.

The war changed things a bit. With Selective Service, our hero entered the Medical Corps, where he performed skillful brain operations in the swamps of New Guinea. Thousands of miles away, back home, our heroine was accepting her ration books like a game trouper—no complaints. She was forced to get along on a major's pay, to be sure, but she had the children, and, since there was no direct communication between finishing school and the Solomon Islands, no young rivals to worry about. With the end of the war, these literary lemon meringues were restored to the original recipe, and our lady romancers were back at their old stand, supplying American fiction with its perennially favorite Blue Plate Specials.

A second variety of light fiction that bloomed during the 30's was the detective story. Where Kathleen Norris and her school operated within the framework of conventional morality, the high priests of mystery fiction worked outside that framework. They tended, by and large, to strip the police of any pretensions to virtue, and the criminals of any ineradicable wickedness. The commission of the crime, its investigation, and the unmasking of the murderer, became a mechanical game with scientific rules to be observed by both sides. The detectives won, not because they were symbols of an all-conquering law and order, or because they were better men ethically, but because they were shrewder and had the ingenious resources of scientific detection on their side.

This was true of nearly all the mystery writers, from Agatha Christie at one end to Raymond Chandler at the other. Miss Christie and Dorothy Sayers wrote social comedies around which their murders were drawn. They stemmed from the Trollopes of an earlier generation, but their criminals, with few exceptions, have justifiable motives and are otherwise decent people. Their sleuths, Hercule Poirot and Lord Peter Wimsey, are brainier and more charming than the creatures they pursue, but not much more angelic. The same is true of Nero Wolfe, whose intricate passion for money, beer, and orchids makes him a more interesting figure than his victims, but no more concerned than they with preventing crime. S. S. Van Dine,[3]

[3] Some of these writers began their careers in the 20's, but, in the main, their influence reached its climax in the 30's.

who learned his craft from Conan Doyle, created Philo Vance, a kind of Sherlock Holmes with an aesthetic varnish, who rather admires the men he brings to justice, and holds the law in such profound contempt that he tries whenever possible to keep the murderers he unearths from falling into its clutches, permitting them to take their own lives without interference from the police.

What applies to these relatively polite practitioners applies with even greater force to the hard-boiled school. The world in which the private detectives of Hammett, Chandler, Jonathan Latimer, and Peter Cheyney move is stripped of everything except the tensions and libidos of the combatants. It was a world perfectly suited to the new order of European values that came to a head in the late 30's, where threats, toughness, a complete abandonment of every kind of ethics, public and private, filled the vacuum after the flight of morality. It was a world in which Hitler and Mussolini, the yeggmen of the Japanese Empire, and the growing number of people everywhere who were coming to believe that strong-arm tactics were, after all, the most effective, would have felt perfectly at home. It caught with impressive accuracy the strains of the new time, and as a microcosm of the jungle universe into which Europe and Asia were being transformed, it took hold of the American imagination (in the movies as much as in books) at the very moment that events in Europe began to occupy the center of everyone's attention.

Nothing more sharply indicated the forces battering at law and order, at conventional stability, in the years just before the second World War, than the contempt which mystery story writers and their amateur sleuths had for the police. This contempt is expressed in a variety of ways. Philo Vance sneers at them. Perry Mason uses illegal methods to keep one jump ahead of them. Peter Wimsey tolerates them as junior partners. Sir Henry Merivale and Dr. Gideon Fell are constantly exposing by superior example the crudeness of their methods. Hercule Poirot is always giving them lectures on elementary logic. As for the detectives of the hard-boiled genre, they regard the police as enemies only one degree less dangerous than the murderers they pursue; and the war between them and the police rarely ceases. Working outside the boundaries of law and accepted tradition became, as in Hemingway, the accepted standard, and reflected the growing world-wide reliance on force. Indeed, few literary phenomena proved how symptomatic the printed word can be of the state of civilization as did the mystery story in the last stages of the decade.

III

Less symptomatic of the times were the movies of the 30's, which relied, to a considerable extent, on the light fiction texts for their themes and orientation. Distinguished and original pictures were produced, but these were exceptions in the great mass of formula films to which the talents and exchequers of Hollywood were largely devoted.

The light romances were one of the great sources of supply. Scores of pictures on the boy-meets-girl theme were turned out, vying with one another not so much in the perception of the characters of the young people involved, but in mechanical ingenuities which led to an ever greater complication of plot. Occasionally, a picture of this type would blossom into sudden and unexpected radiance, and produce a host of envious imitations. *It Happened One Night*, perhaps the best, and certainly the most memorable of this genre, began as another "newspaper reporter in pursuit of a story, chasing the spoiled rich girl running away at the last minute, for no reason other than boredom, from a suitable marriage" kind of comedy. At an early point in the picture, it is difficult to say precisely where, this jaded formula sprang to life, shed its triteness, and began to deal with figures on the screen who had become real in a very personal way. The trip on the bus, the hitchhiking scenes, even the romantic byplay, acquired a spontaneous motion rarely in evidence in a formula movie. A whole stream of films dealing with bus trips and train or ocean trips followed *It Happened One Night*, without coming close to equaling its vitality; and, within the sphere of film comedy at least, its principal players, Clark Gable and Claudette Colbert, have never acted so well or been so happily cast.

The historical novels were another rich source of film material, and lavish screen spectacles were made from many of them. *Cimarron, Drums Along the Mohawk, So Red the Rose, Northwest Passage*, and, as a climax, *Gone with the Wind*, were produced in Hollywood at great expense, with very few changes from the original literary versions, and practically no originality.

Still another popular Hollywood product was the domestic triangle, in which the three principal figures were the successful business executive (or professional), his wife, and her somewhat younger rival (a secretary frequently, or a débutante, or a young artist to whom he is attracted because she is so "different" from the women in his set). They went through the same maneuvers that their prototypes in the light romantic novel had perfected, their story differing only in the fact that their surroundings were usually plushier. A variation upon this was the movie centering around the young male writer (or composer or painter) who becomes infatuated with a rich young Park Avenue beauty who seeks to turn him into a success; he saves his artistic integrity by returning to his Greenwich Village garret and marrying the girl down the street (who runs a bookstore, or has a good job in an office, and shares a room with a female who comes home in the evening and always says, while taking off her shoes, "My feet are killing me.").

A corollary of this basic triangle was the career woman film, which invariably portrayed a female executive, glamorously dressed, having to choose either between a career and domesticity, or between two men, one a sound, practical man who has been her faithful friend for years, and who wouldn't think of interfering with her career, the other some young, romantic fellow who sweeps her off her feet. One way or another, her career comes off second best and she discovers her essential femininity, thereby illustrating Hollywood's insistence that women, to be happy, must be feminine, that they want secretly to be "mastered," and that this mastery can be exercised only by the romantic male. Ruth Chatterton and Kay Francis played the leading career woman rôles at the beginning of the 30's, Rosalind Russell at the end, and among them, practically all the respectable professions for women, from law to the management of factories, were spanned.

In the main, these particular cinematic recipes were aimed at the larger cities. For the small towns, especially the huge juvenile market in the small towns, other bills of fare were prepared. The most popular was the Western picture. As in other types of light fiction, the Western had a basic triangular pattern, but it altered the pattern in ways peculiar to itself. The three main characters were the rancher's daughter, the foreman, and the young unattached cowboy. In reel one, the cowboy (fleeing from Montana or Texas, or some place far away, for killing a man, in self-defense as it turns out later) rides up to the ranchhouse and asks for a job. He discovers that the girl, with whom he falls instantly but silently in love, is engaged to the foreman, and that a good deal of rustling has been going on. The next four reels pit the girl and the foreman against the cowboy. At the beginning of reel five, the girl discovers that the foreman is secretly the head of the rustler gang, and switches sides. The last four reels pit the girl and the cowboy against the foreman and his gang. After a series of gun duels, fist fights, and assorted violence, the cowboy and the girl are cornered in a shack. He picks off one rustler after another, suffering only small flesh wounds himself, until his ammunition runs out and their plight becomes desperate. At this point, the cowhands from the ranch come riding up (or the U. S. cavalry if the Western has a military background), seize the rustlers, and send hero and heroine riding, in the last scene, into the sunset. The young man has been unable all this time to declare his love, mainly because he is a man of action and not of words. Now he must declare it, and the tension twists his facial muscles into an effort far greater than he has been called upon to exert so far. At last, after an agony of tongue-tied silence, when we know that he is struggling with passions too powerful to be controlled, he utters what is undoubtedly the supreme illustration of bathos in the films of the 30's: "Well, I guess I kinda like ya, gal."

Very occasionally, a Western would appear which escaped the formula. The most outstanding film of this sort was *Stagecoach* (1939), directed by John Ford who, together with Frank Capra, was perhaps the decade's most original director. The horse operas turned out on low budgets, even more than the musicals [4] (which kept growing more elaborate and expensive), were the bread-and-butter products of Hollywood, reaching a vast audience in the rural areas, and requiring little or no advertising.

The detective story, too, came in for its share of attention. In the beginning 30's, this took the form of the gangster movie, with liquor barons, hijackers, girl friends in mink who sang in swank night clubs, all more or less based on the Al Capone script. *Scarface* and *Little Caesar* were

---

[4] The ones in which Fred Astaire and Ginger Rogers were teamed were among the freshest and most delightful.

among the more famous of this type, and James Cagney and Edward G. Robinson the most persistently cast as gang chiefs. The gangster movies, which were frequently based upon actual episodes from Prohibition days, were followed by the G-man films which dealt with the exploits of the F.B.I. and used the same general formulas and actors. They stood in about the same relationship to the actualities of the criminal world as the Westerns did to the actualities of the frontier.

Later in the decade, they branched off into two familiar subdivisions. One was the international jewel thief story, starring Marlene Dietrich chiefly, in which the relationship between the crooks and police was indistinguishable from that in the gangster film, and in which the police triumphed in the end to the same tune of "crime does not pay." The other subdivision was the classic detective story in which the private sleuth was the hero, and the criminal, always more intelligent than the police, his worthy competitor. The story, sometimes based on the slick texts of S. S. Van Dine, sometimes on the tough ones of Hammett and Chandler, followed without change the three-pronged rivalry of the literary original. There were the suave versions like the Thin Man series,[5] based on the characters created by Dashiell Hammett, or the hard-boiled ones, of which *The Maltese Falcon* was the most convincing. As the war drew nearer, and the ethics of normal life grew weaker, the tough mysteries began supplanting the

[5] With Myrna Loy, William Powell, and Asta, one of the better-known cinematic canines.

soft-shelled kind, and the thin, bored face of Humphrey Bogart, who became the screen's favorite hard-boiled private detective, was displayed from coast to coast.

Finally, there were the Shirley Temple pictures, which were a genre all to themselves. Little Miss Temple, the child star of the 30's, sang, danced, cut adorable capers, and made millions. Her films were small miracles of inoffensive sentimentality.

Of movies that dealt seriously with the experiences and emotions of the American people during the 30's, that sought to comment on life or come to grips with reality, there was only a relative handful. Hollywood's treatment of the depression was especially gingerly. In the screen version of the waifs in Central Park, taken from Robert Nathan's *One More Spring*, sentimentality and a miraculously happy ending sweetened such small miseries as were permitted entry. Another depression movie, *Man's Castle*, began with the hero living in a shack near a garbage dump, then got sidetracked onto the theme of the romantic soul defying fate and rationalizing unemployment into a heaven-sent opportunity to prove that the will of the individual, if strong enough, can triumph over anything. Still a third attitude toward the depression was defined in *My Man Godfrey*, in which the wealthy, having lost their money, are rescued by Godfrey, the ingenious and resourceful butler, a character who traces his long and honorable dramatic ancestry to Jeeves, the Admirable Crichton, Molière's Scapin, and the clever slaves in Plautus and Terence. Perhaps the most serious of the movies dealing with the economic misfortunes of the early 30's was *Little Man, What Now?*, from the novel by Hans Fallada, which communicated poignantly the grim effects of unemployment on a young couple in Germany during the last chaotic years of the Weimar Republic. For the most part, the movies tended to avoid the depression as a theme, particularly the depression in America, no doubt partly on the theory that people do not attend the movies to be reminded of the harsh facts of life.

Hollywood's conception of poverty was, and indeed remains, professionally cheerful. The poor are either happier than the rich because they are free of the worries attendant upon the acquisition of money, or they are sure to be saved by some miraculous windfall. In nearly every instance, the family life of the poor is more affectionate and emotionally satisfying than that of the rich, an attitude best illustrated by the screen version of *You Can't Take It with You*, based on the play by Moss Hart and George S. Kaufman. This skillfully produced comedy expressed Hollywood's final word on the subject of the depression: since money destroys our sense of the real values in life, why worry about its lack, especially since we can be so much happier and gayer without it?

Some of the other serious experiences of the decade were treated rather scantily. A number of pictures about anti-Nazi Germans were turned out, but with the exception of Charlie Chaplin's *The Great Dictator*, these had a tendency to transform daring escapes from concentration camps into thrillers of a purely melodramatic kind. One movie, *Blockade*, sympathetic to the Loyalists, was produced on the Spanish Civil War. In general, with the single exception of the Nazis, Hollywood avoided foreign politics on the ground that they were controversial, just as it tended to avoid films dealing with domestic politics on the ground that somebody important was sure to be offended.

The 1930's had its share of memorable movies, covering a wide variety of themes and moods. *It Happened One Night* was one of them. *The Informer*, perhaps the best of the lot, projected with unforgettable realism revolutionary scenes from the Black-and-Tan period in Ireland. *Fury* dealt with lynching (a white man was the intended victim) with an intensity that in some scenes became terrifying. *Mr. Deeds Goes to Town* described the adventures of a small-town tuba player who inherits a large fortune, and, with naïve and characteristically American idealism, seeks to give most of it away to the needy. For this he is accused of insanity, and defends himself with the vigor and effectiveness also commonly associated with America in times of practical emergency. In another famous film dealing with idealism, *Mr. Smith Goes to Washington*, the scene shifts from a tuba player to a Boy Scout leader who is elected senator by the machine and refuses to play ball when he gets to the capital. His ensuing difficulties, and his famous and triumphant use of a filibuster for a democratic end, suggested what Hollywood could do when it rid itself of its timid formulas. This was demonstrated further by the film treatment of Robert E. Sherwood's noted play, *Abe*

Lincoln in Illinois, in which democracy as a living idea was dramatized with forthright candor. It was demonstrated for the last time during the decade when the movie version of *The Grapes of Wrath* appeared, and transferred to the screen with very moving skill the events and characters of Steinbeck's novel.

For the most part, however, the movies continued to reiterate in the talkies of the 30's the familiar, threadbare themes of the silent 20's: that the rich, too, have their troubles and are not to be envied; that a woman's life, however useful, acquires meaning only in romance; that ladies of easy virtue, of whom Mae West was the most prominent, can have hearts of gold; that even bankers, however crotchety and hard-hearted they may appear at the beginning, redeem themselves before the end; and that the cure for all the ills of existence lies in preserving an unquenchable optimism. The mores of Hollywood remained more or less the same, though its technique advanced with great leaps, and the lavishness of its budgets grew astronomic.

It has been the fashion to attack Hollywood for all the bad pictures it produces, the illusions it nurtures, and the censorship codes it adopts so eagerly. In the process, Hollywood's achievements, occasional though they are, tend to become lost in the argumentative shuffle. The 30's, for example, in addition to the first-class pictures already mentioned, witnessed the spectacular rise of Walt Disney, whose films, from *The Three Little Pigs* to *Snow White and the Seven Dwarfs* and *Fantasia,* were national events, and whose Donald Duck, when introduced in 1934, soon grew into an international figure. Charlie Chaplin produced *Modern Times* and *The Great Dictator*. It was a period of fine historical biographies, headed by *The Life of Louis Pasteur* and *The Life of Emile Zola*, and of faithful renditions of literary classics, like *Romeo and Juliet*, *David Copperfield*, and *Wuthering Heights*, and modern novels like *Arrowsmith* and *The Good Earth*. Toward the end of the decade, Hollywood made a few tentative gestures in the direction of consciously defending democracy, gestures summarized by Will Hays in his 1939 report to the Motion Picture Producers and Distributors of America, when he spoke of "a succession of pictures which dramatized present-day social conditions, which exposed slum areas in many of our great cities . . . which dealt with issues of war and peace . . . which discussed the values of our present-day democracy and emphasized the traditions that have made this nation great . . ." Though films of this type were not sustained, they were effective while they lasted, as *Mr. Deeds* and *Mr. Smith* proved in sufficient measure.

Despite the enormous popularity of the movies, and the relaxation provided millions of moviegoers, they failed in any continuous way to live up to their promise. They remained a discreet distance removed from the emotional experiences of the country, almost as though afraid that these experiences were a fire in which they might be consumed. Yet one never lost the feeling that Hollywood had developed a tremendous instrument, as effective in its way as great literature or music, for the mature communication of the world, and that, when freed from its squeamishnesses, self-imposed censorships, and fears, it would produce with greater frequency works of art whose stature was in keeping with its potentialities.

IV

As the writers of light fiction, and their Hollywood counterparts, remained largely within their safe and narrow formulas, the poets sought refuge in modes of expression that were significant to fewer and fewer people. The older poets, Carl Sandburg, Robert Frost, Edna St. Vincent Millay, Robinson Jeffers, remained for the most part in their familiar grooves; but the younger ones, partly under the influence of T. S. Eliot,[6] partly under the impact of a world thundering toward another World War, began to write in a difficult idiom that reflected somehow the difficulties of the contemporary scene or else abandoned poetry altogether. Instead of bringing them closer to the rest of the country, these tendencies drove them farther away, and some, drifting on the horizonless sea of obscurantism, lost contact with everything except their own souls. The semilucidity of a figure like James Joyce can be explained on the ground that he had to invent a new language to express the subconscious mind, a new phase of human ex-

---

[6] Who, in *The Love Song of J. Alfred Prufrock, The Waste Land,* and other poems, had inveighed against the sterility and impotence of the twentieth century.

perience in his day. The obscurantism of the new poets had no such excuse. It suggested that the chaotic world was too much for them, and they were taking flight in unintelligible rhetoric to conceal the inadequacy of their insight.

One result of this was an increase in the popularity of the versifiers, those lighter and more easily digestible poets who filled the middle level between the Hart Cranes and E. E. Cummingses at one extreme, and the Edgar A. Guests at the other. The versifiers used language much closer to everyday speech than the serious poets, though not as close as the syndicated ones. Their feelings, though often as intense, were simpler, and hence more communicable. For this reason their talents were better suited to topical poetry, for example, than those of writers with more difficult techniques and more complicated states of mind. When, for a variety of reasons, the serious young poets of the 30's failed to grapple in any sustained way with the problems and passions of the time, the public turned to the versifiers even more eagerly than usual.

One of the typical successes of the decade was Alice Duer Miller's *The White Cliffs*, a long poem that deals with the virtues and glories of England. Coming as it did not long before our entry into the war, it served as a propaganda weapon on the side of those favoring all-out aid to Britain, standing alone against the Nazis. Without being a memorable work, it was still a moving one, and for want of anything better in poetry on the subject of national feeling with regard to the war, it enjoyed a tremendous success. As for the lightly satirical verse which had been turned out so deftly by Dorothy Parker in the 20's, there was a steady stream of it in the 30's, produced mainly by Margaret Fishback, Phyllis McGinley, and Ogden Nash, each of whom found a ready market and a large audience.

There appeared in America in the 30's no poet of the proportions and the perception that the several varieties of prose produced, no figure who exploited the resources of his craft as did Wolfe and Steinbeck in fiction, and Odets, Anderson, Behrman, Sherwood, and Lillian Hellman in the drama. The nervousness, the tension of the decade, are in nearly all the verse; but its sweep, its surges of passion, its sequential waves of despair and buoyancy, are strikingly absent. Hart Crane had shown signs of developing an idiom suitable to these larger themes before he committed suicide in 1932. At about the same time Archibald Mac-Leish wrote a number of vigorous and masculine poems, notably *Conquistador* and *Frescoes for Mr. Rockefeller's City*. He also turned out one of the period's significant dramatic poems, *The Fall of the City*, in which many of the threads of the time come to a synthesis. It was a play designed for radio, the newest of the complex modes of communication devised by science.[7] It was devoted to the

---

[7] Stephen Vincent Benét was another poet of the 30's who wrote effective radio plays. But the great figures in this new form of drama were Norman Corwin and Arch Oboler. Both were radio technicians and writers with strong anti-fascist convictions, as were indeed MacLeish and Benét, but most of their plays were fantasies, comedies, burlesques, and educational skits that had nothing to do with politics. Oboler introduced the stream-of-consciousness technique into radio dialogue. Corwin had a flair for lyric speech, and his vivid fusion of music, poetry, and narration has made radio history.

thesis formulated by President Roosevelt during his first inaugural address when, speaking of the depression, he remarked that "the only thing we have to fear is fear itself." It applied this observation to the onrush of fascism that began in the middle 30's. The people of the city are demoralized by the propaganda of fear and capitulate without resistance to the approaching tyrant. But when they look upon their conqueror at close range, they find inside his glittering armor no face, no substance, only nothingness—a discovery which drives home with paralyzing impact the poet's argument about the nature of the foreign danger menacing the country.

He's there in the end of the street in the shadow. We see
    him!
He looks huge—a head taller than anyone:
Broad as a brass door: a hard hero:
Heavy of heel on the brick: clanking with metal:
The helm closed on his head: the eyeholes hollow.
He's coming! . . .
                    He's clear of the shadow! . . .
                                        The sun takes him.

They cover their faces with fingers. They cower before him.
They fall: they sprawl on the stone. He's alone where he's
    walking.
He marches with rattle of metal. He tramples his shadow.
He mounts by the pyramid—stamps on the stairway—
    turns—
His arm rises—his visor is opening. . . .

There is an instant's breathless silence: then the voice of the Announcer low—almost a whisper.

There's no one! . . .

There's no one at all! . . .

No one! . . .

The helmet is hollow!
The metal is empty! The armor is empty! I tell you
There's no one at all there: there's only the metal:
The barrel of metal: the bundle of armor. It's empty!

The push of a stiff pole at the nipple would topple it.

They don't see! They lie on the paving. They lie in the
Burnt spears: the ashes of arrows. They lie there . . .
They don't see or they won't see. They are silent. . . .

The people invent their oppressors: they wish to believe
in them.
They wish to be free of their freedom: released from their
liberty: —
The long labor of liberty ended!

They lie there!

The Fall of the City, though heard by a considerable
number of people, did not reach a wide enough audience
to satisfy its author.[8] Shortly afterward, he withdrew from
poetry, and began his campaign to arouse the public to
the imperative need of preparing itself for war against Germany. Verse, to MacLeish, had become an inadequate me-
dium of communication in times of peril. With his retire-

---

[8] The professional radio playwrights found audiences which, on special
occasions, ran to huge size. The largest of these, estimated to be sixty million or more, listened to the broadcast of Corwin's *We Hold These Truths*
the week after Pearl Harbor. The play, based on a narration of the articles
in the Bill of Rights, was widely regarded as the author's masterpiece, and
benefited (as far as the size of its audience was concerned) by President Roosevelt's speech from Washington which served as an epilogue to the play.

ment, the poetry of the 30's lost another of its climactic voices. MacLeish, who had already been appointed Librarian of Congress, went on to become an Assistant Secretary of State, working with the Division of Cultural Relations, set up by the State Department to promote better understanding among the United Nations.

The relationship between poetry and its times is nearly always more tenuous than with other forms of literary expression. It is hence futile to search for hard-and-fast social principles which shape a poet's, or for that matter, any artist's work. Edna St. Vincent Millay, for example, during the late 30's, began writing poems about the Nazi evil and the concentration camps, the iniquities of appeasement and the "Munich Men," the pretenses of Marshal Pétain and his Vichy régime. They appeared in various magazines and Sunday newspaper supplements during the bitter months before and after the war's beginning, when the democracies were suffering so many defeats. These poems were passionately but badly written, and did far more credit to her heart than to her talent. Was it that politics is not a suitable subject for verse that caused Miss Millay to falter? Or that after twenty-five years of writing poetry on love, youth, and death, of sojourning in the pastures of "Euclid alone has looked on beauty bare," she was unpracticed in polemical verse? Or were her most fruitful years behind her? Or was it simply a matter of temperament, that incalculable element which sets aside all theories? Obviously, no flat or final statement can be made, but the personal explanation in this instance seems more convincing than the social or thematic. Quite incidentally, Miss Millay was demonstrating in her topical poems what the proletarian writers had already demonstrated in a more pronounced way: that having the "correct" political opinions was not enough to produce great art.

Other poets who had grown to maturity in an earlier time continued, in the 30's, to write on the whole as before. The rise of the common man in the age of Roosevelt stimulated Sandburg to continue reaffirming the greatness of the democratic tradition in such well-known collections as *The People, Yes.* Robert Frost went on pursuing his quiet, quasi-philosophical meditations in the stillness of the New Hampshire landscape, which appeared to many of his readers about the only place in a chaotic world to have retained its serenity. Mark Van Doren, in a quiet way, and William Ellery Leonard, in a stormily personal way, proceeded on their already established courses, as did Countee Cullen and Langston Hughes, in their sensuous and robust articulations of Negro life. And from his cliff in California, Robinson Jeffers, who, in the 20's, had already repudiated materialist society, continued to repudiate it in the peculiar blend of sex, anatomy, and evolution that comprised his special language. Even the approaching war had no special meaning for Jeffers who, like Santayana, regarded it as merely another incident in the long turmoil of history, and was for this reason accused of being isolationist and pro-Nazi in the days when the angry voices of '40 and '41 were rising to their crescendo. Stephen Vincent Benét, writing half under Sandburg's influence, carried on in *Western Star* [9] the impulses that beat so vividly in *John Brown's Body* (1928), one of the few authentic epics based on an American theme. He, together with the historical novelists, searched the past in order to illuminate the present, with occasional effective excursions, as in *Litany for Dictatorships,* into the field of anti-Nazi polemics.

The other established poets, of a more specialized genre, contracted, during the 30's, into their already lovely cocoons. Wallace Stevens, practicing the glass blower's art in words, continued to produce without interruption the delicately filamented poems associated with his name.

> The light is like a spider.
> It crawls over the water.
> It crawls over the edges of the snow.
> It crawls under your eyelids
> And spreads its webs there—
> Its two webs.
>
> The webs of your eyes
> Are fastened
> To the flesh and bones of you
> As to rafters or grass.
>
> There are filaments of your eyes
> On the surface of the water
> And in the edges of the snow.

His landscapes remained full of "rosy chocolate" and "paradisal green," "mallow morning" and "bronze rain." His

---

[9] And earlier, in many brilliant short stories, of which *The Devil and Daniel Webster* was perhaps the most widely read.

flawless images remained flawless, and wholly within the moods and dimensions of the style he had perfected a generation before.

Marianne Moore, within a greater emotional range, turned out her verbal counterpoint, stripped of connectives and powdered with the light ironies and mathematically tilted tensions that first established her reputation. The restraint that she practiced to such good effect was admirably suited to her favorite themes of poetry: Ireland, England, Virginia, and literature; and to her favorite images of snails, cats, mice, fish, pelicans, monkeys, and unicorns. She did not venture into areas of experience outside the bounds of the intensely personal life which she versified so skillfully, and, to quote Eliot, "in which an original sensibility and alert intelligence and deep feeling have been engaged in maintaining the English language."

As for E. E. Cummings, as late as 1940 he was still writing:

> i am so glad and very
> merely my fourth will cure
> the laziest self of weary
> the hugest sea of shore
>
> so far your nearness reaches
> a lucky fifth of you
> turns people into eachs
> and cowards into grow
>
> our can'ts were born to happen
> our mosts have died in more
> our twentieth will open
> wide a wide open door

> we are so both and oneful
> night cannot be so sky
> sky cannot be so sunful
> i am through you so i

with the tantalizing verbal acrobatics of 1925, within the framework of the passionately private world that had become Cummings's imprimatur.

Of the poets who sought to take hold of the specific configurations of the decade, and worked at their profession sustainedly, Horace Gregory, Kenneth Fearing, and Muriel Rukeyser achieved the greatest measure of success. The success was minor in each instance. Each caught single veins and angles of the period. In Gregory, it is the voice of the mass, the emergence of the crowd that impacts.

> *Regret, return, do not return, retreat,*
> the mouthpiece siren at my ear
> speaks from a million faces in the street
> shouting,
> > *We are alive and do not die,*
> *not die, give us the power*
> *not to die but to return*
> *at each imperishable hour.*

In Fearing, the agitation of the big city, the city of the 30's, pelts at us:

What have you won, plunger, when the 20-to-1 comes in; what have you won, salesman, when the dotted line is signed; irresistible lover, when her eyelids flutter shut at last, what have you really, finally won;

And what is gone, soldier, soldier, step-and-a-half marine
    who saw the whole world; hot-tip addict, what is al-
    ways just missed; picker of crumbs, how much has
    been lost, denied, what are all the things destroyed,
Question mark, question mark, question mark, question
    mark,
And you, fantasy Frank, and dreamworld Dora and hal-
    lucination Harold, and delusion Dick, and nightmare
    Ned,
What is it, how do you say it, what does it mean, what's
    the word,
That miracle thing, the thing that can't be so, quote, un-
    quote, but just the same it's true,
That third-rail, million-volt exclamation mark, that ditto,
    ditto, ditto,
That stop, stop, go.

    In 1938, the year in which Nazism won its great blood-
less triumphs, Fearing wrote a savage little poem called
Ad, a precise statement of what the rest of the country was
to feel five years later.

WANTED: Men;
Millions of men are WANTED AT ONCE in a big new field;
NEW, TREMENDOUS, THRILLING, GREAT.

If you've ever been a figure in the chamber of horrors,
If you've ever escaped from a psychiatric ward,
If you thrill at the thought of throwing poison into wells,
    have heavenly visions of people, by the thousands, dy-
    ing in flames—

YOU ARE THE VERY MAN WE WANT
We mean business and our business is YOU
WANTED: A race of brand-new men.

Apply: Middle Europe;
No skill needed;
No ambition required; no brains wanted and no character
    allowed;

TAKE A PERMANENT JOB IN THE COMING PROFESSION
Wages: DEATH.

Muriel Rukeyser was the most socially conscious of
the younger poets of the 30's, as was Genevieve Taggard
among the older. Miss Rukeyser's first volume, *Theory of
Flight*, was one of the numerous poems dealing with air-
planes that appeared during the decade.[10] But her chief
distinction was the zeal with which she tackled in verse
the problems of political and economic injustice. In *The
Trial*, she treats the case of the Scottsboro boys. In *City of
Monuments*, she contrasts the conditions of rich and poor:

> Blinded by chromium or transfiguration
> we watch, as through a microscope, decay:
> down the broad streets the limousines
> advance in passions of display.

> Air glints with diamonds, and these clavicles
> emerge through orchids by whose trailing spoor
> the sensitive cannot mistake
> the implicit anguish of the poor.

> The throats incline, the marble men rejoice
> careless of torrents of despair.

[10] Others were Selden Rodman's *The Airmen*, Fleming MacLeish's
Exploration by Air, Reuel Denney's *Elegy on the Pilot*, and Archibald Mac-
Leish's verse play, *Air Raid*.

Split by a tendril of revolt
stone cedes to blossom everywhere.

As in Fearing, the hard world of the big city of the 30's peers out of her *Citation for Horace Gregory*:

The brass voice speaks in the street

STRIKE STRIKE

the nervous fingers continue elaborately
drawing consciousness, examining, doing.
Rise to a billboard world of Chesterfields,
Mae West hip-wriggles, Tarzan prowess, the little
nibbling and despicable minds.

Despite these vivid projections of single aspects of the times, Miss Rukeyser, Fearing, and Gregory remained essentially minor figures, snippeting at an age whose ultimate dimensions escaped them. This was also true of the more personal and less topically conscious poets of the time, like Louise Bogan and Robert Penn Warren, whose verse revealed so much fine craftsmanship. There were a great many other serious young American poets who appeared during the 30's and left small indentations on the public mind. Among the better known of these were Paul Engle, Marya Zaturenska, Edward Weismiller, and Delmore Schwartz.[11] It was an age whose intensities, crosscurrents, and rapid alternations of mood invited the accents

[11] Shortly after Pearl Harbor, Karl Shapiro made his début with *Person, Place, and Thing,* and gave signs of developing in the 40's into the major poet that the 30's so conspicuously lacked. At any rate, he displayed in that first volume some of the qualities necessary for a major poet: among them, an intensity of feeling and a mastery of the language in its idiomatic and connotative meanings.

of a major poet. No such poet appeared. A cross-pollination of Sandburg and Eliot might have produced one ideally equipped for the occasion, but eugenics has not yet been extended to the arts. The closest approximation in the 30's to such a figure turned up in England in the person of W. H. Auden, with his swing from a passionate flirtation with Communism to a passionate embrace of the High Church, his gift for parody, his wry, twisting irony, and a rhetorical equipment uniquely modern.

Reasons for the nonappearance of a great American poet during the 30's remain speculative and elusive. Are they to be looked for in the pressures of the contemporary scene? Was fascism too immediate and ugly a matter to be suitable for poetry? Was the depression too smothering an experience? Is there any necessarily close topical relationship between the poet and the times? It seems very doubtful. There have been too many instances of writers who lived through periods of great dramatic change without reference to them for any permanent correlation to be established. Jane Austen is, perhaps, the most illustrious example. Living through the Napoleonic wars at the beginning of the nineteenth century in a country threatened with invasion, she makes no mention in her novels of provincial manners of the turbulent times. The same principle was true a few years later of Keats.

A great deal of good poetry was written in the 30's by a considerable number of poets young and old; not much of it appears likely to survive as a major part of our literature. Why there should have been an outpouring of notable verse during the second decade of the century [12] and not during the fourth, may be due at bottom simply to the accidents of birth and temperament: a group of impressionable and gifted figures happened to grow to maturity at one particular time and not another.

Whatever the explanation, whether it lies in the nature of the contemporary scene or in the less predictable factors of heredity, the poetry of the 30's, unlike the fiction, and to a lesser degree the drama, failed to realize its vast and glittering potentialities.

[12] When Miss Millay, Vachel Lindsay, Sandburg, Frost, Edgar Lee Masters, and T. S. Eliot, made their spectacular débuts.

11: LAST ECHOES OF AMERICA FIRST

EVERYONE was preparing for the great debate. Under the menace of a resurgent Germany, the New Deal had begun battening down its hatches and abandoning further measures of special reform, a process that began at the end of 1937 and was virtually complete by the time Hitler seized what was left of Czechoslovakia, in March, 1939. The President was beginning to arouse the country to the foreign danger, in part from a loathing of the indecencies and cruelties of Nazism, but far more from a realization that the defeat of Britain would imperil the strategic position of the United States. He was also one of the few who realized that a successful attack by Germany on the Soviet Union (to which Chamberlain and the advocates of appeasement seemed by no means averse) would make Hitler, with Russian resources at his command, invulnerable.

The isolationist camp was a *smörgåsbord* of diverse and centrifugal elements. All the Anglophobes, headed by Colonel McCormick and his *Chicago Tribune*, were enthusiastically enrolled, as were the sympathizers with the Third Reich, led, fittingly enough, by the German-American Bund. Many groups violently antagonistic to the Soviet Union, spearheaded by the Hearst press, joined with banners flying. Charles A. Lindbergh was there, partly because the German Air Force, under the leadership of Goering, had given him a tumultuous reception on a recent trip to Germany, partly because his wife in a series of books (*North to the Orient* was the best known) had been advocating a mystical "Wave of the Future," which to many readers seemed like a spiritual acceptance of fascism. Senator Wheeler was prominent in the front ranks; he had for some time now ceased to be the mugwump radical who had run for Vice President on the Progressive ticket with Fighting Bob La Follette, in 1924. John L. Lewis, his anger at the President's "plague on both your houses" attitude during the sitdown strikes still warm inside him, was among those present.[1] As was Charles A. Beard, the famous historian, who had never forgotten Washington's precept about no entangling alliances and keeping out of Europe; he was an isolationist from intense intellectual conviction. Late in August, 1939, on the occasion of the Nazi-Soviet Pact, the Communists, with their slogan, "the Yanks are not coming," joined the ranks, and worked furiously for the isolationist cause until Hitler invaded Russia. They left then as abruptly as they had arrived.

The debate was one of those furious, brass-knuckle affairs into which nearly everybody was drawn sooner or

---

[1] Another reason for Lewis's pique, according to Frances Perkins in her *The Roosevelt I Knew*, was that Mr. Roosevelt had refused to accept the mineworkers' leader as his Vice Presidential running mate in the campaign of 1940.

later. Few events in the 30's aroused such burning passion, none split the country from end to end so thoroughly. Though it had been going on in various places almost since Hitler came to power, it began on a nationwide scale when he seized Prague, if an official date can be set at all. The debate, which had been growing since the Spanish Civil War and the Munich Agreement, gathered momentum slowly during the summer of 1939 with the development of the Polish crisis, rose to a climax with the Nazi-Soviet Pact and the German invasion of Poland, and subsided into angry mutterings during the first winter of what was then regarded as the "phony" war. It came to another climax with the fall of France and the air blitz against England, paused for breath during the Presidential campaign of 1940, when both Willkie and Roosevelt turned up on the same side (the all-aid-short-of-war-to-England side), warmed up again after the invasion of Russia, in June, 1941, swelled to its most percussive climax during the long negotiations with Japan that followed, and ended with the enforced defeat of the isolationists at Pearl Harbor.

During these stages, sloganeering and name-calling flooded the air. Senator Wheeler coined perhaps the most cutting slogan when he accused the President of seeking "to plow under every fourth American boy," a devastating reference to the earlier agricultural program of the New Deal which sought to boost farm prices by destroying surplus crops and hogs. Lindbergh, in a series of speeches, argued that Germany was invincible and should be left alone in her part of the world, and that the President was agitating for war so that he might establish a dictatorship and abolish elections, beginning specifically with the one scheduled for 1942; this prediction proved as unfounded as the earlier one by Nicholas Murray Butler, when he claimed that a third term for Mr. Roosevelt would imperil American democracy. In time, Lindbergh became a central figure in the most formidable agency transmitting the isolationist program, the America First Committee.

Blessed with an appealing and patriotic name, large sums of money, and skilled publicity advisers, the America First Committee led the long fight against the country's gravitation toward the Allied cause. It campaigned against the Selective Service Act, in 1940, and in 1941 came within one vote in the House of Representatives of defeating its extension. It struggled against the repeal of the Neutrality Act, which a short time before had been used to strangle Republican Spain. It fought against the destroyers-for-bases deal with England, the Lend-Lease Act, the arming and convoying of merchant ships, the firm line taken in the negotiations with Japan.[2] Each legislative defeat served only to increase its zeal, accelerate its efforts, drive it harder toward its objectives. In the two years before Pearl Harbor, the country was exhorted by communications and literature bearing the America First letterhead, speakers making

[2] The New York *Daily News*, one of the newspapers espousing the isolationist cause, used to refer in its editorials to China as "that great big slob of a country" allowing itself to be beaten up by a neighbor one-sixth its size. Since American sympathies are traditionally with the little fellow, implied the *News*, we should waste no tears on the treatment China was receiving at the hands of Japan.

nationwide tours under America First auspices, and full-page advertisements in newspapers and magazines bearing the same ubiquitous label. No amount of invective from the interventionists could discourage or stem this flood of propaganda. When Hitler was overrunning one European country after another, from Norway to Yugoslavia, Secretary of the Interior Ickes, one of the Administration's chief sluggers in the verbal polemics of the day, dubbed the America First Committee the America Next Committee. The irony took hold, the quip made the rounds, but the isolationists continued to ply their trade as vigorously as ever.

They received aid from a variety of conspicuous quarters. Henry Ford warned against tampering with the Neutrality Act on the grounds that it would lead to war. Herbert Hoover opposed the convoying of our merchant vessels (under U-boat attack) as one step on the road to war and as futile anyway. Senator Henry Cabot Lodge, Jr., following in his grandfather's footsteps, worked hard against the passage of Lend-Lease.[3] Senator Vandenberg came forward, in January, 1941, with the suggestion that the United States initiate peace negotiations between England and Germany. And from England, the noted tennis player, Bunny Austin, arrived to promote the "moral rearmament" plan that the Oxford Group and the diligent followers of Dr. Frank Buchman had been sponsoring through most of the decade. This proposal, which traced

---

[3] Though he changed his mind later, resigned his seat in the Senate, and enlisted in the Army.

its ancestry to the ideas of non-resistance to evil associated with Tolstoy and Gandhi, was an ethical philosophy admirably suited to isolationism. It urged a reduction in physical armament, which was plain enough, and an increase in moral rearmament, which was not so plain. It seemed a rather astonishing program to put forth in the summer of 1939, with Hitler thundering on the doors of Poland, but put forth it was, and added its weight to the arguments of those who insisted, in the words of the founding fathers, that America keep out of European entanglements.

A perfect symbol of the great debate was the visit of the King and Queen of England to the United States, in May and June of 1939. As a demonstration of Anglo-American unity, it was perfectly timed, and calculated to take advantage of the well-known American love of pageantry and interest in the movements of high society. The tour was skillfully managed, the right Senators and bigwigs invited to the British Embassy's garden party in Washington, their Majesties photographed from every angle eating hot dogs and drinking soda pop on the Roosevelt lawn at Hyde Park, the Queen smiling brightly and waving her hand with well-trained insouciance, the King, with his long melancholy face tightly pulled together under the ordeal, the Roosevelts friendly and imperturbable. The isolationists, especially in the Middle West, the traditional center of Anglophobia, let out howls of disapproval, clamored that the visit was a piece of cunning propaganda designed to pull Britain's chestnuts out of the fire, pleaded with the nation's mothers not to be dissuaded by the Queen's kind face from their resolve never to permit their sons to be sent overseas, and behaved in general like people being assaulted in open daylight without the police lifting a finger. The tour did not prevent the war from erupting in September, but it did bring the two English-speaking countries a bit closer together.

At any rate, whether the royal visit had much effect on public opinion or not, it was evident that the America First Committee had cut out for itself a formidable task of persuasion. This was clearly shown by a *Fortune* magazine poll taken three months after the royal visitors left for home, which indicated that two-thirds of the American people were against isolationism.

II

The interventionist camp was filled with as many motley elements as the isolationist. Its chief warriors and armorbearers after the President were Harold L. Ickes, Senator Pepper (who wanted the Navy to seize Dakar before we were at war with anyone), the C.I.O., Secretary of State Cordell Hull, all the Anglophiles, the Committee to Defend America by Aiding the Allies, and two prominent Republicans, Stimson and Knox, who joined the Cabinet in 1940 and were promptly read out of the Republican Party. In some ways, the most remarkable figure in the ranks of the Allied sympathizers was Wendell Willkie, the Republican candidate in the presidential campaign of 1940, who was an ardent partisan of Anglo-American-Soviet friendship in particular and world cooperation in general.

Equally prominent among the interventionists was Henry Luce, publisher of the powerful *Time-Life-Fortune* chain of magazines. In a famous editorial Luce coined the phrase "The American Century," which was to be one of the more ringing captions of the time, and was to suggest that the motives animating those who wanted the country to get into the war were as diverse and heterogeneous as those who were urging it to stay out. Luce was in favor of all-out aid to England against Germany and to China against Japan, not for sentimental reasons, and not only to protect America from ultimate Axis attack. His strategy was wholly offensive. By establishing outposts in Europe and Asia, the United States, already the wealthiest and most industrialized country on earth, could control the channels of power and trade not simply in the post-war period but through the remainder of the century as well.

Side by side with the advocates of "The American Century" were Henry Wallace (the most militant of the New Dealers) and the advocates of the idea contained in his equally famous slogan, "the century of the common man." Wallace and his followers thought of the war not as a means of substituting American domination for the old British imperialism of the nineteenth century, but as an opportunity to end all forms of economic and political imperialism, and raise the standard of living for the "common man" throughout the world.[4] For diametrically oppo-

---

[4] Throughout the 30's, Wallace, one of President Roosevelt's closest associates, was the center of bitter controversy. His friends thought him a

site reasons, they and the devotees of Luce were subscribing to the same interventionist policy in 1940 and 1941.

Luce's prognostication of the future rested upon a good deal of evidence from the recent past. Whether the end of the twentieth century was to witness American global hegemony remained speculative, but the trend during the opening decades of the century seemed to point in that direction. With the end of the first World War, the political and economic dominance of the Western world began shifting from Great Britain to the United States. This was not evident at the time, since the Treaty of Versailles had added to the territorial possessions of the British Empire. But it began growing evident in the 30's with the rise of a resurgent Germany, more powerful than the Kaiser's and with more grandiose ambitions, and became overpoweringly so when, with the fall of France in the second World War, the inability of Britain to reconquer Europe without American aid grew plain to everyone. Now, in the era following the second war, America is playing a dominant rôle in the West, as England did during the nineteenth century.

This shift of political power has been accompanied by profound changes in the culture of the countries. One of the most pervasive phenomena of our time has been America's assumption of leadership in the world of Eng-

prophet living twenty years ahead of his time. His enemies attacked him as an impractical visionary living with his head in the clouds. At the Democratic convention, in 1944, he came within a few votes of being renominated for the Vice Presidency, and by that narrow margin missed becoming President upon the death of Roosevelt the following year.

lish letters. Between the Revolutionary War and 1914, Britain's literary creativity was so abundant that, by comparison, American literature seemed simply in the process of being housebroken. A hundred years of Keats, Shelley, Carlyle, Thackeray, Browning, and Hardy, could with justice look upon a century of Hawthorne, Emerson, Poe (more French than American), Melville, Whitman, Mark Twain, and Henry James (more Anglo-American than American) as a satellite era. Individual exceptions, such as James or Melville, might be argued, but the collective bulk was all on the other side of the Atlantic.

In the first decade of the present century, the play was firmly in the hands of Shaw, poetry in Kipling's, the novel in the grip of Conrad, Butler, Wells, and Galsworthy. American letters had few figures to compare with these. Despite *Sister Carrie, The Jungle,* and the florid energism of Jack London, there seemed little reason to doubt, in the year 1910, that America would linger for an indefinite time to come in the wake of the mother country.

Yet within ten years a virtually complete exchange of rôles had taken place; and, for more than a generation now, the American O'Neills, Hemingways, Wolfes, Sandburgs, and Lewises have monopolized the stage with as much finality as did the Victorians in an earlier day. The westward-flowing tide of literary as well as political empire proceeded at an accelerated tempo through the 30's, and lent weight to Luce's case for "The American Century," and to his enlistment in the interventionist ranks.

III

In the thick of things, as usual, were the literati, headed by the belligerent and articulate Archibald MacLeish. Having abandoned poetry for the duration, he proceeded to declare war on half the important writers of his time for having bred a pacifist spirit in American youth. Dos Passos and Hemingway, who had written novels casting doubt on the usefulness of the first World War, were his particular targets, but Dreiser, Farrell, and Sherwood Anderson, who had referred to that war as an imperialist slaughter, came within the periphery of his attack. The argument that followed was one of the livelier corollaries to the larger polemics involving the nation as a whole with regard to the current wars in Europe and China. MacLeish's opponents, when they weren't arguing that their charges against our entry into the other conflict were perfectly true, claimed that literature, in any case, did not mold the opinions of readers, but only reflected them. On this issue, seldom before so explicitly stated, the contending sides squared off. The battle raged through the magazines, the Sunday supplements, and the topical books; and was still going strong when Pearl Harbor put a temporary end to it, as it did to so many political and aesthetic disputes at the same time.

The issues of the battle can be tested by referring to some of the more significant works of the period. In 1940, for example, Richard Wright wrote his scorching novel

Native Son, about a Negro who goes bad after being cruelly treated by the white world. This brooding and somber story was dramatic enough to absorb even those not interested in race relations. That it jogged the public conscience is hardly to be disputed. But that it precipitated a crisis over the Negro problem, or brought any aspect of it to a head, or vitally influenced public thinking on the subject, is very much open to question. The same thing was even truer of *Uncle Tom's Children,* a volume of Wright's short stories which appeared earlier. Not until the autobiographical *Black Boy* came out near the end of the war, when race riots at home and the issue of the colored soldiers' rôle in the armed forces received wide publicity, did Wright's work begin to coincide with the focus of public thinking on the Negro question.

In 1936, Irwin Shaw's fiery one-act play, *Bury the Dead,* appeared, in which the slaughter of the first World War was attacked as purposeless. Shaw went on to write a longer play, *The Gentle People,* in which two harmless, middle-aged men murder a petty gangster who has fastened himself upon them. The play was intended as a parable on fascism, calling upon the peace-loving citizens of the world to overthrow the new tyrants. In many of his short stories, too, an art which he practiced with increasing skill, Shaw assumed a strongly anti-fascist position. This passage from anti-militarism to anti-fascism encompassed both sides of the reigning argument, and made Shaw a testing ground for the issue raised by MacLeish. The public impact of Shaw's work in the late 30's was small. *Bury the Dead* attracted notice more because of its spectacular stage setting, in which a group of soldiers rise from the trench in which they died to discourse with their survivors, than because of the popularity of the subject. The parable of *The Gentle People*, timely enough in 1939, the year of its production, was not put forcefully enough to make an impression commensurate with the size of its theme. Shaw's topical stories, like *Sailor off the Bremen* and *Main Currents of American Thought*, were read far more for their trenchant narrative style than for their topical references.

In 1939, Lillian Hellman turned out one of the fine plays of the decade, *The Little Foxes*, a penetrating study of a rapacious Southern family symbolizing the new post-Civil War middle class climbing upon the backs of the old aristocracy to wealth and power, the same middle class represented in an earlier stage by the Snopeses of the Faulkner novels. The play was beautifully articulated, presented its social ideas in purely human terms, and was made into a movie that was as good of its kind as the play. Did it influence the political thinking of the tens of thousands who saw it on the stage or the millions who attended the film? Did it create in its audience a revulsion against lives devoted solely to the acquisition of money? It seems questionable. The play was a superb illustration of President Roosevelt's oft-repeated thesis that property rights must not be put above human rights, which was one of the basic tenets of the New Deal. There is little evidence, however, to indicate that *The Little Foxes* did anything more than cement the feelings of those who already felt that way. Those who didn't, enjoyed the play as absorbing theater, and probably remained insulated against the thrust of its moral doctrine.

A year later, after the start of hostilities in Europe and at the height of the polemical ferment in the United States regarding the war, Miss Hellman wrote *Watch on the Rhine*, a play that pressed even more heavily on the topical consciousness of the theater- and movie-going public. In it, the anti-Nazi German dramatizes two ideas which the interventionists were vehemently espousing: the Nazi menace must be met with force; and this must be done even at the cost of temporarily abandoning family ties. The hero of the play, blackmailed by a Rumanian lackey of the Nazis, murders him as the only way out of his difficulty, then says good-by to his adoring wife and children and returns to the struggle against Hitler. There can be no peace for anyone, the playwright argues, until fascism is destroyed. *Watch on the Rhine* was not as good a play as *The Little Foxes*, not so vigorously structured nor so penetrating in characterization. Yet its political influence appeared greater, largely because a considerable section of the American people had not yet made up its mind about our policy toward the Nazis. The issue was a very real and pressing one. The issue raised by *The Little Foxes* was not in the air; hence its impact was a glancing one. A few years earlier, S. N. Behrman, in *Rain from Heaven*, the decade's most supple and beautifully modulated high comedy, had also dealt with an anti-Nazi refugee and his effect on a variety of unawakened and isolationist Americans. It, too, was a better play than *Watch on the Rhine;* its hero was better drawn than Miss Hellman's. But since, in the middle 30's, the questions it raised had not yet grown to national prominence, its political influence was probably very slight.

The polemics of MacLeish can then be submitted to the test of timeliness. *Three Soldiers* and *A Farewell to Arms* or, for that matter, *What Price Glory* and *All Quiet on the Western Front,* drove home their anti-war sentiments when the question of a militarist spirit was no longer pressing. These novels and plays were published after Versailles when the Western world was already pacifist in feeling, and were popular in part precisely because they confirmed this pacifism. They did not create pacifist sentiment or make it qualitatively stronger. The novels of Dickens, by contrast, coming at the beginning of the legislative reform of the evils they attacked, influenced and hastened that reform. *Uncle Tom's Cabin,* perhaps the most influential piece of propaganda in American literature, helped to solidify abolitionist sentiment while the issue of slavery was still unsettled. Upton Sinclair's *The Jungle* moved Congress to set up a committee to investigate the Chicago slaughter-houses. *The Grapes of Wrath* inspired the *New York Times* to send a correspondent to the Far West to report on the Okies, and both the State of California and the Federal government subsequently took steps to improve their lot. In each case, the book and the problem came to a head at the same time. It cannot be said that MacLeish was wrong, for literature has on occasion exercised a profound influence on society. He was wrong only in the instances he chose, where the works of art were postscripts to the events they emotionalized, and hence could not be held responsible for them.

The most famous play of the 30's, *Winterset*, was another case in point. Written by Maxwell Anderson with more than his usual burning indignation at social injustice, it was built around the famous Sacco-Vanzetti trial which had aroused so much passion in the 20's. It was articulated in the free blank verse which Anderson had developed in many previous verse plays. It had an important theme and a novel, yet comprehensible style. But the play appeared in 1935, eight years after the execution of Sacco and Vanzetti, when the issues of the case, in the public mind at least, were dead. So far as reopening these issues was concerned, the effect of the play was nil; though in the vaguer and more general matter of stimulating the conscience of the public and filling it with a sense of uneasiness at the miscarriages of the law, its effect was probably considerable.

The same was true to a lesser degree of *High Tor*, another blank verse play in which Anderson delivered a scathing attack on the encroachments of materialism and materialist civilization on the integrity of the individual. And of *Key Largo*, in which the dramatist concentrated more intensely on what has always been his chief interest: how a man can resolve the conflicting impulses within his soul and learn to live honestly with himself. The physical springboard in *Key Largo* was the Spanish Civil War where the hero joined the Loyalists, then deserted to the Rebels to save his skin, and struggled with the burden of his cowardice till he died. But the springboard was just that, and the war in Spain soon faded into the tensions within the mind of the hero. It is in these and similar tensions that Anderson flourished and grew into perhaps the most co-ordinated and prolific playwright of the decade.

There came to prominence during the late 30's another literary figure whose writing played a certain rôle in the life of the time. The plays and short stories of William Saroyan, written with great rapidity, seemed at first almost as refreshing in their cries of joy at the pure pleasure of living as Wolfe had seemed in *Look Homeward, Angel.* His characters, however different in age and background, respond in an almost primitively simple way to the rhythm of things. They are caught in a kind of sensuous trance: Armenian boys in California going for a swim, telegraph operators boozily philosophical, prostitutes, barflies, ex-soldiers, tough guys, a whole gallery of eccentrics from the lower middle class. Like Steinbeck's primitives, they are all children of paradise, their mouths open with wonder, their eyes filmy with naïve delight. At their best, they seem like the answer to the long questing of D. H. Lawrence and Sherwood Anderson for people attuned to the natural rhythm of life, free of subservience to the machine age and its inhuman pressures. At their worst, they are shamelessly sentimental, and indulge in tear-jerking tactics that make Dickens seem like a novice.

These adult children of his function outside the framework of the everyday world. Society does not concern them.

They exist only for the ecstasy of the tenuous and ineffable moment, during which their souls are bathed in a dazzled well-being. When Saroyan was wrenched away from this exquisite euphoria and drafted into the rude, dull life of the army, he emerged with a petulant and complaining novel, *The Adventures of Wesley Jackson*, in which his hero angrily denounced the military for intruding upon his privacy, felt no hostility toward the Nazis, and found the second World War an intrusive and meaningless event. Saroyan, of course, was not a political isolationist; he was a psychological one. His characters cry out their need for love, companionship, unity with their fellows, and strike varying attitudes of comradely optimism and affection. But only in their dream idyll, on their own peculiarly temperamental terms, according to the strict laws of the fable they are forever unraveling. Charming and seductive, they are the most intransigent kind of egotists, the egotists of arrested childhood, who are willing to play only when in the mood and then only under rules of their own devising.

In many ways, the figures of Saroyan are like the *paisanos* of Steinbeck, though unlike Steinbeck, Saroyan continued to write in a simple vein. His popularity reached its peak during the late 30's and at the turn of the 40's, when millions of Americans were seeking, with understandable intensity, to wall themselves off from the approaching storm. It was then that Saroyan was composing the liquorish charms of *The Time of Your Life* and the nostalgic blisses of *The Human Comedy*. Though a characteristic writer of that day, he was characteristic of a narrower area of public feeling than Steinbeck, and of a narrower segment of the decade.

IV

The cries and counter-cries on the main question of the day drowned out the passage of many an event that, in quieter times, would have lived conspicuously in the public eye. In January, 1939, Tom Mooney, the most famous *cause célèbre* of the century after Sacco and Vanzetti, was pardoned and released from prison. He had been jailed on the eve of America's entry into the first World War, and was freed on the eve of her entry into the second. A torrent of energy had been poured into campaigns for his release; for twenty-two years, his case had been an ulcer gnawing at the conscience of the country. Had he or had he not thrown the bomb that took so many lives in that bloody San Francisco square? Was he or was he not railroaded because of his militancy as a labor organizer? A vast legal literature had accumulated around his name; poems had been written in his honor; pamphlets by the tens of thousands were distributed in his defense. When at last the long war of attrition between his friends and enemies ended in his favor, the eyes of the nation were fixed on issues even more fateful than his, and the pardoning ceremony in the executive office of Governor Olson of California was a somewhat threadbare anticlimax to an affair that had evoked such tidal waves of temper for a generation.

A second remarkable but no less anticlimactic event, that hung like a bright mirage in the summer of 1939, was the World's Fair, which opened in New York on the first of May. The President, in his welcoming address, described it as a "symbol of the Will to Peace," an observation that was almost as true literally as figuratively, in view of the conspicuous absence of a pavilion representing the new Germany. The millions who attended moved in a trance among the lacquered exhibits of a future dazzling to the senses, that yet seemed to tremble in their grasp. It was still trembling there on September 3, when England and France declared war on Germany, and the President, with pathetic irony, invited the nations of the world back to the Fair in 1940. Most of them returned, as did most of the crowds, but with Norway and Poland gone, the Low Countries and France on their way to join them, the Will to Peace had shrunk to a feeble tic, and the dazzling future had become metamorphosed into a terrifying present.

A third incident, not only remarkable but unique, passed into rapid obscurity for all its uniqueness. On May 15, 1939, a five-year-old girl in Peru had a baby. Five years before, she would have remained on the front pages for months. Ten years before, she and her baby would have gone on an exhibition tour of the United States. The fact that the girl was only three feet, one inch tall, and still had her first teeth, that the baby was normal, that the birth was witnessed by sixty South American doctors willing to sign professional affidavits that they had seen something new in the history of medicine, would have added to the passionate interest of the public. Coming when it did, amid the violent political alarums of that season, it only flicked into the center of the stage and out again.

That was the season, too, when everybody was busy making predictions about what would happen, and the predictions were uniformly inaccurate; when one man's guess was as good as another's, and the experts, who had been uniformly wrong during the depression, remained uniformly wrong during the war. Ten days before the invasion of Poland, the newspapers ran headlines saying that Washington was showing little fear about events in Europe, and that Sumner Welles, the Under-Secretary of State, doubted a crisis was at hand. Two days later, the Nazi-Soviet Non-Aggression Pact was announced to an astonished world, and by way of proving that capitalist commentators had no monopoly on error, the *Daily Worker* made one of the more fatuous comments of the day.

"Fascism," it said, "has received a blow in prestige. . . . By the very act of entering into negotiations, the Soviet Union is seriously weakening Hitler's hold upon the German people."

The next day, Earl Browder, then leader of the Communists, made three observations on the Pact, all of which were proven wrong within a month. He claimed that it was a distinct contribution to the peace of the world, weakened Hitler at home, and, if Poland were invaded, the Pact would be re-examined.

On September 3, Major George Fielding Eliot, the military commentator, observed that Germany was doomed if France and England declared war on her, an observation characteristic of practically all the military prognostications of the war, most of them quite as specious as the famous one that the Red Army would collapse in six weeks under the German attack. On September 16, Lindbergh warned the country that if it entered the war to save democracy abroad, it would lose it at home—an event that failed to come to pass during our nearly four years of active involvement in hostilities. On February 5, 1940, Dorothy Thompson, the columnist and news commentator, observed: "Communism has not made Russia a strong state but an extremely weak one. Hitler has nothing to fear from that quarter." The Fuehrer had evidently arrived at the same conclusion; within two years, he realized the enormity of his mistake, and on one notable occasion subsequently, complained that he had been misinformed about the state of Russian preparedness. But, then, even the Communists guessed wrong about the relations between Germany and Russia. On June 20, 1941, two days before the Nazi invasion of the Soviet Union, the *Daily Worker* was contemptuously dismissing rumors from London of war between Hitler and Stalin as "malicious fabrications."

And so on and on.

The military experts, the columnists, the diplomats, the radio analysts, the inside-this-and-that-country writers, those who knew what was coming and kept telling us what to expect, covered themselves with error and absurdity. It is, of course, difficult to shape the forces of history. It is folly to anticipate them. The years 1939, 1940, 1941, were object lessons in demonstrating the full measure of that folly.

V

With growing momentum, the country—politicians, writers, isolationists, internationalists, the great massed citizenry—slid toward Pearl Harbor. It was in a strange, split state. The straw polls might indicate that two-thirds of the people sympathized with the Allied cause, but the same two-thirds watched our edging into the conflict with sinking hearts. In 1941, the President's every utterance on the war was listened to with an intensity that scarcely cloaked the anguish and dread which stretched across the nation. The pressure of history was forcing it irresistibly to participation in the war; the prospect of Germany organizing Europe and exploiting the resources of Russia, reeling during the summer under the blows of the Nazi army, was too menacing to national security to be tolerated. But there was no enthusiasm, none of the parade-ground fanfare of the Spanish-American War or the huzzahs and band-playing of the first World War. Grimness and anxiety, a constant grasping at straws suggesting a continued neutrality, a hoping upon hope that the next crisis would not bring the final involvement—these were the prevailing moods. When Winston Churchill delivered his celebrated speech in which he cried, "Give us the tools and we will finish the job," the whole country was relieved. Perhaps Britain could win without us. When, in the fall, it became evident that Russia would not succumb as quickly as the experts had predicted, there was a great rush of support for Lend-Lease goods to the Eastern Front. Perhaps the millions of Russian soldiers would spare us the need to send our own. The protracted negotiations with the Japanese were followed with less interest than they deserved, since few thought Japan would be insane enough to attack us. But they added to the tension.

Week after week slipped by, and the country was like a boat that starts in a quiet part of the river, gets whirled into a rougher and rougher current until its occupants can hear the noise of a great waterfall ahead. When the bombs dropped on that otherwise routine Sunday morning at Pearl Harbor and took three thousand lives at one blow, the concussion at home was beyond all measuring. Before its vibrations had ended, the warring elements, isolationists and interventionists, the timid and the bold, Republicans and Democrats, the President and the President's most vituperative enemies, swung into the same bloc, closing the ranks of the country which had been so deeply split.

And so, with many protestations of unity and faith in victory over enemies now officially proclaimed, with feuds temporarily laid aside, and in the grip of that exaltation which comes when a die long agonized over is finally cast, the nation passed, not without restlessness, not without foreboding, into the great war, the war that was to beget the atomic bomb and change the face of the earth.

With that passing, the angry decade came to its violent and perilous close.

CHRONOLOGY

1929   A *Farewell to Arms*
       Stock Market Crash
       Look Homeward, Angel
1930   *The 42nd Parallel*
       Re-election of Franklin D. Roosevelt as Governor
       of New York
1931   Japanese Invasion of Manchuria
1932   Bonus March on Washington
       Election of Franklin D. Roosevelt to the Presidency
1933   Closing of the banks
       President Roosevelt's First Inaugural Address
       Anthony Adverse
       Repeal of Prohibition
       End of ban on James Joyce's *Ulysses*
1934   Frank Capra's *It Happened One Night*
       Tortilla Flat
       Upton Sinclair's EPIC campaign in California
1935   Creation of WPA
       John Ford's *The Informer*
       NRA invalidated by the Supreme Court
       Wagner Labor Relations Act passed
       Studs Lonigan
       Assassination of Huey Long
       Italian invasion of Ethiopia

Tobacco Road begins its record-breaking Broadway run

1936 Outbreak of the Spanish Civil War
Gone with the Wind
Re-election of Franklin D. Roosevelt to the Presidency

1937 The sitdown strikes
The Late George Apley
The business recession
Of Mice and Men

1938 Walt Disney's *Snow White and the Seven Dwarfs*
Hitler's seizure of Austria
Munich Agreement
Death of Thomas Wolfe

1939 *The Grapes of Wrath*
New York World's Fair
Nazi-Soviet Pact
Outbreak of the second World War

1940 Richard Wright's *Native Son*
Fall of France
You Can't Go Home Again
Re-election of Franklin D. Roosevelt for a third term

1941 German invasion of Russia
Pearl Harbor

A Selected Reading List for *The Angry Decade*

SOCIAL

Adamic, Louis, *My America.* New York: Harpers, 1938.

Agee, James, and Evans, Walker, *Let Us Now Praise Famous Men.* Boston: Houghton Mifflin, 1941.

Allen, Frederick Lewis, *The Lords of Creation.* New York: Harpers, 1935.

——*Since Yesterday.* New York: Harpers, 1940.

Angly, Edward, *Oh Yeah.* New York: Viking, 1931.

Any inspirational book by Emmett Fox, Harry Emerson Fosdick, and Henry C. Link.

Arnold, Thurman W., *The Folklore of Capitalism.* New Haven, Conn.: Yale University Press, 1937.

Beard, Charles A. and Mary R., *America in Midpassage.* New York: Macmillan, 1939.

Brande, Dorothea, *Wake Up and Live!* New York: Simon and Schuster, 1936.

Carnegie, Dale, *How to Win Friends and Influence People.* New York: Simon and Schuster, 1937.

Chase, Francis, Jr., *Sound and Fury. An Informal History of Broadcasting.* New York: Harpers, 1942.

Chase, Stuart, *Rich Land, Poor Land.* New York: Whittlesey House, 1936.

Childs, Marquis W., *I Write from Washington.* New York: Harpers, 1942.

Cowley, Malcolm, *Think Back On Us:* A Contemporary

Chronicle of the 1930's. Carbondale, Ill.: Southern Illinois University Press, 1967.

Flynn, John T., *As We Go Marching*. New York: Doubleday, Doran, 1944.

Foerster, Norman, ed. , *Humanism and America*. New York: Farrar and Rinehart, 1930.

Hayakawa, S. I., *Language in Action*. New York: Harcourt, Brace, 1941.

Hayek, Friedrich A., *The Road to Serfdom*. Chicago: University of Chicago Press, 1944.

Howe, Quincy, *World Diary: 1929-1934*. New York: McBride, 1934.

Huberman, Leo, *America, Incorporated*. New York: Viking, 1940.

Lynd, Robert S. and Helen M., *Middletown in Transition*. New York: Harcourt, Brace, 1937.

McWilliams, Carey, *Factories in the Field*. Boston: Little, Brown, 1939.

Mitchell, Broadus, *Depression Decade*. New York: Rinehart, 1947.

MacLeish, Archibald, *The Irresponsibles*. New York: Duell, Sloan and Pearce, 1940.

Pitkin, Walter B., *Life Begins at Forty*. New York: Whittlesey House, 1932.

Rorty, James, *Where Life is Better*. New York: John Day, 1936.

Schlesinger, Arthur M., Jr. *The Age of Roosevelt*. 3 vols. Boston: Houghton Mifflin, 1957–1960.

Sears, Paul B., *Deserts on the March*. Norman, Okla.: University of Oklahoma Press, 1935.

Seldes, Gilbert, *The Years of the Locust*. Boston: Little, Brown, 1933.

Sheean, Vincent, *Personal History*. New York: Doubleday, Doran, 1935.

Steffens, Lincoln, *The Autobiography of Lincoln Steffens.* New York: Harcourt, Brace, 1931.

Swados, Harvey, ed., *The American Writer and the Great Depression.* Indianapolis: Bobbs-Merrill, 1966.

Taylor, Deems, Peterson, Marceline, and Hale, Bryant, A. *Pictorial History of the Movies.* New York: Simon and Schuster, 1943.

Thorp, Margaret Farrand, *America at the Movies.* New Haven, Conn.: Yale University Press, 1939.

Twelve Southerners, *I'll Take My Stand.* New York: Harpers, 1930.

Wecter, Dixon, *The Age of the Great Depression.* New York: Macmillan, 1938.

LITERARY

Fiction:

Allen, Hervey, *Anthony Adverse.* New York: Farrar and Rinehart, 1933.

Any novel by Lloyd C. Douglas.

Any novel by Kathleen Norris, Faith Baldwin, or Temple Bailey.

Basso, Hamilton, *Sun in Capricorn.* New York: Coward-McCann, 1942.

Bell, Thomas, *All Brides Are Beautiful.* Boston: Little, Brown, 1936.

Brand, Millen, *The Outward Room.* New York: Simon and Schuster, 1937.

Buck, Pearl, *The Good Earth.* New York: John Day, 1931.

Caldwell, Erskine, *Tobacco Road.* New York: Duell, Sloan and Pearce, 1940.

——*Stories by Erskine Caldwell.* Selected by Henry Seidel Canby. New York: Duell, Sloan and Pearce, 1944.

Cather, Willa, *Shadows on the Rock.* New York: Knopf, 1931.

Dos Passos, John, *U.S.A.* New York: The Modern Library, 1939.

Edmonds, Walter D., *Drums Along the Mohawk.* Boston: Little, Brown, 1936.

Farrell, James T., *Studs Lonigan.* New York: Vanguard, 1935.

Fast, Howard, *The Last Frontier.* New York: Duell, Sloan and Pearce, 1941.

——*Citizen Tom Paine.* New York: Duell, Sloan and Pearce, 1943.

Faulkner, William, *The Sound and the Fury.* New York: Cape and Smith, 1929.

——*Light in August.* New York: Smith and Haas, 1932.

——*Absalom, Absalom!* New York: Random House, 1936.

——*The Hamlet.* New York: Random House, 1940.

Fitzgerald, F. Scott, *The Last Tycoon.* New York: Scribner, 1941.

Glasgow, Ellen, *The Sheltered Life.* New York: Doubleday, Doran, 1932.

——*Vein of Iron.* New York: Harcourt, Brace, 1935.

Halper, Albert, *The Foundry.* New York: Viking, 1934.

Hemingway, Ernest, *To Have and Have Not.* New York: Scribner, 1937.

——*For Whom the Bell Tolls.* New York: Scribner, 1940.

La Farge, Oliver, *Laughing Boy.* Boston: Houghton Mifflin, 1929.

Lanham, Edwin, *The Stricklands.* Boston: Little, Brown, 1939.

Levin, Meyer, *The Old Bunch.* New York: Simon and Schuster, 1937.

Lewis, Sinclair, *It Can't Happen Here.* New York: Doubleday, Doran, 1935.

Maltz, Albert, *The Underground Stream.* Boston: Little, Brown, 1940.

Fast, Howard, *Citizen Tom Paine*. New York: Duell, Sloan and Pearce, 1943.

Faulkner, William, *The Sound and the Fury*. New York: Cape and Smith, 1929.

—— *Light in August*. New York: Smith and Haas, 1932.

—— *Absalom, Absalom!* New York: Random House, 1936.

—— *The Hamlet*. New York: Random House, 1940.

Fitzgerald, F. Scott, *The Last Tycoon*. New York: Scribner, 1941.

Glasgow, Ellen, *The Sheltered Life*. New York: Doubleday, Doran, 1932.

—— *Vein of Iron*. New York: Harcourt, Brace, 1935.

Halper, Albert, *The Foundry*. New York: Viking, 1934.

Hemingway, Ernest, *To Have and Have Not*. New York: Scribner, 1937.

—— *For Whom the Bell Tolls*. New York: Scribner, 1940.

La Farge, Oliver, *Laughing Boy*. Boston: Houghton Mifflin, 1929.

Lanham, Edwin, *The Stricklands*. Boston: Little, Brown, 1939.

Lewis, Sinclair, *It Can't Happen Here*. New York: Doubleday, Doran, 1935.

Maltz, Albert, *The Underground Stream*. Boston: Little, Brown, 1940.

Marquand, John P., *The Late George Apley*. Boston: Little, Brown, 1937.

—— *H. M. Pulham, Esquire*. Boston: Little, Brown, 1941.

Mitchell, Margaret, *Gone with the Wind*. New York: Macmillan, 1936.

Nathan, Robert, *One More Spring*. New York: Knopf, 1933.

O'Hara, John, *Appointment in Samarra*. New York: Harcourt, Brace, 1934.

Roberts, Kenneth, *Arundel*. New York: Doubleday, Doran, 1930.

Roberts, Kenneth, *Northwest Passage*. New York: Doubleday, Doran, 1937.

Saroyan, William, *My Name is Aram*. New York: Harcourt, Brace, 1940.

Short Stories from *The New Yorker*. New York: Simon and Schuster, 1940.

Steinbeck, John, *Tortilla Flat*. New York: Covici, Friede, 1935.

—— *In Dubious Battle*. New York: Covici, Friede, 1936.

—— *Of Mice and Men*. New York: Covici, Friede, 1937.

—— *The Grapes of Wrath*. New York: Viking, 1939.

Stribling, T. S., *The Store*. New York: Doubleday, Doran, 1932.

Suckow, Ruth, *The Folks*. New York: Farrar and Rinehart, 1934.

Swanson, Neil H., *The Forbidden Ground*. New York: Farrar and Rinehart, 1938.

Wolfe, Thomas, *Look Homeward, Angel*. New York: Scribner, 1929.

—— *The Web and the Rock*. New York: Harpers, 1939.

—— *You Can't Go Home Again*. New York: Harpers, 1940.

Wright, Richard, *Native Son*. New York: Harpers, 1940.

Zugsmith, Leane, *The Summer Soldier*. New York: Random House, 1938.

Drama:

Anderson, Maxwell, *Winterset*. Washington, D. C.: Anderson House, 1935.

—— *High Tor*. Washington, D. C.: Anderson House, 1937.

—— *Key Largo*. Washington, D. C.: Anderson House, 1939.

Behrman, S. N., *Rain from Heaven*. New York: Random House, 1935.

Corwin, Norman, *Thirteen by Corwin*. Radio Dramas. New York: Holt, 1942.

Federal Theatre Project. National Service Bureau Publication, 1937, 1938:

No. 3. *1935; a Living Newspaper Play*, by Arthur Arent.

No. 35. *Triple-A Plowed Under.*

No. 44. *One-Third of a Nation*, by Arthur Arent.

Gassner, John, and Nichols, Dudley (eds.), *Twenty Best Film Plays*. New York: Crown, 1943.

Hart, Moss, and Kaufman, George S., *You Can't Take It with You*. New York: Farrar and Rinehart, 1937.

Hellman, Lillian, *The Little Foxes*. New York: Random House, 1939.

—— *Watch on the Rhine*. New York: Random House, 1941.

Kingsley, Sidney, *Dead End*. New York: Random House, 1936.

Lorentz, Pare, *The River*. Harrisburg, Pa.: Stackpole, 1938.

MacLeish, Archibald, *The Fall of the City*. A Verse Play for Radio. New York: Farrar and Rinehart, 1937.

Oboler, Arch, *This Freedom*. Thirteen New Radio Plays. New York: Random House, 1942.

Odets, Clifford, *Awake and Sing, Waiting for Lefty*, and *Golden Boy*, in SIX PLAYS. New York: Random House, 1939.

Peters, Paul, and Sklar, George, *Stevedore*. New York: Covici, Friede, 1934.

Saroyan, William, *The Time of Your Life*. New York: Harcourt, Brace, 1939.

Shaw, Irwin, *Bury the Dead*, in TWENTY BEST PLAYS OF THE MODERN AMERICAN THEATRE. Edited by John Gassner. New York: Crown, 1939.

Sherwood, Robert E., *The Petrified Forest*. New York: Scribner, 1935.

—— *Idiot's Delight*. New York: Scribner, 1936.

—— *Abe Lincoln in Illinois*. New York: Scribner, 1940.

Engle, Paul, *Worn Earth*. New Haven, Conn.: Yale University Press, 1932.

Fearing, Kenneth, *Collected Poems*. New York: Random House, 1940.

Frost, Robert, *A Further Range*. New York: Holt, 1936.

Gregory, Horace, *Poems: 1930-1940*. New York: Harcourt, Brace, 1941.

Hughes, Langston, *The Dream Keeper and Other Poems*. New York: Knopf, 1932.

Jeffers, Robinson, *The Selected Poetry of Robinson Jeffers*. New York: Random House, 1938.

MacLeish, Archibald, *Frescoes for Mr. Rockefeller's City*. New York: John Day, 1933.

Millay, Edna St. Vincent, *There Are No Islands Any More*. New York: Harpers, 1940.

Miller, Alice Duer, *The White Cliffs*. New York: Coward-McCann, 1940.

Moore, Marianne, *What Are Years*. New York: Macmillan, 1941.

Rukeyser, Muriel, *U.S.1*. New York: Covici, Friede, 1938.

Sandburg, Carl, *The People, Yes*. New York: Harcourt Brace, 1936.

Schwartz, Delmore, *Shenandoah*. Norfolk, Conn.: New Directions, 1941.

Stevens, Wallace, *The Man with the Blue Guitar & Other Poems*. New York: Knopf, 1937.

Warren, Robert Penn, *XXXVI Poems*. New York: The Alcestis Press, 1935.

Weismiller, Edward, *The Deer Come Down*. New Haven, Conn.: Yale University Press, 1936.

Criticism:
Adams, J. Donald, *The Shape of Books to Come*. New York: Viking, 1944.

Rukeyser, Muriel, *U.S.1.* New York: Covici, Friede, 1938.

Sandburg, Carl, *The People, Yes.* New York: Harcourt, Brace, 1936.

Schwartz, Delmore, *Shenandoah.* Norfolk, Conn.: New Directions, 1941.

Stevens, Wallace, *The Man with the Blue Guitar & Other Poems.* New York: Knopf, 1937.

Warren, Robert Penn, *XXXVI Poems.* New York: The Alcestis Press, 1935.

Weismiller, Edward, *The Deer Come Down.* New Haven, Conn.: Yale University Press, 1936.

Criticism:

Adams, J. Donald, *The Shape of Books to Come.* New York: Viking, 1944.

Beach, Joseph Warren, *American Fiction, 1920-1940.* New York: Macmillan, 1941.

Cargill, Oscar, *Intellectual America.* New York: Macmillan, 1941.

DeVoto, Bernard, *The Literary Fallacy.* Boston: Little, Brown, 1944.

Geismar, Maxwell, *Writers in Crisis.* Boston: Houghton Mifflin, 1942.

Gregory, Horace, and Zaturenska, Marya, *A History of American Poetry, 1900-1940.* New York: Harcourt, Brace, 1946.

Hicks, Granville, *The Great Tradition.* New York: Macmillan, 1933.

Kazin, Alfred, *On Native Grounds.* New York: Reynal and Hitchcock, 1942.

Krutch, Joseph Wood, *The American Drama Since 1918.* New York: Random House, 1939.

INDEX